Advanced Praise for
Houston Astros: Armed and Dangerous

"No reporter is more plugged into the Astros' players, coaches, front office and ownership than Jesus Ortiz, and *Houston Astros: Armed and Dangerous* is the result of his journalistic doggedness. This is a painstaking, probing account of the two most eventful seasons in the history of Texas baseball, from the behind-the-scenes maneuvers that brought Andy Pettitte and Roger Clemens to Houston, to the everyday dramas of the regular season, to the bright lights and bunting of October. Ortiz has crafted an expert, minutely detailed book; always informed, always compelling."

—Daniel Habib, *Sports Illustrated*

"If anyone can write a book about Andy Pettitte, Roger Clemens, and Nolan Ryan, it is Jesus Ortiz, a columnist and staff writer for the *Houston Chronicle*. Jesus is a conscientious and thorough reporter, a terrific writer, and, most importantly, a clear and objective thinker. Beyond that, however, Jesus has covered the Houston Astros as a beat reporter for years, and he knows where the bodies are buried. I highly recommend him for this book based on my 40 years as a writer of such books as *A False Spring* and *A Nice Tuesday.*"

—Pat Jordan, author of *A False Spring*

HOUSTON ASTROS
ARMED
AND
DANGEROUS

Jose de Jesus Ortiz Jr.

Foreword by Brad Ausmus

SportsPublishingLLC.com

Cover photos by Rich Pilling/Getty Images (Oswalt, Pettitte) and Jed Jacobsohn/Getty Images (Clemens).
Interior photos by Stephen O'Brien, courtesy of the Houston Astros.

Publishers: Peter L. Bannon and Joseph J. Bannon Sr.
Senior managing editor: Susan M. Moyer
Acquisitions editor: Noah Adams Amstadter
Developmental editor: Elisa Bock Laird
Art director: K. Jeffrey Higgerson
Cover design: Joseph Brumleve
Interior layout: Kenneth J. O'Brien
Imaging: Kenneth J. O'Brien
Photo editor: Erin Linden-Levy

Printed in the United States of America

Sports Publishing L.L.C.
804 North Neil Street
Champaign, IL 61820

Phone: 1-877-424-2665
Fax: 217-363-2073
SportsPublishingLLC.com

Library of Congress Cataloging-in-Publication Data

Ortiz, Jose de Jesus.
    Houston Astros : armed and dangerous / Jose de Jesus Ortiz ; foreword by Brad Ausmus.
        p. cm.
    ISBN 1-59670-071-8 (softcover : alk. paper)
    1.   Houston Astros (Baseball team)—History. I. Title.

GV875.A3O78 2006
796.757'6409764141--dc22

2006001894

To Megan and Kathleen Maria,
my conscience and soul

Contents

Foreword

People outside of the baseball world always assume that players have inside information or, even more erroneous, are consulted throughout the course of team personnel moves. This couldn't be further from the truth. The great majority of the time the players get their information the way the whole country does—through the media. If we do get a whiff of a possible roster move, we love to bounce scenarios back and forth between teammates like gossiping teenage girls. In November 2003, Jeff Bagwell (or "Baggy" as I know him) called me with whispers of a possible Andy Pettitte signing, that Andy wanted to come home to Houston. Well, I didn't hold my breath. I did hold out hope. Even while vacationing on Maui a few weeks later, scanning the AP wire on ESPN.com, and reading the reports that the Astros were poised to announce the signing of Andy Pettitte to a three-year deal the following day, I was wary. I knew, or maybe in some stretch of reverse superstition, I forced myself to believe that Mr. George Steinbrenner and the New York Yankees would swoop down and snatch Andy Pettitte away from the Astros in their "too good to be true contract" talons and fly away with one of the best pitchers, and certainly the best big-game pitcher, in baseball.

The press conference was held, Andy Pettitte had signed, and the baseball landscape in Houston would never be the same. The city and players were about to be swept up by baseball fever in a city and state where football reigned supreme. Baggy called again and asked if it would bother me if Roger Clemens was allowed to leave the team, at times, to visit with his family.

"Hell no, not if that will get him to sign with us."

Rocket signed, too. From that point, everything began to really accelerate. I suddenly couldn't wait for the first day of spring training. At a time when I normally enjoy my family and surf, I couldn't get my mind off of spring training. "This team is good," I keep telling myself. "This team is good," I keep telling Baggy. "This is our chance. This team has the chance to win it all. Forget making the playoffs, forget making the World Series, we can be world champions." The pundits agreed. We were picked by everyone to make the playoffs and by many to win the World Series.

Spring training was great. The lights of the baseball media had never shined brighter on the Houston Astros. Everything was going smoothly until the day Andy mentioned some elbow pain. Elbow pain in our new star pitcher was not a good thing. The cloud began to cast its shadow over the Houston Astros. It was a shadow that would get even darker.

Over the course of the next two seasons, the players, managers, coaching staffs, employees, and fans would ride a roller coaster of emotions following and rooting for the Houston Astros. The early offensive struggles of the power-packed 2004 lineup and the injuries to both Andy Pettitte and Wade Miller would test the mettle of the entire organization, and cost Jimy Williams his job. There was the utter misery in 2005 of starting 15–30 that caused even some players in the clubhouse to doubt the team's ability to get back in the pennant race and made them wonder aloud who would be traded before the July 31 deadline. Then there was Baggy, one of the two Astros pillars, succumbing to shoulder pain so fierce that he sometimes needed help putting a shirt or jacket sleeve on his right arm.

There were times of hope, times that lit a spark under our proverbial asses, and times that put the strut back in our walks. The trade for Carlos Beltran brought promise in a five-tool package. Rocket's mastery of his new league, his ascension on the all-time strikeout list, and his All-Star start made us proud. Jeff Kent's breaking the second baseman home-run record let us crack smiles. In 2005, Craig Biggio took another hit for the team, only this time he set a record. Roy Oswalt, Brad Lidge, and Morgan Ensberg all went to their first All-Star games. (By the way, Roy, a bunch of us were on the Internet punching in your name on ballot after ballot.) Then there was Rocket's performance against the Marlins in a must-win game the day his mother passed away. I will forever have the image of both teams standing on the field after the game to watch the video the Astros had prepared about Bess Clemens. A classy move all the way around.

The baseball season is 162 games for a reason. I am a firm believer in statistics and probability, especially when it comes to baseball. Over the span of 162 games, statistics in baseball always return to where they are supposed to be. If you are a career .250 hitter, regardless of how hot or cold you start, you will generally end up hitting in the neighborhood of .250. I think this applies to a team, as well. If you are a playoff-caliber team, regardless of how hot or cold you start, you will make the playoffs.

That being said, the probability of the Houston Astros starting so awfully, being so far out of the playoff race, and finishing in record fashion to clinch a postseason berth on the final day of the season in consecutive years, was unlikely, at worst.

When you spend the better part of a year with three dozen guys all working toward the same thing on a daily basis, a family bond is formed. You will fight, you will laugh, you will probably even cry. When I read *Houston Astros: Armed and Dangerous,* I had a flood of memories and images as if I were flipping through the family photo album. I see Rocket gritting his teeth, Baggy on one knee in the on-deck circle, Bidge wiping the dirt off the front of his jersey, and a batter staring at the sky, wondering what happened after another Lidge-induced strikeout.

The one thing that stands out in my mind more than any other memory of the 2004-2005 Houston Astros is the deafening hum in Game 5 of the 2005 NLCS, just before Albert Pujols hit his infamous home run. Minute Maid Park had turned into a black hole of noise, and any noise made inside of it was swallowed and became part of it. It was the only time in my career that stadium/fan noise felt like it was rattling my brain. And, within seconds, following the Pujols home run, that deafening hum became a deafening silence. A silence even louder than the hum moments before.

Jesus Ortiz was the beat writer covering these two teams, these two seasons, daily. He did more than just eat popcorn and keep a scorebook. He built relationships, although sometimes confrontational, and knew the players. He was in the clubhouse keeping record. He was there when we were losing and answered questions with a stare of disbelief and a robotic tone. He was there when we were winning and too superstitious to talk about it. I hope you enjoy *Houston Astros: Armed and Dangerous* as much as I did. If you're an Astros fan, it reads like a memory.

—Brad Ausmus

Acknowledgments

I t's nearly impossible to thank every person who helped with this project. I must begin with Megan Ortiz, my bride, colleague, and part-time writing coach. Brian McTaggart, my fellow Astros beat writer at the *Houston Chronicle,* deserves an assist for helping me understand the psyche of Houston fans. He still won't forgive me for the 1981 Los Angeles Dodgers of my youth beating the Astros of his youth. Since you've joined the beat in 2004, it's been nothing but a joy. You've made what can be a stressful job fun, even providing laughs during force plays in softball. I wouldn't work at the *Houston Chronicle* if not for deputy managing editor Daniel Cunningham, the man who helped guide my career and eventually lured me back to Houston from New York in 2001. Special thanks goes out to sports editor Fred Faour, who understands the commitment needed to cover baseball. Much gratitude goes out to *Houston Chronicle* editor-in-chief Jeff Cohen, a former Astros bat boy who follows baseball as closely as anybody in Houston. With Cunningham, Faour, and Cohen, Houstonians can rest assured that baseball will have a prominent place in the *Houston Chronicle.*

Mark Gonzales, one of the premier beat writers in America, was invaluable with all of his help. As the Chicago White Sox's beat writer for the *Chicago Tribune,* Gonzales provided most of the research and background on the White Sox for this project. Gonzales, a veteran reporter who covered the World Series champion Arizona Diamondbacks in 2001 for the *Arizona Republic* and has worked extensively covering Major League Baseball for nearly two decades, left Arizona for Chicago just in time to cover the 2005 World Series champions from the first day of spring training until the final out against the Astros at Minute Maid Park. Although Gonzales has covered the White Sox for only one season, nobody has a better pulse on that organization than he does.

Assistant sports editor Carlton Thompson and Joseph Duarte, who helped recruit me to Houston, were invaluable because of the knowledge they carried as former Astros beat writers. To David Barron, thanks for teaching me what being the ultimate team player is all about.

Richard Justice, John P. Lopez, Fran Blinebury, and the rest of the *Chronicle* sports staff also have been tremendous help. Of course, the *Chronicle* sports staff would not run without Terry Hayes.

None of this could be possible without the help of Drayton and Elizabeth McLane, who truly understand customer service. Thank you Mrs. McLane for not yelling at me when I've called to speak to Mr. McLane at all hours of the morning and night and during Thanksgiving, Christmas Eve, Christmas, New Year's Eve, New Year's Day, and countless other holidays over the last few years as I searched for one story or another. You are the epitome of class, and I can never repay you for your tremendous insight on your husband and family. Special thanks goes out to the McLane children—Drayton III; Amy and their son Robert Drayton McLane IV; and Denton, Amy, and their son, Jefferson Blaylock McLane.

With owners such as Drayton and Elizabeth McLane it's no surprise that the Astros have what is considered one of the best media relations staffs in baseball under the direction of Jay Lucas. Jimmy Stanton, Lisa Ramsperger, Leah Tobin, Charlie Hepp, Sally Gunter, Candice McCallie, and Nathan Coffey were always ready to facilitate interviews or research material during the Astros' run to the World Series. Thanks to the entire Astros, front office, including Pam Gardner, Tim Purpura, Tal Smith, David Gottfried, John Sorrentino, Rosi Hernandez, Paul Ricciarini, Enos Cabell, Ricky Bennett, and Nolan Ryan.

Thanks to Phil and Carol Garner and the Astros' coaching staff, especially Doug Mansolino and Jose Cruz. To all the Astros players and their wives, many of whom provided countless hours of interviews. Special thanks go out to Roy and Nicole Oswalt and Roy's father, Billy. To Jeff Bagwell, quite simply the most accountable man I have ever had the privilege of covering. There's a reason your teammates consider you the team leader. Despite all of the Houston children wearing No. 5 Astros jerseys, the city of Houston will never really understand just how much Bagwell has given of his body and soul to help Houston baseball thrive. This project would not be possible without Roger Clemens, Andy Pettitte, and their families. To Brad Ausmus and Jose Vizcaino, thanks for providing much insight throughout the years. Thanks to Lance Berkman, Brad Lidge, Russ Springer, and Morgan Ensberg for giving intelligent perspectives and sincere answers through good times and bad times. Unofficial Astros historian Mike Acosta, who joined the Astros in 1999 as an intern in the broadcast department and has since worked his way to the ticket office, was a godsend with his wealth of knowledge on the franchise.

Elisa Bock Laird, my editor on this project, deserves a special mention for leading me through this rookie experience as an author. Thanks for holding my hand through this process. It was a special experience to work with an Astros fan who showed tremendous interest and passion for this project.

Thanks to Jeremy Rakes and Andrew Ferraro, two of my Houston-based researchers who served as my ears when I couldn't be everywhere at once.

Last and certainly not least, thanks to the folks who made it easy to spend so much of my time covering baseball. To Donna Manfull, the best mother-in-law a guy can have. Other than being a Cubs fan, you're all right, especially because you fly in from Washington, Iowa, to take care of Kathleen at any time as long as we give you about seven hours of notice. To Sid Manfull, for not having a problem with Donna spending more time in Houston than Iowa. To Patricia Lynn Heck, Kathleen's godmother and emergency babysitter. To my parents, Angela and Jesus Ortiz, for giving me the work ethic and appreciation for everything that God has given us. To my brother Horacio, who flew in from Las Vegas on September 21, 2005, to board up my house in advance of Hurricane Rita. Gracias to the rest of my siblings—Jose Ascension Ortiz, Joel, Edith, Antonio, Angelica, and Silvia—for keeping me humble with your biting criticism. Thanks to Miguel and Adela Estrada, my godparents, for taking me to many of the first baseball games I ever saw at Dodger Stadium.

Thanks to Kathleen Maria for keeping me smiling and telling stories about your latest exploits. At age two, you still don't realize that every Astros player isn't named Roy, but that was fine on the day after Game 5 of the National League Championship Series because I will never stop telling the story of the time you told Mr Drayton McLane that all will be fine because "Roy wins. Go Astros." After Roy Oswalt won Game 6 of the NLCS a day later to push the Astros to the World Series, Mr. McLane and I laughed at that conversation you two had because you had predicted the victory.

1

Monument Park

"We'll be looking at a tape job and fill-ins and no marquee additions in the offseason [preceding the 2004 season]."
—former Astros closer Billy Wagner, who was traded to the Phillies on November 3, 2003

L istening to Yankees games on the radio as a child in the 1950s in Temple, Texas, Astros owner Drayton McLane tried to visualize himself at Yankee Stadium's Monument Park. He always found it difficult to envision the monuments of Babe Ruth, Lou Gehrig, and Miller Huggins in fair territory near left-center field at Yankee Stadium.

So on June 11, 2003, before the Astros' second regular-season game in franchise history against the Yankees, McLane went in search of Ruth, Gehrig, and Huggins. He arrived early to the stadium with his wife, Elizabeth, and their two sons and daughters-in-law. Together they toured Monument Park with Astros president of baseball operations Tal Smith, the architect of Houston baseball and a former vice president of the Yankees.

The monuments are no longer in fair territory—they now sit behind the left-center field wall in Monument Park—but they still evoke the same awe.

"There's a lot of history," McLane said. "I grew up in the 1950s, and you listened to baseball on the radio then. They talked about the monuments being in play, and you just couldn't visualize having monuments in play. Coming here is like going to the Smithsonian Institute."

McLane found more than monuments in Monument Park that day. He visited the future of his franchise and the men who would build his legacy for generations of Astros fans.

Not far from Ruth, McLane saw future Hall of Famer Roger Clemens and Andy Pettitte milling about. At that time, each of Clemens's starts was front-page news throughout the country as he tried to become the 21st pitcher in major league history to record 300 victories. McLane noticed Clemens and Pettitte and told them the people of Houston and the Astros were proud of them. In their brief chat, McLane wished the hard-throwing Clemens luck in his quest for his 300th victory and 4,000th strikeout, which he collected two days later against the St. Louis Cardinals.

A few hours after McLane visited with Clemens and Pettitte, the Astros dominated the Bronx Bombers by throwing the most improbable game in the history of both franchises. That night Roy Oswalt left after one inning with a right groin strain, and relievers Pete Munro, Kirk Saarloos, Brad Lidge, Octavio Dotel, and Billy Wagner followed with eight no-hit innings. In only their second game ever at Yankee Stadium, the Astros had thrown the first six-pitcher no-hitter in major league history and handed the Yankees their first no-hitter defeat at Yankee Stadium since August 25, 1952, when Detroit's Virgil Trucks accomplished the feat.

The Yankees, who have been no-hit only seven times in their glorious history, had not been held without a hit in a game since Hall of Fame knuckleballer Hoyt Wilhelm of the Baltimore Orioles held them hitless on September 20, 1958. The Yankees had played 6,980 games between Wilhelm's gem and the Astros' combined no-hitter, which broke the longest active no-hit streak in the majors.

After the game, temperamental Yankees owner George Steinbrenner stormed out of his suite at Yankee Stadium furious at his team and offended by Astros manager Jimy Williams. Steinbrenner later accused Williams of "rubbing it in." Never mind that the then-Yankees' $150-million payroll was twice the size of the Astros'. Never mind that Steinbrenner's payroll would surpass $200 million in 2004 and 2005, making them the richest bullies in baseball.

"I will not be critical of the other team; they're a great team," Steinbrenner told *The New York Times*. "But I thought their manager kind of rubbed it in on our guys, one reliever after another. He was on a mission. I've always liked Williams. He's a good manager. He was good in Boston. I don't think he should have been let go. Whatever. I don't like what he did to our troops."

Williams defended his moves the next day by noting that he was just trying to win the game and that his relievers weren't exactly ready to pitch multiple innings. Away from New York, Williams felt free to give his real thoughts on Steinbrenner, whom he has disparagingly referred to publicly as "Georgie Porgie" in the past.

"If Steinbrenner gives one two-by-four to the Ladies of the Poor, he'll call the media to write about it," Williams said, making it clear he had no use for Steinbrenner's manipulation of the New York media.

Six months later, Steinbrenner was dealt another surprising blow by McLane's organization. In a span of 32 days, McLane stunned Steinbrenner and the Bronx with two moves that had repercussions from New York to Houston and throughout the baseball world. For the first time in a long time, the Yankees lost at their own game—free agent signings. On December 11, 2003, McLane signed Pettitte, taking advantage of Steinbrenner's inability to understand Pettitte's desire to pitch close to home or to finally receive some appreciation from "The Boss" for a stellar and loyal career in New York.

McLane and Gerry Hunsicker had met with Pettitte and Randy and Alan Hendricks for the first time on November 18, and McLane wasted little time in asking the Hendrickses about possibly signing Clemens, if he could also sign Pettitte.

"When Gerry and I were talking to them, I mentioned Clemens. And they said, 'Let's get Andy done and then we'll talk about that,'" McLane said.

With Pettitte now interested, suddenly the 2003 farewell tour for Roger Clemens had the possibility of being only a journey back to his hometown team. It was a completely different scenario than what McLane remembered only months before.

It had been a moment unlike any other in major league history, and McLane had watched it in stunned silence on his television at his mansion in Temple. Although appreciative of the historic moment, McLane could not stop thinking about what could have been—a lost opportunity, a failed bid that had been his for the taking five years earlier in December 1998.

With $1.2 billion in net worth and both George Bushes on his speed dial, McLane is a man accustomed to getting what he wants. McLane prides himself on being as good a salesman as anybody, but his hopes of ever landing Roger Clemens in Houston seemed to vanish with every tear strolling down the big right-hander's cheek. It all seemed to end as Clemens walked off the Pro Player Stadium mound during Game 4 of the 2003 World Series against the Florida Marlins, as 65,934 fans stood on their feet honoring the future Hall of Famer and his illustrious career. Clemens had made it perfectly clear to anyone who would listen that the 2003 season with the New York Yankees would be his last.

On that stroll on October 22, 2003, nobody could have predicted what would occur exactly two years later. Two years after walking off the mound for the last time in the World Series with the New York Yankees, Clemens took the mound for his hometown Houston Astros in the first World Series game ever played by a Texas team. In their 44th season, the Astros were finally playing for it all on October 22, 2005, at Chicago's U.S. Cellular Field, facing a Chicago White Sox team that had gone 46 years between World Series appearances.

Back in 2003, however, hardly anybody in Houston was talking about the Astros and the World Series in the same sentence. All of the attention in Houston was focused on adoptive son Roger Clemens, the Astro who could have been. McLane had had his chance at The Rocket five years earlier, and he never got over losing that bid. He had always wondered what if. What if his then-popular general manager, Gerry Hunsicker, had not harshly criticized Clemens's agents, Randy and Alan Hendricks, in December 1998, ruining the backroom deal McLane was working on with them to bring The Rocket home to Houston?

Watching Clemens pound his glove and slowly march off the mound toward the visitors' dugout in Florida, McLane finally understood what he had lost and what the Astros had failed to deliver to the people of Houston. The missed opportunity of landing one of the best pitchers in Major League Baseball history was made clearer as the ovation for Clemens grew louder and louder and camera flashes enveloped the stadium like a mass of fluttering butterflies.

Clemens had received ovations throughout the season during his farewell tour of the major leagues, from Tampa Bay's Tropicana Field to his first major league home at Boston's Fenway Park, where the fans had learned to love him and hate him. This was the World Series, though, and even the normally composed Clemens was caught off guard.

After reaching the dugout, Clemens noticed the Marlins standing together in praise. Marlins catcher Ivan "Pudge" Rodriguez, who had tapped him on the leg and offered up a simple "nice career" early in the game, cheered from home plate. Jack McKeon, the Marlins manager, paid his tribute near the home team's dugout. Most of the Marlins were lined up behind McKeon, clapping and thanking the living legend for his 310 career wins and six Cy Young Awards (then a major league record).

"When you battle like I have over my career and you get the respect from your peers, that's all you can ask for," Clemens said on that night. "I appreciate that a lot. It really shows, I think, that everybody understands what was going on after the fact, and I think it shows that they love to compete, too. I can only appreciate that fact—that I love to compete, and I wanted to make sure that I tipped my cap back to them. I think Pudge knew. When I went to the plate for the first time, he mentioned something to me. You get down to business."

Even Clemens's detractors had to stop and appreciate the moment as Rocket tipped his hat, raised his arms, and acknowledged the tribute. Yankees fans, some of whom needed a few years before embracing the former hated Red Sox ace, had another moment to cherish in the history of the storied franchise—a moment right up there with Don Larsen's perfect game, Lou Gehrig's tear-jerking speech, and those 26 World Series championships.

How could Rocket ever turn back after such a powerful yearlong sendoff?

"I guess he's retired now," McLane told his wife, Elizabeth.

As a hopeful comment more than anything else, McLane allowed himself to dream.

"Wouldn't it be great if we had an opportunity in all this for Roger to pitch in Houston?" McLane told Elizabeth.

McLane dispelled that notion as quickly as he said it, acknowledging to his wife that there was no reason to believe Clemens would come back. Like most baseball fans in Houston and New York, McLane believed Clemens when the veteran right-hander said that his 20th season would be his last.

It was time for Clemens to focus on his family—his wife, Debbie, and the four Ks: Koby, Kory, Kacy, and Kody.

Sitting with his father in what was considered Clemens's final postgame press conference, nine-year-old Kacy offered this parting remark, "Thank you for watching over my dad for the last 40 years. I mean 20 years," he said amid laughter from his father and the hundreds of media surrounding them. "And we'll take it from here."

Clemens wanted to spend time with his children because, as he often said, "With my two oldest, I'm going to blink and they're going to be gone."

He was also concerned about his ailing mother, Bess, who had been battling emphysema for the past several years. Clemens dreaded the idea that she might not be there when he would finally be inducted into the Hall of Fame in Cooperstown, New York. For that reason, Debbie and the children thought Clemens was finally home for good after the Marlins beat Andy Pettitte and the Yankees in Game 6.

Clemens assumed Pettitte, his good friend and fellow Houstonian, would re-sign with the Yankees, and they'd hang out in Tampa during spring training or during the regular season in the Bronx a few times a year. Clemens had spoken to the Yankees about potential broadcast opportunities. Even Pettitte assumed he'd be back in New York.

Everything had seemed as though it would work out as planned. But just a few months later, the baseball world was turned upside down and baseball in Houston was changed forever.

McLane had a simple plan to woo Pettitte and his agents, Randy and Alan Hendricks: Don't insult them and don't set the market. If it was going to be about the money, McLane knew he couldn't compete. George Steinbrenner, the principal owner of the Yankees, could overwhelm the Astros and any other major league team in any bidding war. Steinbrenner's massive $200 million payroll in 2005 was proof that he would stop at almost nothing in his quest to bring another championship to the Bronx. Pettitte was willing to listen to the Astros, so a meeting was set up by Astros general manager Gerry Hunsicker and Alan Hendricks.

McLane, Hunsicker, and Astros president of baseball operations Tal Smith had discussed how much money they could possibly offer Pettitte, and they decided $10 million a year for possibly three years would be respectful parameters for an offer. Astros first baseman Jeff Bagwell heard about the meeting and didn't even bother to get his hopes up. As far as he and several of the Astros were concerned, those negotiations might as well have been a publicity stunt to try to show Astros fans that they were attempting to build a winning team. Some critics assumed the flirtation with Pettitte was no different than when the Astros came in second when they lost Darryl Kile to the Colorado Rockies after the 1997 season and when they lost Randy Johnson to the Arizona Diamondbacks after the 1998 season.

Actually, few people in Houston believed the Astros were serious about landing Pettitte, especially with the disappointing trade of the popular Billy Wagner fresh on the minds of Astros fans and players. Even fewer people in New York assumed Pettitte would leave the Yankees, although a small faction of Yankees insiders knew Pettitte genuinely wanted to be closer to his wife, Laura, his parents, in-laws, and extended family in Deer Park. With the $30 million figure on their minds, McLane, Hunsicker, and Smith met with Pettitte and his agents November 18. In that meeting, McLane became enamored with Pettitte's four World Series championship rings and six trips to the Series over nine years in New York. Equally important, Randy and Alan Hendricks went over the entire Astros roster and asked questions. They even asked about some players in the farm system, making sure that McLane was serious about fielding a World Series contender.

McLane's parameters for a deal were good enough to get the Astros into the competition. It didn't take long for McLane to realize why he wanted and needed a man like Andy Pettitte on his team. Pettitte had everything the Astros didn't—a résumé full of success in the postseason.

Considered one of the clutch performers of his era and a building block for the Yankees' resurgence in the 1990s, Pettitte has more postseason victories than any pitcher in Yankees history and more postseason victories than any other pitcher in major league history except Atlanta's John Smoltz.

"When I had an opportunity to get to know Andy and visit with him and I asked him to say a little about his career, he said he had been a New York Yankee for nine years and he had six World Series [trips]. I thought, 'Boy, I'm in the right place at the right time,'" McLane said.

At six feet, five inches tall and 225 pounds, with solid posture and a firm handshake, Pettitte poses an authoritative figure. He also had cultivated a strong reputation in New York and at his father-in-law's church in Deer Park as a person of faith. Even the cynical New York media endorsed the soft spoken Pettitte as a person "who absolutely cannot lie." In the game of baseball, Pettitte's traits put him in rare company, and McLane understands leadership abilities better than most.

"This is a historical time for the Houston Astros," McLane said. "Our goal since I've been involved with the Houston Astros in 1993—you've heard me say this many times, but I'm going to say it again—our goal is to be the champion, to be the best."

Randy Hendricks, as a longtime resident of Houston, knew the Astros roster well. If Pettitte were to have success in the National League, he would need a good catcher to help guide him through a new league. Catcher Brad Ausmus, who had won the previous two Gold Gloves in the National League, was a key figure in Randy Hendricks's roster breakdown after the 2003 season. Ausmus, a Dartmouth graduate who essentially runs the Astros clubhouse, was a free agent flirting with the San Diego Padres because he wanted to play close to his offseason home.

But on the same day Pettitte and the Astros met for the first time, the Astros' chances of re-signing Ausmus received a major boost because the San Diego Padres moved closer to acquiring All-Star catcher Ramon Hernandez and outfielder Terrence Long from the Oakland A's. Until then, Ausmus and the Padres had settled on the parameters of a contract for him to return near his year-round home. Ausmus was preparing for a four-day surfing trip to Baja California, Mexico, when the opportunity to land in San Diego essentially closed on him. Meeting with Pettitte, however, the Astros didn't have much time to negotiate with Ausmus. But 24 hours after meeting with Pettitte, McLane reached a two-year, $4 million contract ($1 million in 2004, $3 million in 2005) with Ausmus, admitting that he hoped the deal would serve as a sign to Pettitte.

"Our pitchers are comfortable pitching to Brad," McLane said. "In attracting a good free agent pitcher, he is a good selling point because everybody respects Brad Ausmus."

Pettitte definitely took Ausmus's signing as a positive indication, realizing that McLane was bringing back every member of the starting lineup from the 2003 team that finished only a game behind the Chicago Cubs in the National League Central.

McLane and his Astros are definitely in the right place: Houston, Texas. A native of Baton Rouge, Louisiana, Pettitte was raised in Deer Park, where his in-laws, parents—Tommy and Jo Ann, and extended family live. Pettitte and his wife, Laura, have three young children—Josh, Jared, and Lexy Grace, who turned three years old a month after her father signed—and the young ace was interested in opportunities to pitch closer to home.

The Astros, Pettitte, and the Hendrickses met again on November 25, clarifying some matters. McLane intended to keep the meeting a secret, denying that they had even met. But word of the meeting leaked out to a local television station. McLane denied the story, and Randy Hendricks told the station that they had met with Houston officials to clarify some matters previously discussed. Suddenly, some Astros officials and the Hendrickses were privately wondering if somebody within the organization was trying to sabotage the deal by leaking a supposed offer.

Not wanting to build false hope for the fans of Houston, McLane vehemently denied the television report. He didn't just deny making an offer to Pettitte's agents; he said serious negotiations had not even started. He also admitted that he expected the veteran left-hander to re-sign with the Yankees.

"The market leader is the Yankees because he's played there nine years," McLane said. "I would think the Yankees have more capacity, and they know him better. He's been there nine years. There's always an edge [to the player's former team], because a player has played with that team."

Asked specifically if the Astros had made a preliminary offer to Pettitte, McLane said he and the Hendrickses hadn't even had a serious negotiation session.

"They called and wanted to come out," McLane said of the Hendricks brothers. "Where they got [that an offer was made] got blown out of proportion. That wasn't a real negotiation session at all. When [the Hendrickses] were there the Tuesday before, they were there with Andy. They wanted to come back and talk business without him. There's not been a serious negotiation [with the Hendrickses]. We talked more about baseball in general and the World Series than anything else. This was not a negotiation session. They wanted to know our impression of Andy, and they wanted feedback. If anybody was saying that was a negotiation, they're wrong. We're not down to negotiations."

Those comments ran in the *Houston Chronicle*'s 2003 Thanksgiving edition, and it stunned Pettitte and the Hendrickses, making them wonder if McLane wanted to back out of the negotiations. Thanksgiving dinners were interrupted with tense conversations between Astros officials and Pettitte's agents. Asked to give assurances that he was serious about his interest in Pettitte, McLane, through his general manager, assured Alan Hendricks that he wasn't trying to bail out of the Pettitte sweepstakes.

"Alan called Gerry [Hunsicker a day after Thanksgiving], and we assured him that Gerry and I were excited about trying to get something done with Andy," McLane said.

While McLane was having Thanksgiving dinner with his family in Texas, his chances of landing Pettitte were getting a tremendous boost across the Southwest. In Arizona former Astros pitcher Curt Schilling, who credits Roger Clemens's tough counsel in the early 1990s during a workout at the Astrodome as a key to his ascension as a major league ace, played host to Boston Red Sox general manager Theo Epstein. The Red Sox had been interested in Pettitte, even making an offer that dwarfed the eventual deal he got from the Astros and the offer he received from the Yankees. But Epstein's recruiting pitch paid off with Schilling, who waived his no-trade clause in his contract with the Diamondbacks to head to Boston.

With Schilling on the Red Sox, the competition for Pettitte's services became a two-team race. With that in mind, McLane headed on his annual winter business trip to Poland vowing to monitor the negotiations via email and cellular phone. If Pettitte truly wanted to pitch closer to his wife and children in Houston, as many folks in baseball now believed, McLane said he was excited about finding the Deer Park resident a home at Minute Maid Park.

"Even though this is a complicated deal and he's a free agent and will have an opportunity with the Yankees, it's going to be a hard deal to get done," McLane said at the time. "We're optimistic that Gerry and I will look at every angle to get this deal done. We have a high motivation to get a deal done, but it has to be the right deal for the Astros and the right deal for Andy Pettitte. We're optimistic, and I can almost see Andy Pettitte pitching for the Houston Astros. But we have to wait to see where this takes us."

Pettitte's desire to play at home proved to be too powerful for the Yankees to overcome despite an offer of $39 million over three years from Yankees owner George Steinbrenner. Everything seemed set by

December 9, but the talks almost broke down between Hunsicker and the Hendrickses over minor language in the contract. Ultimately, McLane stepped in, driving from Minute Maid Park up Interstate 45 to the Hendrickses' offices. McLane and the Hendrickses went into the conference room and sat down on opposite sides of the table. McLane sat on the right corner, and Randy and Alan Hendricks sat toward the left corner.

"Do you really want to lose out on Andy Pettitte over this language?" Randy Hendricks asked.

"No," McLane replied emphatically.

Pettitte gave the Yankees one final shot to improve their offer, but Pettitte essentially had made his decision by the time he tucked his sons into bed on December 10.

The Astros announced the deal on December 11, sending the city into a craze unlike anything else in Houston since Hakeem Olajuwon led the Rockets to their second consecutive NBA title in 1995. Pettitte's signing sent the city into a tremendous lobbying campaign to lure Clemens out of retirement, capitalizing on the pull Clemens started feeling when Pettitte told him he was signing with the Astros.

Andy Pettitte ultimately chose the Astros so he could pitch closer to home. Here he is after signing with owner Drayton McLane's (left) club, joined by his wife, Laura, and their children and general manager Gerry Hunsicker.

"Lefty, this changes everything," Clemens told Pettitte shortly after Pettitte decided on the Astros.

Less than 24 hours after Pettitte was introduced as the newest Astro, a pair of Houston radio personalities got in on the act by offering Clemens a Hummer if he came out of retirement to pitch for the Astros. Dean and Rog were merely playing a prank, trying to have some fun with their Classic Rock station fans. The listeners of the popular morning show on 93.7 KKRW played along perfectly, showing Houston's excitement over possibly having Roger Clemens pitch at home.

Dean and Rog promised to visit Clemens's mansion to lobby him personally, and fans throughout Houston gave them exact directions with calls to their station. It seemed as though everyone knew where Roger and Debbie Clemens lived. Driving to the mansion in Houston's exclusive Memorial neighborhood, Dean and Rog received directions the whole way from their listeners. Dean remembered listeners saying, "Go this way. Turn here. Go there."

When they finally arrived, Debbie Clemens was already expecting them. Dean and Rog had figured they would see a front gate, talk into a speaker system, and go home patting themselves on the back for a genuinely clever prank. Instead, the shock jocks were the ones shocked by the jock. Dean and Rog were taken aback when they saw the gates to Clemens's mansion open right up.

"It was like going to Graceland," Dean said. "They were very gracious, and they love the city. I like the house. I want them to adopt me."

Clemens played along, saying that if he signed with the Astros, he would probably have to return the burnt orange Hummer his 2003 Yankees teammates, led by Pettitte, presented him with as a farewell gift. The problem was solved when prominent Houston car dealer Lee DeMontrond telephoned Dean and Rog to offer one of the Hummers from his dealership.

"This is getting very interesting," Clemens told the station. "I didn't know [by] making a comment like that you guys would show up in my front driveway with a burnt orange H2."

Asked if he would be in an Astros uniform in April 2004, Clemens said, "Maybe."

Soon after Pettitte signed with the Astros, McLane put on the charm, visiting with Clemens's family twice at the Clemens mansion which is 15 minutes from, Minute Maid Park. The final home visit, complete with 200 business cards with the words *Roger Clemens, Astros starting pitcher,* fell on December 23, the same day Clemens's older children were actually

Shortly after Pettitte signed, former teammate Roger Clemens joined him in Astros pinstripes. Here Clemens announces his signing with the support of Kody, his youngest son.

buying their father an Astros cap to be presented to him on Christmas day.

After visiting Clemens's home and seeing his six Cy Young Awards above the fireplace, McLane chose a military analogy to describe the hard-throwing right-hander's place in baseball history.

No matter how full of himself a brigadier, major, or lieutenant general might feel, he defers when the four-star general walks in a room, McLane pointed out. In the world of Cy Young Awards and victories, no active player is more accomplished than Clemens. Nonetheless, McLane wanted Clemens for more than the 310-160 career record and 4,099 strikeouts he posted through the first 20 seasons of his career.

"Part of the reason I wanted him was his leadership," McLane said. "Can you picture Roger helping the other guys? Have I not mentioned that leadership is the most important thing in the world? I told Roger, 'I hope I don't insult you, but only 50 percent of the reason we want you is your ability. The other is your leadership.'"

Clemens wouldn't have it any other way. He had enlisted Pettitte into his demanding workout routine in 1999, and McLane knew he would do the same with the other Astros starters.

"Roger is 41 years old, and he's going to be out there running extra," the Astros' Craig Biggio said at the time. "Are you just going to watch him run extra, or are you going to join him? Are you going to let an older man work harder than you? It's the little things like that that are going to be huge in helping those pitchers out."

With the permission of his family and an agreement from the Astros that he could miss road trips on days he wouldn't pitch, Clemens accepted McLane's one-year, $5 million contract on January 12, 2004. The deal came with a 10-year personal services contract worth $2 million and the gratitude of Astros fans, who packed Minute Maid Park for each of his starts.

After the signings, Houston fans literally sprinted to the Minute Maid Park box office. Current Astros vice president of business development John Sorrentino, the Astros' ticket manager at the time, kept dialing for help. He had already added four salespeople in December to cope with the extra volume for ticket requests after Pettitte signed with the team. The heavy season in the Astros ticket office is usually late February, but Christmas came early and late for Sorrentino and McLane.

Pettitte's signing prompted Sorrentino to open the ticket office on Saturdays, which was rare during the winter. Staff members even came into work on Sundays, but nothing in the history of the franchise prepared them for January 12, 2004. With each story in the *Houston Chronicle* updating the negotiations between Clemens and the Astros, the phones in the ticket office rang more consistently, Sorrentino recalled. Once word of the signing began circulating throughout the city early on January 12, Sorrentino found his office's phone system ill equipped to handle the volume of calls.

The phone system at Minute Maid Park was overloaded, making it impossible for club officials to make outgoing calls until late that night. McLane ordered more telephone lines and allowed Sorrentino to hire temporary personnel to help field calls. By the time Sorrentino left his office at about 10 p.m., the Astros had sold nearly 1,000 season tickets—in one day.

By the time the season started, Sorrentino's staff had sold a little more than 20,000 season tickets, and the Astros were on their way to drawing three million fans for only the second time in franchise history.

"I've never had anything like today in my 18 seasons with the franchise," Sorrentino said on January 12, 2004. "Our phones haven't stopped ringing since 10 a.m."

The defections of Andy Pettitte and Roger Clemens filled the back pages of New York's famous tabloids, drawing disparate reactions. After the signings, Yankees fans ripped Steinbrenner for letting the beloved left-hander go. Even the great Whitey Ford, whom Pettitte was being compared to as the top left-hander in Yankees history, aired his disappointment.

In Houston, Pettitte and Clemens were welcomed back as conquering heroes. The tape job disgruntled closer Billy Wagner predicted for the roster could not have been further from the reality of the 2004 Astros season, a year in which McLane landed two of the top free agent pitchers on the market and the top player on the trade market in June when All-Star Carlos Beltran was acquired from the Kansas City Royals in a three-team deal.

Shortly after Pettitte signed, the people of Houston began a lobbying campaign unlike any other in the city's history to try to get Clemens into an Astros uniform. Quite simply, the city of Houston could not get enough of Clemens and Pettitte, both of whom grew up within a short drive of the Astrodome and currently live within 15 to 30 minutes from the ballpark.

With Clemens joining the Astros, Bagwell, Biggio, and Pettitte believed that they should win the National League Central in 2004. Clemens welcomed the responsibility of trying to contribute to Houston's first World Series appearance. That was a lofty goal for a franchise that had never won a postseason series before Clemens and Pettitte landed in Houston and had not even been in the playoffs since the Atlanta Braves swept them in the 2001 division series. But the World

Series talk grew loud around Houston once Clemens signed with the Astros.

"We're trying to get to the playoffs, and that's not the only goal," Clemens said. "The first thing [McLane] said when he went to my house was, 'I've been to the playoffs. I want to win the World Series.' I hear him loud and clear."

Clemens settled into his Astros pinstripes with two World Series rings, both with the Yankees, and five trips to the World Series (four with the Yankees, one with the Red Sox) over the first 20 years of his career.

"The things I've had with my [former] teamates, you can't re-create those moments." Clemens explained. "Starting today [with the Astros], we got to create some new memories."

With Clemens, Pettitte, Roy Oswalt, Wade Miller, and Tim Redding, Astros manager Jimy Williams opened the 2004 season with what was considered one of the most impressive starting rotations in baseball.

"We expect to win. I can promise you that," said Pettitte, whose 14 postseason victories place him second on the all-time postseason victories list. "With adding Roger, and if we can all stay healthy, we expect that we should be able to win this division and go on from there."

Even future Hall of Famers such as Bagwell and Biggio were turned into fans when they first saw Clemens don an Astros uniform the day he was introduced as the team's newest pitcher.

"Like I told [Bagwell], I'm a fan today," said Biggio, who has long had an autographed Clemens jersey hanging at his home. "I'm sitting over there, and you get goosebumps when you get to walk out to the mound and take a picture [with Clemens, Pettitte, and Bagwell]. That's Clemens. I mean, that's Clemens—Roger Clemens is going to be on your team!"

The reaction in New York wasn't as positive. In New York, the phone lines were busy with angry calls to sports talk radio shows. The tabloids had a blast, trying to outdo each other with critical headlines on the back pages.

"Roger the Rat" cried out the *New York Post* on its front page. On the back page, the *Post* ran a picture of Clemens in an Astros uniform and an Astros cap with the headline: "What an ASStro! Traitor Roger Unretires, Joins Pettitte in Houston."

The (New York) *Daily News's* headline on the front page was "Traitor! Roger Clemens Unretires to Sign with Houston—Yankees Fans Tell Him What They Think." On the back page, *The News* declared: "Texas Two-Face. Turncoat Clemens Becomes Pride of the Astros."

Yankees officials, who could have made it difficult for the Astros to sign Clemens by offering the right-hander salary arbitration a month earlier, were a bit more restrained.

"Did I talk to him about retiring? Yeah," Yankees general manager Brian Cashman told the New York media. "He said he was taking it to the house. ... He doesn't need to justify his decision to me. If I talk to him, I'll ask how his family's doing and how he's doing. We're going to concentrate on the 2004 Yankees, and obviously, he's going to concentrate on the 2004 Astros. They're going to get one of the greatest competitors of all time."

Steinbrenner praised Clemens in a statement: "Roger Clemens was a great warrior for the Yankees—a teacher and a leader. He told the world he was retiring, and we had no choice but to believe him."

Many in New York accused Pettitte, Clemens, and their Houston-based agents of conspiring with the Astros to land both pitchers in Houston. If that were the case, this story wouldn't be so interesting.

These deals were far more complicated, involving some people needing to rebuild bridges before beginning serious negotiations. The story is far more fascinating considering the hard feelings between Hunsicker and the Hendrickses. When the Astros traded popular closer Billy Wagner to the Phillies in November, hoping to trim the payroll to $65 million, fans in Houston crucified McLane.

After selling only 15,000 season tickets in 2003, down from 22,000 season tickets only three years earlier, the Astros saw a tremendous backlash from season-ticket holders after the Wagner trade. Considering the Wagner backlash, some folks thought the Astros would have been lucky to sell 10,000 season tickets in 2004 even with the hook of the 2004 All-Star Game, which was scheduled to be played at Minute Maid Park.

McLane's critics and even his biggest supporters never imagined after the Wagner trade that he'd walk away with two of the prettiest Houston babes on that winter's free agent market, setting in motion the Astros' drive to their first World Series appearance and changing Houston Astros baseball and the city's bond to the franchise, as Pettitte, Clemens, and young ace Roy Oswalt led the away to the National League pennant in 2005.

2

Biggio and Bagwell

When Roger Clemens considered joining the Astros, he placed two calls. One was to Jeff Bagwell. The other was to Craig Biggio. These two men are essentially the symbols of the Houston Astros organization. Clemens would end his retirement only if he could miss some road trips while devoting time to his four sons. Clemens wanted to make sure that agreement wasn't a problem, so he went to the team's two elders to ask. He went on a golf outing with Bagwell to the exclusive Shadow Hawk Golf Course, where Bagwell claims to have been leading their game before they cut the outing short of 18 holes. That outing followed a dinner with Clemens at Biggio's home days earlier.

Biggio and Bagwell gave their permission, realizing the 2004 season might be the Astros' last opportunity to do something special with this core of players. By the end of the 2003 season, Bagwell already knew his and Biggio's baseball days were nearing an end. Yet, it is not easy for him to embrace the thought of playing on an Astros club without Biggio.

"It's very difficult to think of the Astros without [Biggio] when [he has] been here for [18] years," said Bagwell, who has teamed with Biggio since 1991. "That said, there's going to come a time when Craig isn't going to be here and I'm not going to be here."

To many people in Houston, Biggio isn't just part of the organization. He is the Astros, the person many young adults grew up idolizing in Houston.

"It's weird," said Biggio, who made his club record 17th opening-day start on April 3, 2005. "Sooner or later it's going to happen. Who knows when that's going to happen? For me, personally, I know how much

Veterans Craig Biggio and Jeff Bagwell anchored the Astros through the 1990s. They led the team as new Astros stars like Morgan Ensberg have risen up the ranks.

longer I want to play. I'm just focused on going out there and playing this year and doing the best job I can and hopefully something special will happen for us as a team and a city."

For much of their careers, Bagwell and Biggio had to carry the Astros on their own. If they struggled, so did the team. In 2004 and 2005, however, Bagwell and Biggio no longer had to carry their teammates. Guys like Carlos Beltran, Lance Berkman, and Jeff Kent carried the team's offense in the 2004 postseason. In 2005, Roy Oswalt, Clemens, Andy Pettitte, and Brandon Backe carried the burden on their shoulders all the way to the World Series as Berkman sparked the offense all the way through the World Series while Morgan Ensberg played well through the first two rounds despite tissue damage on his right hand.

Kent became an important presence in the middle of the Astros order, and Richard Hidalgo was the team MVP in 2003 after consecutive disappointing seasons in 2001 and 2002. Although much of Kent's two-year, $17.5 million contract was deferred, the annual average value of his deal is $10 million, which was a $2.5 million raise over 2003. Hidalgo's 2004 salary was $12.5 million, but he was traded midway through the 2004 season. Hidalgo's four-year, $32 million deal goes down as one of the worst contracts ever given by general manager Gerry Hunsicker.

Conversely, Kent lived up to his deal. But the Astros declined a $9 million club option on Kent for the 2005 season with a $700,000 buyout, losing the man that likely would have made the difference in a year they missed at least one other run producer for a team with only Berkman and Ensberg as consistently legitimate threats in the middle of the order. Jason Lane became a serious offensive threat toward the end of the season. But there's no doubt Kent's ability to annually produce 100 RBI would have forced pitchers to reconsider their decisions to pitch around Berkman throughout the 2005 postseason.

When talking about the Astros, though, it starts with the Killer B's, especially Biggio and Bagwell.

Although baseball has meant Biggio and Bagwell in Houston for a generation of fans, it never would have worked out this way if the good folks of Boston could rewrite history. Bagwell, a Boston native who grew up in Connecticut, was bred to play for the Red Sox. His swing was perfectly suited to conquer the Green Monster at Fenway Park. Janice Bagwell, Jeff's mother, was certain her son was meant to play for her beloved Red Sox. As far as she was concerned, the Astros might as well have been in the minor leagues, because that is what she thought of the National League.

She raised her son just the way her dear father, Robert Hare, had raised her: to love the Red Sox. Hare, a labor relations manager for the Raytheon Company, which made electronics, took his eldest daughter Janice to Fenway Park at least three times a year. Six years older than her brother, Robert, and 17 years older than her sister, Kathy, Janice got plenty of baseball lessons early. At a time when girls weren't encouraged to play sports, Robert Hare always played catch and baseball with Janice outside their home in Newton, Massachusetts, which Janice quickly tells you is only about 10 minutes from Fenway.

Janice was only eight in 1949 when her father took her to Fenway for the first time to see his favorite player, Ted Williams. She had just celebrated her first birthday in 1941 as Teddy Ballgame was closing out the last .400 (.406) season in major league history. Some of Janice's best childhood memories are of her father taking her to Fenway on her birthday, especially her first visits to the stadium.

"I was kind of in awe," says Janice, who was actually born exactly 22 years after Teddy Ballgame. "The size of it, all the people, all the fans, the openness. For me as a young girl growing up, going to Fenway was a real treat. My father would buy some kind of a souvenir for me, whether it was a pennant or a cup. He would always buy me something from the Red Sox. You know, he probably saved up for a while to take me. Sometimes when it came around my birthday, he would surprise me and say, 'We're going to go to Fenway.' It was something to look forward to. That was kind of like a present. That was very nice. As a child, you look forward to these things. Obviously, these memories last through life. I still love going to baseball games. I kind of grew up with the love of baseball, basically. My dad, of course, loved Ted Williams, and Jeff loved Carl Yastrzemski."

Robert Bagwell, Jeff's father, also built fond memories at Fenway early in his life. He was born in Boston and spent the early part of his life in Beantown. Bernard Bagwell, known as Barney, started taking a young Robert to Red Sox games in the late 1940s.

"I was a big Ted Williams fan," Robert Bagwell said. "I used to go to college at Northeastern, and sometimes I'd sit in the bleachers. Baseball is a big part of my life."

Together, Robert Bagwell and the former Janice Hare married and soon passed on their devotion to their son, Jeff, a star baseball and soccer player at Xavier (Connecticut) High. Like every loyal Red Sox fan, Jeff Bagwell has watched a few games at Fenway behind some of those poles that obstruct the view.

"About 20 or 30 years ago, they used to play doubleheaders on Sunday," Jeff Bagwell remembered. "My dad used to take me to those games just so we could see two games. We'd go early to see batting practice. I remember Bo Jackson [of the Kansas City Royals once] make a throw from the outfield wall to home plate on a line. I also remember sitting behind one of those poles on the first base side."

After graduating from high school, Bagwell started drawing attention at the University of Hartford, where he hit better than .400 in each of his three seasons there and hit safely in 87 of his 112 games. He played in tryout camps and college all-star games at Fenway in the late 1980s. He also visited Yankee Stadium for a tryout camp in 1989.

"I told him, 'Well, you don't have to do well today,' because I didn't want him to have anything to do with the Yankees," Robert Bagwell said.

When the June 1989 draft rolled around, three rounds passed before the Red Sox picked the man who would become the National League Rookie of the Year two years later and the National League Most Valuable Player five seasons later. The Red Sox, who picked Biggio's former Seton Hall University teammate, Mo Vaughn, in the first round of the 1989 June draft, picked Bagwell in the fourth round. Bagwell played five games in the Gulf Coast League in 1989 before jumping to Low-A Winter Haven, where he had 65 hits in 64 games. The next year he was the Class AA Eastern League Most Valuable Player after hitting .333 at New Britain. He lost the Eastern League batting title by a point, despite leading the league with 160 hits, 220 total bases, and 34 doubles. That

1990 season definitely caught the attention of the Astros, who pounced when Boston asked for veteran reliever Larry Anderson down the pennant stretch. With Wade Boggs entrenched at third base for the Red Sox, Bagwell seemed dispensable.

August 31 had always brought up great memories for Janice Bagwell. As a child, it was always the day after the wonderful birthday trip with her father to Fenway. But on August 31, 1990, there was no joy because that's the day her dear Red Sox dumped her kid to the Astros.

The Astros? In the National League?

"I was thinking, 'Who are the Astros?' I'm an American League fan, and I just watched the Red Sox. Unless it was the World Series, I didn't see the National League teams," Janice remembered. "That tragedy—it felt like a tragedy to me—turned out to be a wonderful moment with the Astros. He got to the major leagues as opposed to languishing in the minors. I think I cried off and on for a week.

"I thought it was the end of everything. He's a nice guy. He truly is easy to get along with. He never says, 'It all about me.' It's always a team effort for him. He was a wonderful boy growing up. That translates to a wonderful man. They would have loved him at Fenway. The left field wall would have been perfect for him. As I look back now, I'm glad it didn't happen."

Robert Bagwell's initial reaction to the trade also was disappointment, but he ultimately became the voice of optimism for his dejected son. Robert compared the Astros and Red Sox rosters and realized the trade would be a blessing in disguise. The Red Sox had Boggs, a perennial American League batting title threat and ultimate Hall of Famer, starting in the majors in 1991. Houston, absent from the playoffs since 1986 and in the middle of a rebuilding process, had youngster Ken Caminiti at third base, but an opening at first base.

Bagwell, helped by coach Matt Galante, made the switch across the diamond with ease during his first spring training with the Astros and started opening day 1991 at first base. Bagwell finished his rookie season with a .294 batting average, 15 home runs, 82 RBI, and 75 walks to become the Astros' first and only National League Rookie of the Year. He earned all but one of the 24 first-place votes from the Baseball Writers Association of America. He also was the Astros' 1991 MVP, *Baseball America*'s Major League Rookie of the Year, and a member of *The Sporting News*' postseason All-Star team. Not bad for a guy who would have been stuck in Boston's farm system that year if he had not been traded to the Astros.

"After that, I was thrilled because he was Rookie of the Year in 1991," Janice said. "He loved the people. After that first year, I thought it was a very good move. I was so happy for him. Fourteen years is a long time for anybody."

In this era, Bagwell's long tenure with one organization is definitely rare. To have two players with at least 15 seasons together is a credit to Astros owner Drayton McLane, Bagwell and Biggio, and their superb agent, Barry Axelrod. No active pair of teammates has played together longer than Biggio and Bagwell have.

"It's definitely important to have players with the same team for a long time," Bagwell says. "In today's game with all the people saying it's not about the money when it's really all about the money for the players and the teams, you don't see many people stay with the same team anymore. When you were a kid, you always had people with the same organization a long time. I had Carl Yastrzemski, and my dad had Ted Williams. I don't compare myself to those guys, but I think it's important. I used to hit like a right-handed Carl Yastrzemski when I was a kid. Now maybe kids hit like me or Bidge or even later Lance Berkman. I think those things are important."

Biggio and Bagwell have done their part to fill the seats at the Astrodome and later at Enron Field-turned-Minute Maid Park. Biggio leads the Astros franchise in hits, games played, doubles, and several other categories.

Perhaps more than any of his Astros teammates, Biggio makes his children a part of every milestone he sets. His sons, Conor and Cavan, are two of the most beloved presences in the Astros' clubhouse, often playing catch with their father or with other players hoping to warm up. When a coach needs to throw batting practice, it is not uncommon for him to ask one of Biggio's boys for assistance. Craig and Patty Biggio have even developed a system in which Biggio divides his most prized mementoes among his children. Each time Biggio collects a ball from his latest achievement, he passes it down to the child whose turn it is on the memento rotation.

On the day the Astros won the 2005 National League wild card, Biggio signed a four-year, $4 million contract to return in 2006. Barring injury, he is on pace to collect his 3,000th hit early in the 2007 season. And there's no doubt he'll re-sign with the Astros to continue that quest if he remains healthy and willing.

Biggio, the Astros' first-round pick out of Seton Hall in 1987, has done almost everything the organization has asked while staying in the important middle of the field. He broke into the majors in 1988 as a catcher, becoming the first Astros catcher to make an All-Star team in 1991, the same season his teammate Bagwell was a rookie. The next season, Biggio moved to second base, becoming the first player in Major

League Baseball history to make the All-Star team as a catcher and second baseman. A seven-time All-Star, Biggio made his final switch at the age of 37 when he moved to center field in 2003. Two years later, he didn't switch as much as he returned home to start at second base for the NL champions after Kent left via free agency.

Bagwell has remained at first base throughout his career, but it has been anything but easy. He has played with an arthritic right shoulder since 2001 and with pins attaching his labrum since 2002. Bagwell jokes that his five-year-old daughter, Bryce, and three-year-old daughter, Blake, throw farther than he can, and he is not far off in his assessment. Nonetheless, Bagwell has never made excuses or alibis. He merely kept marching toward 500 home runs, which he was on pace to reach by the end of the 2005 season or the start of the 2006 season until his right shoulder finally gave out and landed him on the disabled list in May 2005.

Life definitely would have been different if he had remained in Boston, where Red Sox players can hardly walk around without being bugged. Bagwell doesn't have such a problem in Houston, where Southern hospitality and manners provide a calm existence for people like Bagwell and Biggio away from the field.

"I'm perfectly happy with the way my life has transpired and with how my status is in Houston," Bagwell says. "I don't need it any other way. It's very easy to walk around this town. I get recognized, but people don't say anything. The funny part is, for years people would say, 'Hey, Biggio! I'd say, 'Come on. I'm taller and I can grow facial hair.' But that's the interpretation people have here when they see me or Biggio. They know it is Biggio or Bagwell."

3

The Friendship

"I wouldn't be here if it wasn't for you."

—Roger Clemens to Andy Pettitte on the day Clemens surpassed Steve
Carlton for second on the all-time strikeout list

A ndy Pettitte has grown accustomed to congratulating Roger Clemens for special feats, but he still cannot fully embrace what impact he has had on his good friend. Ever since Clemens signed with the Astros, he has repeatedly said he would still be retired if Pettitte had not signed first. Clemens said as much on January 12, 2004, when he was introduced as an Astro, and he repeated that comment almost a hundred times before that opening day. Yet, after Pettitte congratulated Clemens for passing Steve Carlton for second place on the all-time strikeout list on May 5, 2004, Clemens responded by saying, "I wouldn't be here if it wasn't for you."

"When I think about him saying he's coming over here just because I signed, I didn't really understand it that much," Pettitte said that day. "I appreciated that. I felt like if we were both able to come over here, we wanted to try to do something special. That was the whole reasoning behind it. We want to have a chance to maybe try to get to another World Series with me, him, Roy [Oswalt], Wade [Miller], and Redding. It's very flattering, I guess."

Pettitte was in the Yankees dugout for Clemens's 300th victory on June 13, 2003, at Yankee Stadium against the St. Louis Cardinals. He was there for the sixth Cy Young Award and the two World Series rings with the Yankees. He had been there through the grueling workouts in Houston and the tough losses in New York, developing a bond comparable to any formed by close friends. Yet, Pettitte was always humbled and

Roger Clemens and Andy Pettitte changed the entire landscape of baseball in Houston.

surprised every time Clemens said he joined the Astros only because of Pettitte's decision to do the same.

"It's awesome to see everything that he's been able to do and all the records and all the stuff he did in New York while he was there," Pettitte said. "I'm used to it, and I feel like he let me be a big part of it all just because of all the work we've done together. We've kind of used each other to push each other. It's a long season and a hard season, so you get tired. But he's always let me be a part of everything that he's done. It's been cool for me, obviously."

Since Clemens joined the Yankees for the 1999 season, both Houston residents quickly developed a bond. Pettitte, 10 years younger than Clemens, bought into Clemens's tough workout regimen. They were seemingly always together in the Bronx during the season or in Houston during the offseason. But it would be a mistake to think Pettitte always liked Clemens. Sure, as a baseball fan growing up in the Houston suburb of Deer Park, Pettitte definitely respected Clemens. Clemens was to Pettitte what Nolan Ryan was to Clemens's generation of baseball players from Houston: an icon worthy of admiration. Pettitte even attended San Jacinto College in 1991, 10 years after Clemens earned All-America status at that school. Clemens had reached stardom and was headed for his third Cy Young Award with the Boston Red Sox by the time Pettitte signed with the Yankees as a draft-and-follow guy on May 25, 1991, after being selected the previous June in the 22nd round.

After reaching the majors in 1995 with the Yankees, it didn't take Pettitte very long to develop the dislike most Yankees had for the mean, hard-throwing right-hander who hurled for the Yanks' archrival Boston Red Sox. The Yankees hated Clemens's menacing nature and the unapologetic way he owned the inside part of the plate.

"I always liked him because of just growing up in Houston, but I think it's kind of like an ongoing joke that when you're competing against him you learn to hate him," Pettitte said. "The first time I ever met him was in 1996. I was pitching against him at Boston and walking to the bullpen, and he just gave me a little pep talk. I can't even remember what he said, but you know the way Roger talks. He said something about bringing a championship to the American League. I think it was his last start at Fenway Park."

Clemens suffered the second losing season of his career in 1996, going 10-13 with a 3.63 ERA in 34 starts. Even though Clemens led the American League with 257 strikeouts that season, then-Red Sox general manager Dan Duquette thought The Rocket was in decline and let him get away after that year. Clemens signed a four-year contract with the Toronto Blue Jays on December 13, 1996, and he wasted no time proving

Duquette wrong by winning his fourth Cy Young Award in 1997 after going 21-7 with a 2.05 ERA in 34 starts. He won the Cy Young Award again in 1998, finishing that stellar season with a 20-6 record and a 2.65 ERA. Equally important, Clemens had a handshake deal with the Blue Jays, allowing him to bail out of the contract after two years if he wished. He took them up on that offer, and the Hendrickses tried to work out a trade to the Astros. The Astros refused to give up right-hander Scott Elarton and right fielder Richard Hidalgo, so Clemens landed in the Bronx in exchange for left-handed starter David Wells, reliever Graeme Lloyd, and utility man Homer Bush.

Clemens earned his first World Series ring in 1999 when the Yankees beat the Atlanta Braves. He won his second ring the next season in the Subway Series against the New York Mets. Clemens, who won his sixth Cy Young in 2001 with the Yankees, was credited with helping Pettitte grow as a pitcher. But it would be a mistake to think Pettitte wasn't a star in his own right by the time Clemens joined the Yankees.

Pettitte had two World Series rings, a 21-win season, and 67 major league victories under his belt before Clemens ended up in the Bronx. He was a major part of that 1996 Yankees club that gave the Bronx Bombers their first World Series appearance since 1981. Along with Bernie Williams, Derek Jeter, Jorge Posada, and Mariano Rivera, Pettitte will go down as a key member of the core of young players who helped reestablish the winning tradition at Yankee Stadium. With 149 victories as a Yankee, Pettitte was making a run at the team's all-time victories record. He was already in ninth place and within close range of leader Whitey Ford's 236 victories. His 13 postseason victories in New York are the most in the Yankees' rich history.

"It was my first team," Pettitte said of the Yankees. "Obviously that was special for me. I guess it was special that I was a big part of the start of it all again because we were so bad for so many years there. Then in '95 I was able to get in the rotation and as a young kid be put in a serious, serious, pressure-packed situation where I was pitching on three days' rest to try to make the wild card spot—me and three different guys in the rotation. It was me and [Jimmy] Key and [Jack] McDowell and David Cone. We went to a four-man rotation toward the end of the year, trying to make the playoffs. I was able to make it. I was able to start Game 2 of the playoffs, and I started nine straight years in Game 2 of the division series. Then in 1996, me and Cone were the guys there. That's the year [Cone] had an aneurysm and came back. Young in my career, I was thrown into the fire and was able to get through it. That's where I grew as a big league guy. Everything else is just called maturing and getting stronger, fine-tuning, trying to fine-tune the edges to be as consistent as you possibly can."

It only takes one day in Yankees pinstripes to realize and understand the significance of that uniform. And Pettitte embraced his place in history, which is why one can sense a tinge of disappointment in his voice for not being a Yankee anymore.

"I'd be lying if I said I didn't want to [chase some of the Yankee records]," Pettitte said. "A lot of that had to do with Roger and seeing how he goes about the game and the things that he does. I started paying a little bit of attention. Then all of a sudden, they started telling me I was fifth on the all-time strikeout list in Yankees history. All of a sudden they started telling me all the guys I was passing up and stuff over the last few years. Then, all of a sudden, you start thinking about that stuff.

"I realize what I've done there, and I'm proud of what I've done there. What else can you ask for? Nine straight years of going to the play-offs and going to the World Series six times. It's just always going to be a special, special place."

And what about his favorite moment?

"No doubt the first time we won it. Probably, on a personal level, it was going to Atlanta and pitching Game 5 after pitching Game 1 and getting beat up like I did, and then being able to come back against [John] Smoltz and win that game 1-0," Pettitte said. "That gave us a 3-2 victory. We won three in a row at Atlanta, and went home and won Game 6. That's definitely my most memorable moment."

But Pettitte got off to a much rougher start in Houston. With 50 of Andy Pettitte's friends and relatives amid the crowd of 40,660 at Minute Maid Park for his Astros debut April 6, 2004, Pettitte struggled as the San Francisco Giants had their way. Pettitte lasted only $5\frac{1}{3}$ innings, giving up 11 hits and six runs with two walks and three strikeouts on the way to a 7-5 loss. Even worse, he suffered a strained left elbow in his first at-bat with the Astros. With the bases loaded and no outs in the bottom of the first inning, Pettitte checked his swing and felt a twinge in his elbow right away. He tried to shake off the pain, but he couldn't. He eventually was called out on strikes. Craig Biggio gave the Astros a 1-0 lead with an RBI walk, but Brett Tomko escaped by striking out Adam Everett and Jeff Bagwell to set the tone for a game in which the Astros stranded 16. But the Astros loaded the bases in the fifth with three consecutive singles. Everett led off with an infield single to short. Bagwell followed with a single to center, prompting Giants manager Felipe Alou to pull Tomko. Trailing 4-1 in the bottom of the fifth, Jeff Kent greeted reliever Jim Brower with an RBI single to center. Lance Berkman kept the rally going with a walk, loading the bases for Richard Hidalgo, who was robbed when Neifi Perez made a leaping grab on a line drive to short. Mike Lamb's sacrifice fly to center field cut the Giants' lead to 4-3, and Brad Ausmus reloaded the bases with a dribbler to third. Pettitte was allowed to hit for himself and stranded the bases loaded by striking out on three pitches. Jimy Williams might as well have called for a pinch hitter with the bases loaded, because the ailing Pettitte gave up two more runs while failing to get out of the sixth. Marquis Grissom led off with an infield single to third, and Perez followed with an RBI double to center. Pettitte was finally lifted after giving up pinch hitter Pedro Feliz's RBI single to left field.

"To pitch [5⅓ innings] and give up six runs, that's terrible," Pettitte said. "It was very disappointing."

Nonetheless, Pettitte quickly realized he was no longer in the Bronx as the near-sellout crowd gave him a standing ovation when he walked off the mound.

"No matter how I did, I was probably going to get that [ovation]," he said. "Give me a few more starts like that, and they'll probably be booing. Again, there was so much buildup and excitement for the fans. It's disappointing to go out there and really to feel like you had gotten into a pretty good groove in the first three innings."

The Astros knew Pettitte's recent history of elbow problems, and they felt comfortable giving him his three-year, $31.5 million deal after reviewing copies of past magnetic resonance imaging exams that had been taken on his left elbow. Nonetheless, there was definitely some concern in the Astros front office after Pettitte acknowledged tenderness in his elbow a day after losing to the Giants. Two days after the loss, he had an MRI exam that revealed inflammation in his left elbow and a strain in his flexor tendon. Considering the more devastating possibilities, the diagnosis was seen as a positive. But Pettitte didn't feel much better that afternoon while playing catch at Minute Maid Park before the Astros flew to Milwaukee. He played catch again the next afternoon at Milwaukee's Miller Park with knuckleballer Jared Fernandez, who said he didn't notice any problems. By April 9, however, the Astros decided to put Pettitte on the 15-day disabled list after he cut short the session of catch with Fernandez. That stint on the disabled list was the third of his career with elbow problems. Although he also was on the disabled list in 1999 from April 4 to 17 and in 2002 from April 21 to June 14, he never bought into the rumors that concern about his left elbow was the reason the Yankees failed to overwhelm him into re-signing after nine successful seasons in the Bronx.

Pettitte was 21-8 with a 4.02 ERA in 33 regular-season starts with the Yankees in 2003, winning 17 of his final 20 decisions after a career-high four-game losing streak. The 33 starts were his most since he made 35 in 1997. He followed that regular season with a 3-1 record and 2.10 ERA that postseason.

"They offered me $40 million (actually $39 million) over three years," Pettitte said of the Yankees. "If they thought I had that bad of an elbow, why would they offer me that? I just look at [the fact that] I threw the best postseason of my career. It's not even an issue to me. I don't even talk about it. What more do they want me to do? I won 24 games. It's frustrating, because I just spent the whole offseason taking batting practice to make sure my back was going to be ready. It's frustrating. That's part of it now. It just happened. For me, it's going to be a long two starts waiting. But in the long scheme of things, hopefully I won't have any more problems."

Unfortunately for Pettitte and the Astros, his stint on the disabled list in April was only the start of his elbow problems in 2004.

Clemens urged the four other members of the rotation to help pick up the slack while Pettitte was on the disabled list. Although Jared Fernandez and Brandon Duckworth weren't very good in spot starts in place of Pettitte, the Astros won in all three of the turns in the rotation Pettitte would have taken if he had not been on the disabled list. More impressively and importantly, Pettitte returned from the disabled list on April 29 and beat Pittsburgh 2-0. He followed that outing with a 4-3 victory over the Pirates on May 4. Five days later, he beat Atlanta at Turner Field 2-1 in a pitchers duel against Braves ace right-hander Russ Ortiz.

The victory over the Braves set a perfect hook for the New York media heading into the Astros' series against the Mets. Of the six New York-area newspapers that follow the Mets, only *The New York Times* and *The* (Westchester) *Journal News* didn't send two reporters in to set up coverage for Clemens and Pettitte versus Mike Piazza and company. Even *Sports Illustrated* sent its lead baseball writer to Houston for the series. The confrontation against the Mets was of only minor importance for Pettitte, though. He had truly more important concerns as a family friend, R.D. Crumley, 65, was on his deathbed. Pettitte was 15 when he met Crumley, a deacon at Second Baptist in Deer Park, where Pettitte's father-in-law is the pastor.

Pettitte co-owned a hunting ranch in South Texas with Crumley, and he had never been hunting or to their ranch without his close friend. (In fact, Crumley had taken him hunting since he was 15 years old.) They always finished the hunting season by going to the ranch a final time before spring training. Their 2004 trip was no different until Pettitte noticed that Crumley continually coughed up blood as they drove back home to Deer Park.

"Go get that checked out," Pettitte told Crumley, who was diagnosed to have a cancerous tumor behind the esophagus. Further tests revealed cancer in both lungs and the lymph nodes.

"Here we are almost three months later," Pettitte said, "and it just ate him up."

Crumley's health deteriorated rapidly, and he landed in the hospital for good on May 9 as Pettitte was beating the Braves in Atlanta. The Astros returned to Houston late on May 9, and Pettitte rushed to the hospital to be with Crumley's family. He remained there most of the night and visited him daily to pray as Crumley hung on through life support. Crumley never regained consciousness.

Only a few of the Astros knew Pettitte's burden as the hype grew for the upcoming series against the Mets. On the outside, everything seemed fine as Pettitte cheered on his teammates during the three-game series against the defending World Series champion Florida Marlins. Pettitte even brought out his sense of humor on May 15, asking a conference room full of New York media whether he was addressing them before a World Series game. Pettitte seemed at ease, jovial even as he answered questions about life at home and Clemens's tremendous start to the 2004 season. Inside, however, Pettitte braced for the inevitable. He returned to Minute Maid Park on May 16. Then he got a call from Crumley's wife, Joyce, at about 2 p.m., four hours before he was set to start against the Mets.

"The doctors basically said they knew there was nothing else they could do for him," Pettitte said. "They called me, and their family thought that I needed to be there. I was like, 'I can't come. I've got to pitch.' I just told them that as soon I got pulled out of the game, I'd be there. I guess they turned the [life support] machines off, they said, around five o'clock."

Ausmus approached Pettitte before the game, and Pettitte assured his backstop he'd be fine. Pettitte sure was. He gave up six hits and four runs with eight strikeouts in six innings before a sellout crowd of 42,581. He retired the first 11 batters in a row.

"Pettitte's awesome," Mets left fielder Cliff Floyd said. "He knows how to pitch. It's a great pickup for the Astros. He's a competitor. He got through some tough innings out there. We almost got him, but that shows you how poised he is. That's a good pitcher there."

As fate would have it, Pettitte didn't give up a hit until about the time Crumley's family called Pettitte's wife, Laura, in the fourth inning to tell them Crumley had just succumbed to cancer. Pettitte had been leading

4-0 in the fourth when Floyd hit a one-out single to center field for the Mets' first hit. Mike Piazza followed with a walk, and Shane Spencer added an RBI single to center. Jason Phillips cut the deficit to 4-3 with a two-run double to left-center.

The Astros increased their lead to 5-3 with a run off right-handed reliever Orber Moreno in the fifth. With two outs, Morgan Ensberg set up the run with a single to second. Ausmus followed with a single up the middle. Pettitte, who entered the at-bat zero for eight for the season and had stranded two runners earlier in the game, came through with a single to center field for his first RBI of the season and only the third of his career. The Astros won 7-4, but nobody celebrated as Pettitte improved his record to 4-1 and 4-0 since coming off the disabled list.

"As soon as the game was over, I went to my wife and asked her if she had heard anything, and she said he had passed in the fourth inning," said Pettitte, who left the stadium immediately and remained with Crumley's family until 1 a.m. "He's like a father to me."

Crumley's death was the most devastating blow Pettitte endured in what became a frustratingly disappointing first season in Houston for a veteran left-hander.

4

Steinbrenner's Warrior

"I was real comfortable with my decision. Because I had told so many people that I was done and what they were seeing was it, to have this opportunity and this privilege to come back and put the uniform on again because of all the circumstances that figured into this decision, it's been pretty neat. To do it here at home and to drive 15 minutes and have my [four] boys here and be able to share time with them and do the things that I promised them—to be able to keep my word there, it makes it even more meaningful."

—Roger Clemens

Despite all the fuss in Houston, Roger Clemens's mind was still somewhere in the Bronx, the place where he had won his two championships and further secured his legacy among the greatest of all time. The buzz was already building around Minute Maid Park, where 42,863 of Clemens's neighbors would converge that April 7 night to give ovation after ovation, five in all, to the only six-time Cy Young Award winner in major league history.

The start to Clemens's seventh Cy Young season got underway with him on the mound hoping to avoid a three-game sweep in the first series of the Astros' much-hyped 2004 season.

As if Clemens's debut with the Astros wasn't enough of a draw, San Francisco Giants slugger Barry Bonds and his Hall of Fame godfather, Willie Mays, also were in town, threatening to put on a torch-passing ceremony at home plate. Yes, a ceremony at home plate if Bonds hit his second home run of the series, tying his godfather—and the Astros were damn pissed about the mere suggestion. Brad Ausmus, Jeff Bagwell, and Jeff Kent weren't just pissed—they were damn angry, actually, forcing Mays to back off this request a little.

Mays had already had a bittersweet celebration in Houston on September 13, 1965, when he hit his 500th home run off the Astros' Don Nottebart in the fourth inning. Houston resident Sallie B. Norman caught that historic home run, and she was in no mood to give it up when Mays offered to give her an autographed ball in exchange for the cherished memento.

"She can keep it," Mays, who gave Norman an autographed ball anyway, told Houston media in 1965. "I'm just happy to hit it. I just hope I hit another one tomorrow."

Bonds also had already collected a magical moment in Houston, tying the single-season home run record with his 70th on October 4, 2001, against hard-throwing rookie left-hander Wilfredo Rodriguez. Before a Minute Maid Park-record crowd of 43,734—most of them there to cheer Bonds—Rodriguez gave up the historic home run on a 1-1 fastball that was ripped into right-center field to tie the record St. Louis Cardinals first baseman Mark McGwire set in 1998.

In 2001, Astros manager Larry Dierker was dismayed at how the crowd turned against the Astros. On April 7, 2004, the crowd of 42,863 was firmly on the side of Clemens and the home team. But it was up to Clemens to send the Bonds and Mays show on the road without the momentous 660th home run of Bonds's career. For the first time in major league history, a 300-game winner would face a 600-home run hitter. With 659 home runs, Bonds was one home run shy of tying Mays for third on the all-time home-run list. Only a guy named Babe Ruth and another named Hank Aaron stood in front of Mays and Bonds.

Bonds even issued a vague threat, telling the media that Clemens should make sure he focused on his pitches.

Clemens heard about Bonds's little trash talking, but first things came first. Although Clemens had taken a shot at Yankees principal owner George Steinbrenner and his minions for not making a better run at retaining his good friend Andy Pettitte in December, there was still plenty of admiration between Clemens and Steinbrenner. After reading a letter he had received from The Boss, Clemens just knew he had to call Steinbrenner.

About four hours before throwing his first pitch in Astros pinstripes, Clemens picked up the phone and called Steinbrenner. Both men nearly cried, an incident that served as a prelude to Steinbrenner's crying episode a day later during a television interview before the Yankees' home opener.

"You're my warrior," Steinbrenner told Clemens, who responded by telling his former boss just how much he appreciated being able to spend five glorious years in Yankees pinstripes.

With their voices already cracking, Clemens ended the conversation before both men broke into tears, Clemens recalled.

The chat with Steinbrenner was only one of the things tugging at Clemens, whose ailing mother, Bess, had made the two-hour drive from Georgetown, Texas, to Houston the day before. For the first time since he pitched his last season at Spring Woods High in 1980, Clemens was set to pitch a meaningful game a short drive from his Houston home. He had started and been the Most Valuable Player of the 1986 All-Star Game at the Astrodome, but that was an exhibition. This time it would count, and the city of Houston was abuzz.

Everybody who was anybody in Houston was at Minute Maid Park on April 7, and nobody is bigger in Houston than Alvin's own Nolan Ryan. After a 15-year detour with the Texas Rangers, Ryan had been lured back to the Astros in February 2004 with a five-year personal services contract from Astros owner Drayton McLane. For the first time since Dr. John McMullen low-balled him, threatening to cut his salary 20 percent and essentially driving him to the Texas Rangers, Ryan was an employee of his hometown Houston Astros.

Ryan knew exactly what Clemens was going through. He had been in those shoes 24 years earlier, when he made his debut with the Astros in 1980 after 13 years with the New York Mets and California Angels. Until Clemens signed, the biggest moment in Astros history was Ryan's signing. The second biggest, and the one most Houstonians still lament, was Ryan's departure on December 7, 1988.

Ryan attended the entire three-game series against the Giants, but there was little to celebrate in the first two games. Bonds ruined Roy Oswalt's brilliant opening-day start with a three-run home run in the eighth inning. The Giants drove in the winning run in the ninth off new closer Octavio Dotel. Game 2 of the season, Andy Pettitte's homecoming after nine strong years with the Yankees, was actually worse.

Clemens was one of the few people who knew about Pettitte's injury. There was little doubt the hype surrounding the Astros' season would quickly die if the Giants completed the three-game sweep against Clemens. After 20 seasons in the majors, however, his first game with the Astros would pale in comparison to some of the big outings Clemens had made.

"His experience of pitching in so many big games will help him control his emotions," Ryan predicted during that day's batting practice. "Starting in the World Series last year, thinking it was his last start, I'm sure he's glad to be back out there. I think it makes for a very interesting game tonight. The fact that we've gotten out to a little bit of a slow start and that Barry is in town and needs one home run to tie Willie. And

[with] Roger's first start, I mean, there are a lot of factors that come into play.

"It's very interesting from the fan's standpoint and from baseball's standpoint. I'm just thrilled to be here and to get the opportunity to watch them."

If nothing else, Clemens was pleased to get the season started after a winter's worth of hype. And after 20 years in the American League, the future Hall of Famer began his 21st season in style. Reaching the mound at 7:06 p.m., he had to delay for nearly a minute as San Francisco leadoff man Ray Durham stepped away from the plate to let the sellout crowd give The Rocket a second standing ovation of the night. Clemens rewarded the crowd with seven scoreless innings, holding the Giants to one hit in the 10-1 victory.

Clemens, who struck out nine and walked three, collected his 4,100th career strikeout when Jerome Williams struck out leading off the third.

"Here we go again," Clemens said after claiming his 311th victory to tie Hall of Famer Tom Seaver for 16th on the all-time list. "Right when I thought I was done and I had reached all the guys I was going to touch, [Seaver is] another one of those guys that I think about that paved the way for me and gave me some encouragement to go out there and be great. I know all the hard work [it takes]. When I catch these guys, it's like, 'Wow, this is unbelievable.' To catch him and now to see how determined he was and all the hard work that he had to go through to get 310, 311 wins, it's pretty amazing."

Unlike the Giants' visits to Houston in the previous three seasons, Bonds was not even the main attraction at the plate on April 7, 2004, at Minute Maid Park. Clemens, who singled in his first National League at-bat, actually outhit Bonds.

"Roger's got six Cy Youngs, [and] I've got six MVPs," Bonds said after drawing an intentional walk in his first at-bat and striking out looking in his final two. "Come on. It's not like we're both young kids here. We're both up in age. We're both going to struggle at times. We're both playing against the odds, and I think we're both doing a pretty good job at it."

Jimy Williams ordered Clemens to intentionally walk Bonds in the first inning, but Clemens was free to challenge Bonds in the fourth. Clemens began his sequence in the fourth inning against Bonds with a 94-mph fastball that was called a ball. Bonds fouled off the next pitch down the first-base line. Clemens followed up with a 95-mph fastball that Bonds took for a strike, drawing a roar from the crowd. The next two fastballs, 96 mph and 95 mph, were out of the strike zone. But Clemens got Bonds out on a 94-mph fastball for a called third strike.

"Barry, he's awesome," Clemens said. "I don't think a lot of people realize—or maybe they do—what they're seeing with this guy being one of the best hitters if not the best hitter in the time that I've been playing. We kind of came up together. So when he says something, you take note of it. I think he said I better make my pitches, so I tried to make them on him."

Bonds led off again in the seventh, and Clemens went right after him. Bonds took an 83-mph backdoor slider for a strike and swung through an 89-mph splitter before taking an 89-mph fastball low and out of the strike zone. Clemens finished off Bonds with a 94-mph fastball on the outside corner for a called third strike.

Afterward, Bonds insinuated that Clemens got more than the benefit of the doubt on both of the called third strikes. Bonds, who entered the season under the cloud of a steroid scandal brewing with his former trainer, actually found the nerve to complain about the potential of Clemens getting the edge.

"Roger knows what happened out there," Bonds said. "That's all that matters."

Clemens was more gracious.

"He's dangerous," Clemens said of Bonds. "Good for him. Instead of doing it here, he needs to go home and do that in San Francisco to tie Willie. Do that in front of the people that have seen him grow up and what he's done for the fans of San Francisco.... He can get that tying home run and go-ahead run out there in front of the fans that cheered for him and loved him. That's the way it should happen."

The Astros and their fans expected Clemens to create some wonderful moments, but they never imagined his spectacular start garnering him the National League's Pitcher of the Month award for April 2004 after going 5-0 to become the first Astros pitcher to ever win five games in April. The drama continued with each start. On May 5, he made more impressive history by striking out Raul Mondesi in the fifth inning for his 4,137th career strikeout, surpassing Hall of Famer Steve Carlton for second on the all-time strikeout list behind leader Nolan Ryan.

The Astros could never have envisioned Clemens would get off to such an impressive start in his 21st major league season and first as an Astro. But at 41 years old, Clemens collected milestones and ovations almost everywhere he went as he started the season by winning his first seven starts. He followed his victory over the Giants with a 5-3 victory over the St. Louis Cardinals, receiving a standing ovation after his final pitch on his first trip to Busch Stadium since he squeezed under a gate as a child. On April 18, he beat the Milwaukee Brewers 6-1. Six days later, he beat the Colorado Rockies 8-5, receiving another standing ovation on the road after he made his last pitch at Coors Field.

"Do you know how lucky you are to be seeing what you're seeing out here? You have to cherish these moments and see what's happening. It's very special, and it's happening in Houston," Williams said after Clemens beat the Marlins 6-1 on May 11 to run his perfect start with the Astros to 7-0.

Although Clemens left that game trailing 1-0 to the Marlins, he picked up the win when the Astros got to Marlins starter Brad Penny in the bottom of the seventh. Lance Berkman's double scored Kent to tie the game, and Morgan Ensberg singled Berkman home to set up Clemens for career win No. 317.

Craig Biggio put the Astros ahead 3-1 in the eighth when he hit the second pitch from reliever Justin Wayne over the left field wall for his team-leading seventh home run. The Astros pushed three more runs across in the inning to lock down the victory.

"It was a well-played game, and our hitters finally persevered and broke through at the end and made the game a little more comfortable than it really looked early," Clemens said. "I tip my hat to the hitters. They really battled hard.

"I look to Morgan's at-bat [in the seventh] as the biggest, obviously to push us ahead, but you have look at what J.K. did and what Lance did to set that table and be able to push those runs across."

He won his first nine decisions with the Astros and earned the starting nod at the All-Star Game that year at Minute Maid Park, joining Kent, Berkman, and Carlos Beltran as representatives of the Astros in the third All-Star Game ever held in Houston and the first since Clemens started for the American League in 1986 at the Astrodome.

5

A Bumpy Start

With each wrong turn, the change was finally sinking in for Andy Pettitte. He and his good friend were no longer Yankees, no longer at their old spring home of Tampa, Florida. Although Roger Clemens put off retirement to help Pettitte chase a championship for their hometown Astros, Pettitte could not feel more alone late on February 21, 2004, as he searched for the house he rented for that spring training. Each turn was the wrong one, it seemed, sending him on a discouraging voyage through Orlando and Kissimmee, Florida, before even participating in his first workout as an Astro.

Pettitte eventually found his destination after more than an hour. But he and Clemens were barely starting their trek to help end the Astros' history of discouraging voyages through the postseason. Pettitte and Clemens didn't come alone. They carried expectations, and, more importantly, the broad shoulders to embrace the challenge of bringing some of that New York Yankees magic to Minute Maid Park.

"It's just strange, being accustomed for so many years to doing one thing continually, and now it's all different," Pettitte said. "Whether it's finding my way to the ballpark or finding my way to my house and getting lost. Or getting to meet the guys."

If Astros owner Drayton McLane had his way, Pettitte and Clemens wouldn't ever have to change a darn thing. When McLane visited Clemens's mansion in Memorial twice in December 2003, he practically bowed to a pitching shrine unlike any other in the world. The record six Cy Young Awards were right there, as if signaling McLane what was in store for his franchise if he landed Clemens. McLane was just bold enough to predict Clemens could win another Cy Young in Houston, and Clemens came through by winning his record seventh overall and first in the National League in his first season with the Astros.

Houstonians with a pulse and interest in baseball knew about Clemens's 310 career victories heading into his first season in Houston. Once Pettitte signed with the Astros on December 11, it was only a matter of time before Clemens's family gave its blessing for the veteran right-hander to come out and play his 21st season at the tender age of 41.

The Yankees had Lou Gehrig's famous speech declaring himself the luckiest man in the world. Some day the Astros might look back at these famous words, "Lefty, this changes everything."

That's exactly what Clemens told Pettitte shortly after the left-hander from Deer Park signed with Houston. By January 12, a citywide lobbying effort had paid off, prompting Clemens to put off retirement after spending all of the 2003 season with the Yankees saying it would be his last.

"Life has changed in Astroland," general manager Gerry Hunsicker said. "We're not flying under the radar screen anymore."

With that said, Hunsicker acknowledged that anything less than a trip to the World Series would seem like a failure to many Houston fans. Those were lofty goals to place on an Astros organization that had never won a postseason series. Whether fair or not, veteran first baseman Jeff Bagwell could not remember entering a season with the high expectations that awaited them with Clemens and Pettitte on the roster in 2004. Clemens's new teammates had to go all the way back to 1980, Nolan Ryan's first of nine seasons with his hometown team, to find the last time there had been so much excitement for baseball in Houston entering a season. The July 31 trading deadline trade that brought Randy Johnson to Houston from Seattle in 1998 also captured the city's imagination, but Johnson wasn't enough to overcome hard-throwing right-hander Kevin Brown and the San Diego Padres in the division series that year.

Clemens and Pettitte don't shy away from the expectations. They never have, actually. Pettitte and Clemens have grown accustomed to playing for a team that views a season as a failure if it doesn't earn a championship parade down the Canyon of Heroes.

Spend a day with the Yankees and you realize there is something special in the Bronx. The lore is more than just about the record 26 World Series trophies. It's about the men who have worn the famed pinstripes: Babe Ruth, Joe DiMaggio, and Mickey Mantle, to name just a few.

"There's no doubt playing for the Yankees we knew everybody was trying to shoot after us," Pettitte said. "Everybody tried to measure themselves up to us. 'If you could just beat the Yankees.' We knew that every series that we played it was like their World Series. That's something special.

"If we didn't come every night to play, we were going to get our ticket punched because that other team was ready. We were the New York Yankees, and they wanted to beat us. So you just knew playing teams day in and day out that there was something different about playing for the Yankees."

The Astros definitely had the talent to make 2004 special. The entire starting lineup returned from the 2003 season, putting together what on paper was an impressive middle of the order with Bagwell, Lance Berkman, Jeff Kent, and Richard Hidalgo. It remained to be seen if Octavio Dotel had what was needed to replace closer Billy Wagner. By June doubts had started to creep in about Dotel's ability to close, but Brad Lidge was on his way to becoming one of the most feared closers in baseball. More importantly, Dotel was just valuable enough for the Oakland A's to take him from the Astros in the three-team deal that brought Carlos Beltran from Kansas City to Houston while the Astros sent catcher John Buck to the Kansas City Royals.

On paper, the starting rotation definitely seemed improved from 2003 to 2004 with ace right-hander Roy Oswalt, Pettitte, Clemens, right-hander Wade Miller, and right-hander Tim Redding. Redding followed Clemens around Osceola County Stadium most of the 2004 spring training. He seemed committed to joining Pettitte as another follower of Clemens's intense workout regimen. Oswalt wasn't sure if he was made out for Clemens's workout, but he and Miller were definitely ready for healthy competition with Clemens and Pettitte.

Oswalt, Miller, and Redding hoped to learn from Clemens and Pettitte. They were ready to lean on them for tips on the mental aspects of the game. But Oswalt, who started opening day for the second consecutive season in 2004 and came through with 20 victories to earn his third consecutive opening-day nod in 2005, won't defer to his more celebrated mates on the rotation.

"I don't consider anybody better than me," Oswalt says. "Once you get into the big leagues, you're on the same level as everyone else. You should go into a game expecting to win. You should go into the game not wondering if you will win, but by how much you will win."

Oswalt, the only pitcher in the majors to win 20 games in 2004 and 2005, may be the No. 1 starter on the Astros, but he is far from achieving what Clemens or Pettitte has achieved. But he moved in their direction with his first All-Star nod in 2005 and the Most Valuable Player award in the 2005 National League Championship Series against the St. Louis Cardinals.

The Astros' payroll will likely never compare favorably to the Yankees' $200 million payroll. But at $83 million in 2004 and about $85 million in 2005, McLane's payrolls those seasons were higher than the Anaheim Angels needed in 2002 and the Florida Marlins needed in 2003 to win the World Series. Both those teams beat Pettitte, Clemens, and the Yankees on the way to the World Series title.

"When I think of the Yankees, I think money, championships, and George Steinbrenner," Oswalt said before the 2004 season. "That looks like a formula for success. But the thing about baseball is that you don't have to have big money to win. You need pitching, and right now I think we have the team to win."

The Astros had four players who knew exactly what it takes to win a World Series. Backup outfielder Orlando Palmeiro played with the Angels in 2002, and backup infielder Jose Vizcaino was a teammate of Clemens and Pettitte in 2000 with the Yankees.

"The great thing about it is that I have some horses on the mound," Clemens said. "We had a great pitching staff in New York. I told Andy, if we can just get a little piece of that feeling we had in New York as Yankees, the passion that's there.... Everything that we do is measured by our success, and the success, obviously, we had in New York. There are so many teams that are measured against greatness and what happened in New York."

Much like that wacky trip through Kissimmee on Pettitte's drive the night before his first spring training at Osceola County Stadium, the Astros would make countless wrong turns before finally landing at the World Series with Pettitte and Clemens. Although Clemens won his first nine decisions in 2004 en route to an 18-win season and his seventh Cy Young, he and Oswalt were left to carry the starting rotation after Pettitte had season-ending left elbow surgery that August and Miller was lost for good after a loss against the Texas Rangers on June 25. Despite Clemens's help and the numerous openings in the rotation because of injuries, Redding couldn't pitch well enough to remain in the starting rotation.

The tremendous expectations brought upon by the signings of Pettitte and Clemens appeared to smother the Astros, eventually costing Williams his job because, as Bagwell put it, you cannot fire all the players. Nobody can deny Williams's ability to teach. His imprint was left throughout the organization, paying dividends for the Astros all of the way to the 2005 World Series. Williams was the one who put in the extra time in the back fields at Osceola County Stadium in the spring trainings of 2002, 2003, and 2004 working with shortstop Adam Everett and third baseman Morgan Ensberg, giving them the confidence and fundamentals on defense that would help them become key contributors in 2005.

Talking baseball with beat writers who traveled with the team, Williams was extremely helpful. He loved to talk about the game. He'd sit in his office for hours explaining the intricacies of one play or another. He'd expound on his theories for holding runners, bunting, defense, and base running. He'd tell stories about his days managing in Mexico, breaking into a rare smile as he'd recall the time he went out to pull Mexican legend Fernando Valenzuela in what proved to be an extremely unpopular move during a winter league game in Mexico in the early 1980s. Williams had no use for idle talk with the media, though. He'd much rather be hitting hundreds of grounders to his infielders, which he did often, than talking to local talk radio or television reporters who didn't travel with the club. His quotes didn't transfer well to radio or television, especially on the rare instances in which he invoked his infamous "manager's decision" line. To his credit, he hardly used the "manager's decision" line after his first season in Houston, and he genuinely treated the beat writers with class and dignity.

Nonetheless, Williams could not stop the Astros' spiral downward in the first half of the 2004 season. He never managed to build on the success Larry Dierker had achieved. Dierker, a popular former Astros pitcher and broadcaster before coming out of the broadcast booth to lead his former team, won four National League Central titles in his five seasons in the dugout. In large part because the Astros under Dierker never benefited from the clutch postseason hitting of Berkman, Kent, and Beltran as displayed in the 2004 postseason, his Astros never got out of the division series. Hoping to take the next step, the Astros let Dierker go after suffering the 2001 sweep in the division series against the Atlanta Braves. Williams got the Astros' managerial job over Jim Fregosi and Tony Peña. By the middle of his third season, Williams had yet to lead the Astros to the postseason. Even worse, they headed into the 2004 All-Star break with a 44-44 record and 10½ games behind the NL Central-leading St. Louis Cardinals. A .500 mark wasn't exactly what the folks in Houston expected as they entered the 2004 season.

With all of the baseball attention focused on Minute Maid Park during the 2004 All-Star Game, Williams was the ultimate lame duck. Hunsicker had already contacted Phil Garner about becoming the Astros' manager, and Garner had essentially accepted. Hours before Roger Clemens threw the first pitch to start the All-Star Game on the night of July 13 at Minute Maid Park, hundreds of fans formed in lines to receive Garner's autograph across the street at the FanFest being held at the George R. Brown Convention Center. Garner was one of dozens of baseball stars contracted to sign autographs for a fee at that event. To promote the autograph sessions, the event's organizers offered to make the celebrities available to the media throughout the All-Star weekend festivities. For four days, the folks at FanFest lobbied the local media to write about the legends at the autograph booth.

On July 13, however, it was announced that Garner would not be available to the media before or after his autograph session. Garner had long been rumored as a potential replacement for Williams. A longtime resident of the Houston suburb of Kingwood, Garner had been a popular player and coach with the Astros before he began his managing career with the Milwaukee Brewers. He also had a reputation as one of the most media-friendly and accessible managers in baseball despite his lousy teams in Milwaukee and Detroit. So it was strange that he was the only celebrity to boycott the media during FanFest. The security guard posted near Garner tried unsuccessfully several times to usher three reporters away. Local Fox reporter Mark Berman, dogged radio reporter David Dalati, and I refused to budge. We waited patiently at the side of the stage, hidden in a corner behind two black curtains as Garner signed out front at a table on an elevated stage. Over Garner's head, the marquee in shining white lights read: Phil Garner, Houston Astros.

It got so uncomfortable for Garner that he decided against attending the All-Star Game in his own hometown, passing on his tickets because he didn't want anybody to see him in the stands and assume his tickets had been given to him by the Astros. Whatever the case, it had to be an even more uncomfortable situation for Williams and his family. Hunsicker could have easily fired him on the West Coast as the Astros limped to a 2-5 mark on the week before the All-Star break. Instead, Williams was brought back to Houston, where he endured countless questions about his future and one of the rudest welcomes Houston fans have ever given one of their own. When introduced as part of Jack McKeon's coaching staff for the National League All-Star team, Williams received thunderous jeers.

Williams could not have appeared more alone in a building with a sellout crowd of 41,886.

"It broke my heart, it really did," McLane said of the jeers Williams received during the All-Star Game introductions. "Nobody deserves that. He has given his all. I've never seen a manager who's worked harder than he has worked, just like a great player or business leader that gives it his best and it doesn't work as he had hoped for. So it broke my heart."

After the National League lost the All-Star Game 9-4, a throng of media awaited Williams for a comment on his fate and possibly even some words on his opinions about the greeting he received by the home-town fans. Fittingly, perhaps, the manager's office that had belonged to Williams since 2002 was being used by McKeon. Williams would never again use the manager's office at Minute Maid Park, other than to pack his belongings after Hunsicker told him he was fired the next morning. As Williams undressed and headed to the showers in the coaches' room at Minute Maid Park after the All-Star Game, one of the NL All-Star team coaches looked toward an Astros official and did a slashing motion with his index finger across the neck and shrugged his shoulders, silently asking if Williams had already been fired. As of then, Williams had not learned his fate. With more than 20 reporters lining the hallway leading out of the coaches' room, Williams was asked by Astros vice president of communications Jay Lucas if he wanted to comment. Williams declined, so a plan was formulated to get his family to his car while he was smuggled out of the stadium without being seen by the media.

The weight of World Series expectations had claimed the first victim, and the man derided for his trademark "manager's decision" had given his final no comment by sneaking out of his own clubhouse.

"I remember back in December when we announced [the signing of] Andy Pettitte, and in January when we talked about Roger Clemens and we saw the team that last year missed [by] one game tying or winning the National League Central Division," McLane said after announcing Williams's firing. "We thought with one or two additional players it could make a great deal of difference. We saw the city and our fans really get excited when we made these additions. We had great hopes and expectations, and I know the entire team, our manager, and coaches did."

As the Astros started their West Coast trip in San Diego the week before Williams was fired, McLane made it clear that he'd evaluate Williams's job status the day after the All-Star Game. By the start of that three-game series on July 5, all of the Astros were talking about Williams's fate. "What are you hearing about Jimy?" was one of the major questions being asked in the clubhouse. "Is he going to get fired?" many players asked.

The Astros lost the first two games of the three-game series at Petco Park before salvaging the finale against the Padres, and Williams even shut down the clubhouse at one point during the series to implore his players not to worry about his fate. They opened the series with a 2-1 loss. They dropped the next game 5-3 before winning the finale 5-1 with Oswalt on the mound against Jake Peavy. After that series, the Astros drove north to Dodger Stadium and lost three of four with a listless performance in which even Hall of Fame broadcaster Vin Scully noted the Astros' lackadaisical play. At one point during the four-game series against the Dodgers, Orlando Palmeiro drew four balls in an at-bat and failed to take his walk. Not Palmeiro, Williams, nor one single person in the visitors' dugout at Dodger Stadium noticed that Palmeiro was entitled to a walk in that at-bat. Even if the Astros weren't paying attention on the West Coast as their minds wandered toward their All-Star break retreats, the front office was taking notes in Houston.

"It's been a disappointing season for all of us," Hunsicker said. "Over the last 30 days in particular the frustration levels have gotten higher and the anticipation of a turnaround greater. I really believe that last week was the first time as a management team we really started to think about staff changes. That it was time for a change. There are only so many things you can do in management when you see a team struggle like it's struggled for as long as we have. You can't affect what happens on the field day to day. The only thing you really can affect is personnel decisions, be they players or staff. We've tried to make some positive changes to the players' side of the equation. As we watched this team continue to flounder last week on the West Coast, it became more and more apparent for us that it was time for a change. I think for all of us, the clincher was watching us in Los Angeles last weekend, where the team just seemed to take on that defeated, desperate kind of attitude. To me, that's the biggest thing we're looking to change, the attitude of this club."

6

The 2004 All-Star Game

Marlins manager Jack McKeon was certain he was seeing the last of Roger Clemens on October 22, 2003, in Game 4 of the World Series. Clemens had said as much, and most of the baseball world believed the right-hander. So after Clemens struck out Luis Castillo to end the eighth inning, McKeon joined his Marlins players and the crowd of more than 60,000 fans at Pro Player Stadium in giving The Rocket a standing ovation.

As things turned out, Clemens stayed retired for all of 78 days, finally accepting Drayton McLane's offer to pitch at home. Then McKeon, as manager of the world champion Marlins, had to manage against The Rocket during the 2004 and 2005 regular seasons. He also managed him during the 2004 All-Star Game at Minute Maid Park. He even picked Clemens to start for the National League on July 13, 2004.

Five months after what was believed to be his last start in the 2003 World Series, Clemens pitched against the Marlins in an exhibition game for the Astros in Mexico City on March 13, 2004. In Mexico, Clemens was trying to build arm strength and stamina. He gave up seven hits and two runs over his scheduled three-inning stint, striking out three in a 6-1 loss. Almost two months later, though, Clemens emerged as the biggest story and hottest pitcher in baseball. The future Hall of Famer beat McKeon's Marlins 6-1 during his perfect 7-0 run to start the 2004 season.

McKeon had definitely been impressed even before Clemens struck out a season-high 11 and gave up only three hits over seven innings against the Marlins on May 11. Although he didn't make the decision until July 12, McKeon hinted in May that he would likely start Clemens in the 2004 All-Star Game.

"I don't see who could not start him, what he's done, but that's a long way off," McKeon said. "That would be like a dream coming true for everybody in Houston and him pitching the All-Star Game. The way he's going, he's got a pretty good chance."

McKeon wished he could have picked Clemens for the Marlins.

"Absolutely, no question," McKeon said. "That's a great story. The guy retires and comes back, jumps off to a new league, goes [9-0 to start]... I would love to have him. He knows how to win. You're going to hit him occasionally, but he'll win more than he'll lose. He'll give you six, seven good innings all the time. Knows how to pitch. But you've got 20-some years' experience, and to be as successful as he has, you ought to have some kind of idea of what it's all about. He's a horse out there. You like to have guys like that."

Before the 2004 All-Star festivities, McKeon and Clemens had met twice since Josh Beckett beat former Yankee and new Astro Andy Pettitte in Game 6 to win the 2003 World Series. At the New York Baseball Writers' Association of America Dinner in February 2004, McKeon teased Clemens about ending his retirement.

"Here I thought I was going to be in the position to tell my grand-kids after you go to the Hall of Fame that I happened to see his last pitch," McKeon told Clemens, who got a no-decision in Game 4 of the 2003 World Series, a game the Marlins won on Alex Gonzalez's homer in the 11th. "Then you went and blew it!"

Marlins infielder Luis Castillo also lamented losing a place in history when the Astros lobbied Clemens out of retirement.

"When I struck out, I said, 'I'll be in the record books as Roger Clemens's last out,'" Castillo said. "Now he's back, and that's OK with me."

The entire city of Houston shares Castillo's opinion, and Clemens's return seemed perfect as he marched toward the starting nod at the All-Star Game at Minute Maid Park 18 years after he was the MVP of the 1986 All-Star Game at the Astrodome. The 75th All-Star Game in Major League Baseball history was the third Midsummer Classic played in Houston. On July 9, 1968, the National League beat the American League 1-0 at the Astrodome in the first All-Star Game played indoors and on an artificial surface. The National League sent four future Hall of Famers to the mound, beginning with Don Drysdale of the Los Angeles Dodgers, Juan Marichal of the San Francisco Giants, Steve Carlton of the St. Louis Cardinals, and Tom Seaver of the New York Mets. Ron Reed of the Braves and Jerry Koosman of the Mets were the other members of the NL's six-man rotation that held the AL to only three hits. The game's MVP was Willie Mays, who scored the winning run in the first inning on a single, an error, and a double-play grounder from fellow Giant Willie McCovey.

The 1986 game was hyped as a battle of young hard-throwing right-handers: Roger Clemens of the Red Sox versus Dwight Gooden of the New York Mets. Clemens lived up to his billing with three perfect innings in front of his Houston neighbors, family, and friends. Gooden gave up a two-run home run in the second inning. The NL pitching staff also excelled as Los Angeles Dodgers left-hander Fernando Valenzuela tied Carl Hubbell's 52-year-old All-Star record by striking out five consecutive batters, setting down Don Mattingly of the Yankees, future Hall of Famer Cal Ripken of the Orioles, Jesse Barfield of the Blue Jays, and fellow Mexican pitcher Ted Higuera of the Brewers.

The 2004 All-Star Game had a chance to be billed as a battle of George Steinbrenner's old hard-throwing right-handers: Clemens of the Astros versus Kevin Brown, whom the Yankees acquired from the Los Angeles Dodgers that winter essentially to take Clemens's spot in the rotation. Clemens and Brown were their respective leagues' Pitchers of the Month of April, and they led their leagues in victories midway through May before Brown tailed off considerably. Arizona Diamondbacks left-hander Randy Johnson, a former Astro, brought tremendous interest to the All-Star Game after becoming only the 17th person in major league history to throw a perfect game on May 18 against the Atlanta Braves. In Houston, Clemens was brought out as a spokesman for Major League Baseball to begin the All-Star voting process.

As a longtime resident of the Houston area, Clemens appreciates and embraces the impact he has had on the city's baseball fans. He also understands what Jeff Bagwell and Craig Biggio have meant to the Astros. With that in mind, Clemens started his own campaign, urging fans to stuff the All-Star ballot boxes with votes for the guys he simply refers to as "No. 5 [Bagwell] and No. 7 [Biggio]."

"There's two guys that I know that need to be in the All-Star Game," Clemens said. "I meant that when I said it when we talked about the All-Star Game a couple of weeks back. That's No. 7 and No. 5. They've put some time in this organization, and they need to be a part of that All-Star Game."

Other than Clemens, Biggio and Bagwell would have been the most appropriate men to serve as Houston's ambassadors at the 75th All-Star Game. Biggio and Bagwell, after all, are the faces most associated with the Houston Astros. Moreover, Biggio's seven All-Star appearances are the most by an Astros player in the history of the franchise. Playing outfield at the time, though, Biggio was not voted to the National League All-Star team even though he had hit a respectable .301 with 13 home runs and 36 RBI in the first half of the 2004 season. Biggio had hoped to share the 2004 All-Star experience with his three children: sons, Conor and Cavan, and daughter, Quinn.

Biggio made his last All-Star appearance in 1998 at Colorado's Coors Field. Conor was only five years old at the time, and Cavan was merely three years old. Quinn Patricia wouldn't be born until late September 1999. Considering how young the boys were during his last All-Star appearance and the fact that Quinn had not shared in an All-Star appearance with him, Biggio had hoped to make it in 2004. As an added incentive, Biggio had a chance to earn an All-Star bid as an outfielder. The catcher-turned-second baseman had already earned All-Star nods at those positions. An outfield nod would definitely bolster his already impressive Hall of Fame candidacy. His children, however, were the biggest reason he wished to have earned a place in 2004.

"It would have been awesome to make this All-Star Game," he said. "All the [All-Star] games we were at before, [Conor and Cavan] were too young to remember."

Bagwell, who hit .268 with 11 home runs and 40 RBI in the first half of the 2004 season, never even assumed he had a shot at making the 2004 All-Star team. Unlike Biggio, who definitely had put up All-Star-caliber numbers, Bagwell realized his numbers didn't stack up well against the other first basemen who earned spots on the NL team: St. Louis's Albert Pujols (the starter), Cincinnati's Sean Casey, Philadelphia's Jim Thome, and Colorado's Todd Helton.

"There was never a thought I was going to make the All-Star team," Bagwell said. "I don't deserve it. You don't deserve it because it's your home. Look at Lyle Overbay and Eric Milton. They were deserving. If I deserved to be there, I would have loved to have gone, because it's at home. It would have been really nice."

Clemens deserved his All-Star nod, and he accepted his role as an ambassador for the Astros organization and the city of Houston. Clemens and Hall of Famer Nolan Ryan were the official spokesmen for FanFest, so they were around town throughout the entire week's All-Star festivities. Market Information Masters Inc., a consulting firm, estimated the All-Star Game would bring $48 million into the local economy while the state of Texas would gain $4.3 million in sales tax revenue from that spending. In the same year Houston played host to the Super Bowl, the nation's baseball fans turned their focus on downtown Houston's Minute Maid Park—and Clemens more than any other player. The city of Houston allotted $1 million for landscaping to the George R. Brown Convention Center, which held the FanFest event; $158,000 for police and fire services; $280,000 for planting trees around Minute Maid Park; and $280,000 for the Main Event street festival.

All-Star Lance Berkman puts on a power display at the 2004 All-Star Game, finishing second behind Baltimore's Miguel Tejada.

Although Lance Berkman delivered a tremendous power display while finishing second to Baltimore's Miguel Tejada at the Home Run Derby on July 12, there was little doubt which Houston All-Star garnered most of the attention. Houston Astros All-Stars Berkman, Jeff Kent, and Carlos Beltran received tremendous ovations from their home fans on July 13, but the 75th All-Star Game was essentially a Roger Clemens extravaganza with fans and baseball officials pulling the future Hall of Famer in multiple directions.

If the event had anything to do with the All-Star Game festivities, Clemens was probably involved.

Somehow, it always comes back to New York, though, especially in regard to Roger Clemens and Mike Piazza, two figures who seem destined to be tied to each other for life. In one instance, Yankee Stadium fell silent. It happened during a game on July 8, 2000, when a stunned stadium turned all the attention toward home plate, where Piazza, the Mets' star catcher, lay across home plate. Roger Clemens, who had delivered a high fastball that tailed toward Piazza's head, walked halfway in from the mound and watched.

With his hands on his knees and bent down looking in, Clemens was expressionless as then-Mets manager Bobby Valentine and the team's trainers rushed in to help Piazza, who lay on the ground for several minutes. Piazza came into that at-bat on July 8 with three home runs, a double, and three singles in the three previous games against Clemens. So on that Saturday night, Clemens delivered an 0-1 fastball high and tight—too tight. It hit Piazza at the bill of the helmet, nearly killing him. An inch here or there, and it could have been disastrous. Yankees team physician Stuart Hershon examined Piazza and diagnosed him with a slight concussion. Piazza, who was taken to a local hospital for precautionary X-rays, refused Clemens's call from the clubhouse later that night.

Clemens's detractors called him a headhunter, and the Mets yelled at him from the dugout all night. When they met in the Subway Series later that October, Clemens broke Piazza's bat during Piazza's first at-bat in Game 3 at Shea Stadium. As Piazza jogged up the first-base line on the foul ball, Clemens picked up the broken barrel of the bat and threw it in Piazza's direction. Piazza responded by walking toward Clemens and asking him what his problem was. Piazza later called Clemens cowardly, but Clemens dominated on that night. Clemens's critics said he had grown accustomed to intimidating hitters because he pitched in the American League, where the designated hitter rule keeps pitchers from hitting unless they are in an interleague game at a National League park.

Four years later, Clemens and Piazza faced off again without an altercation at Minute Maid Park on May 16, 2004, in a regular-season game in which Clemens dominated through his seven scoreless innings of work against Piazza's Mets. Piazza walked, struck out, and grounded out in three plate appearances against Clemens. Clemens's Astros teammates ultimately saw why it makes no sense to pitch Piazza any way other than inside. If a fastball strays too far inside, it's better to let Piazza try to get out of the way, because a fastball away or anywhere close over the plate is asking for trouble against the perennial All-Star and sure first-ballot Hall of Famer. Only two of the six newspapers that regularly cover the Mets didn't send at least two reporters to cover the series. The hook was definitely Clemens versus Piazza. Clemens allowed only two hits and a walk over seven innings, and he was already icing in the clubhouse when disaster struck. Given a chance to extend The Rocket's perfect record to 8-0, right-handed reliever Octavio Dotel, a former Met, failed. With a man on second, a 2-0 lead, two outs, and Todd Zeile on deck in the ninth, then-Astros manager Jimy Williams visited the mound and let Dotel pitch to Piazza.

"Once I saw they were going to challenge me, I changed my approach a little bit," Piazza said. "I was able to stay behind a fastball over the plate and drive it out of the ballpark. In that situation, I'm not looking for any particular pitch, just a pitch I can hit."

Dotel wanted to show he wasn't afraid of anybody. Williams told him he didn't have to pitch to Piazza, but Dotel's ego got in the way of common sense.

"I'm not afraid of anybody," Dotel said afterward, as if fear has anything to do with making a smart pitch.

With the count 1–2, Piazza got a 95-mph fastball just the way he likes them: away and over the plate. Piazza drilled a similar pitch over the right field wall two days earlier against ace right-hander Roy Oswalt, who was furious afterward.

"I shouldn't have thrown him that pitch," Oswalt said. "I should have thrown the fastball inside. He can't catch up to my fastball inside."

Dotel should have thrown the fastball inside, too. He didn't, and it cost Clemens the victory. Afterward, Dotel walked into the Astros clubhouse and apologized to the future Hall of Famer. Clemens told him to move on and learn from the experience.

"I think [Piazza's] a good hitter," Clemens said. "You have to be careful. That's why you don't let him get extended. There are certain places if you're going to miss, you need to miss with him."

In other words, bust his ass inside and don't ever apologize for pitching inside. Clemens never has apologized for owning the plate, and many New York Mets fans who love Piazza hate Clemens for that fact. Valentine ridiculed Clemens by claiming Clemens pitched the way he did because he played in the American League, where the designated hitter rule keeps the pitcher on the mound. Valentine obviously never could have imagined the zeal with which Clemens would take to hitting once he joined the National League with the Astros. Valentine could have never imagined Clemens leading his pitching group to win the $4,000 pot in a bunting competition during the 2005 spring training.

Clemens shut up those critics who claimed he would never pitch in the National League, and he entered the 2004 season as a marked man. Entering the 2004 season, only 13 pitchers in major league history had hit more batters than Clemens, who hit 141 over 20 seasons in the American League. Walter Johnson is No. 1 on the hit batter's list with 203, followed by Eddie Plank (196), Joe McGinnity (182), Chick Fraser (177), Charlie Hough (174), Randy Johnson (168 entering the 2006 season), Cy Young (163), Jim Bunning (160), Ryan (158), Vic Willis (157), Bert Blyleven (155), and Don Drysdale (154). Entering the 2004 season, Randy Johnson led Clemens in hit batters by only five (146–141). After two seasons, Randy Johnson had added 22 hit batsmen to his total, and Clemens had added only nine.

"Roger carries a reputation, a reputation as a winner and a reputation of a guy that pitches inside," said former Colorado Rockies and

Chicago Cubs manager Don Baylor, who played with Clemens on the 1986 and 1987 Red Sox teams. "And you know that. Plus, it's different now because he has to hit in the National League. When somebody feels like he's being thrown at, retaliation now doesn't have to go to another teammate. They can wait for the pitcher to come up. I mean that's the way they play in the National League. If you move a guy off the plate, the next time up they might have to move that guy off the plate.

"His reputation, I wouldn't say he's a headhunter. Roger and I played together, and he protected me a lot of times. I told him many times, 'Rog, I'll take care of it. I'll break up the double play. I'll slide in hard. You pitch. You take care of the pitching.'"

Once again, Clemens and Piazza found themselves in the center of attention at the 2004 All-Star Game even though both men tried to play down the media's incessant desire to build up their feud as they prepared to serve as battery-mates for the first time in their careers. Both men tried to diffuse the hype long before they arrived at Minute Maid Park.

"As far as Mike and I, I've said a long time ago I was OK with the whole situation. I've reached out and did what I had to do," Clemens said in San Diego a week before that All-Star Game. "I think I made it well known in my career I've hit maybe three people up high when I've tried to pitch them inside. That's old news. I just don't want to take away from the game. I don't want it to be bigger than the game. He's a pro, and I'm a pro. We'll get it done. We'll sit down and talk like I normally do with Brad [Ausmus] or any other catcher depending on what slot I'm put in to pitch. I can tell you I'm glad I'm throwing to him instead of against him because I know that if I do make a mistake, he hurts the baseball. I can tell you that one luxury that I'm going to have is that I don't have to worry about him being in that other lineup."

Noting Clemens was in his hometown, Piazza vowed not to take away from Clemens's moment at home. Indeed, it was again Clemens's moment at home at the Midsummer Classic 18 years after he represented the Boston Red Sox as a 23-year-old starting for the American League at the Astrodome. With a 10-3 record and 2.62 ERA, Clemens made it easy for McKeon to give him the starting nod. This time around, Clemens didn't need to rent out a local sports bar for his family, friends, and intimate supporters to watch him start the All-Star Game at home, as he did in 1986 for many his supporters to watch him then.

"It's my privilege to select a guy that I think is going to be a future Hall of Famer," McKeon said. "He has done a tremendous job his entire career, [is] an outstanding example for all youngsters in baseball, Little League, high school, college, minor leagues. He's a guy that has a tremendous work ethic, has been a proven success for many, many years. And it's a privilege to introduce our starting pitcher, Mr. Clemens of the Houston Astros."

The news caught absolutely nobody by surprise, but the moment definitely provided Clemens's wife, Debbie, an opportunity to reflect on just how much time had elapsed since Rocket faced Dwight Gooden at the Astrodome on July 15, 1986.

Back in 1986, Roger and Debbie Clemens were eagerly awaiting the birth of their first child, Koby, the young man who would become an eighth-round draft choice of the Astros in June 2005. Despite winning his first 14 decisions for the Red Sox in 1986, Clemens had only 30 career victories at that point in his career. Four children, 290 victories, and nine All-Star selections later, Clemens was on his way to his record seventh Cy Young Award in 2004. He earned another All-Star berth in 2005. Clemens shared the 2004 All-Star experience with his entire family, including his proud mother, Bess.

Fighting emphysema, Bess embodied her son's grit as she zoomed through the convention center during FanFest. With great pride she watched Clemens and his four boys hold a batting practice session for underprivileged youth during FanFest.

"We thought he was going to retire last year, but I always compare it to the old horse that used to pull the fire wagon before we got these nice red trucks," she said in July 2004. "They retired the horse when they got the nice red trucks, but every time he heard the bell ring, the old horse wanted to go. Well, that's the way it is. Every spring Roger is ready to go. That's the way he is, and that's the way he does everything."

Each spring brought new challenges, new accomplishments, and another group of pitchers to pass on the all-time victories list. Clemens's first Cy Young and the American League Most Valuable Player award greeted Koby into the world in 1986. Kory followed two years later. Roger and Debbie greeted Kacy in 1994, and Kody a year later. Watching her husband address the media after he was announced as the National League's starting pitcher for the 2004 All-Star Game, Debbie wondered were all the time had gone.

"It's just strange," she said. "It's almost like everything just kept happening. It wasn't really just planned. It's such a blessing. Most ballplayers' children, when the player retires, are young and don't really remember a lot. My kids have been able to experience a lot of it and really watched and really enjoyed what he's offered the world. I was pregnant with Koby, and it was so exciting in 1986. We were so excited 18 years ago when this all was going on. We're just as excited now. It's just that we're a little weathered after so many years of this fast pace. I just can't believe how fast time's gone."

At least by his standards before a start, the pace had never gone faster for Clemens. Legendary for his disciplined regimen between starts, Clemens never had a chance to catch his breath during the All-Star festivities. On the Monday night before his start the next evening, he was up until the wee hours of the night, all in the name of promoting Houston to the baseball world. At the All-Star Gala that night at Houston's Aquarium in downtown, he obliged his good friend Clay Walker, the country music star, and joined him on stage to sing. Joined by Red Sox ace Curt Schilling, Clemens and Walker shook the crowd with a rendition of "Sweet Home Alabama." Schilling and Clemens won't get any record deals anytime soon, but their mere willingness to join Walker on stage proved to be a hit for the hundreds of fans, baseball officials, and Houston civic and business leaders watching at the gala.

Considering Clemens had gone seven innings and given up three runs on July 10 in a 3-1 loss to the Dodgers at Dodger Stadium and had also gone nonstop from one public event to another throughout the entire All-Star week's festivities, it's easy to understand why Clemens wasn't at his dominant best against the American League on July 13. Pitching on only two days' rest—days in which he didn't really get any rest—Clemens gave up five hits and six runs (three earned) with two strikeouts over one inning. He was tagged with the 9-4 loss that night.

The American League was credited with the victory that night, but the people of Houston were the true winners, because of the way Clemens spread himself thin through the All-Star festivities while representing the city and the Astros. During the Super Bowl, Houston's leaders encouraged the city to "Smile, company's coming." There was no such need for a motto during the 2004 All-Star Game. Company came, and Clemens and his family broke out enough smiles for everybody.

7

Scrap Iron

"I have a great deal of respect for Jimy Williams. I have a great deal of respect for the manager's position and what a guy has to go through when he's trying to be a part of a winning organization and ball club. It's tough enough to manage in today's times without a lot of distractions, and these things eventually turn into distractions."

—Phil Garner after replacing Jimy Williams

Phil Garner could appreciate Jimy Williams's predicament. Garner had been fired twice as a manager, and he had only one winning season to show for the 11 years he had managed in the majors. In most other businesses, Garner likely wouldn't have received so many opportunities to test his mettle as a supervisor. As it was, he had been without a managerial job since the lowly Detroit Tigers fired him after losing the first six games of the 2002 season. But his ties to Houston were deep. He had lived in the Houston suburb of Kingwood since soon after the Pittsburgh Pirates traded him to the Astros on August 31, 1981. He and his wife, Carol, raised their three children—Eric, Ty, and Bethany—in Kingwood, educating them in Kingwood schools. They were fixtures at many booster activities throughout Kingwood, especially for the Kingwood High baseball program, which Eric and Ty starred on. Carol Garner even helped with the design of Minute Maid Park as a member of the Houston–Harris County Sports Authority, spending countless hours with Astros president of business operations Pam Gardner discussing the stadium leading up to the ballpark's first season in 2000. Garner's father, a longtime Baptist preacher, also was a fixture in Houston.

As an assistant general manager, Tim Purpura often left tickets for the Reverend Garner to attend Astros games.

"Talking with Gerry [Hunsicker] and Tal [Smith] when talking about Phil Garner, I had to admit I knew his wife, Carol, a whole lot better than I knew Phil," Drayton McLane said. "Carol I got to know—Pam Gardner and I did—[while] she was on the original Houston–Harris County Sports Authority. A great deal of the design that you see at Minute Maid Park, exterior and interior, is Carol's and Pam's. They worked as a team. And we had a budget there just like we do for our baseball team. I had to slow them down every now and then. Whether we're designing a stadium or selecting a manager, that's important. I've also known Phil's father, the Reverend Garner, very well. As I wander through the stadium every game, whether it's on the main concourse or the upper level, I've seen him almost at every game, and we stop and talk. Then, divine guidance, I think, could be a good issue here. Each of you know that at the baseball banquet each year the Reverend Garner would give the invocation. A few years ago, he would always ask for divine leadership for that team in Milwaukee. Now he has to ask it for the Houston Astros."

As a player, Garner was known as a fiery competitor while compiling a .260 career batting average with 1,594 hits and 738 RBI over 2,601 major league games from his debut with the Oakland A's in 1973 to his retirement with the San Francisco Giants in 1988. He never backed down from a fight as a player, and his demeanor hardly changed as a manager. Articulate and affable, he also was politically savvy enough to co-opt his players and the media in Detroit, Milwaukee, and later Houston. He can be politically incorrect at times, but he's smart enough to know when he can get away with his politically incorrect comments. At times he'll lament a player's inability to speak his mind, but he'll contradict himself when a player says something that the players from his era would never say. He wasn't hired to make friends, however. He was hired to shake the Astros out of their despair, and that's exactly what he did.

In the world of Major League Baseball, however, managers are recycled all of the time because front-office folks would rather go with a man who makes team representatives feel comfortable than an unproven manager. Such was the case for the Astros after the 2001 season, when they recycled Williams instead of taking a gamble on Tony Peña, who became the American League Manager of the Year in 2003 with the Kansas City Royals. More often than not, recycled managers live down to their inferior records. Every once in a while, recycled managers prove that they weren't the problem as much as the general managers or owners for whom they worked. Joe Torre proved every cynic wrong with the Yankees, winning four World Series in the Bronx even though he had been fired in previous managerial stops with the Atlanta Braves, New

York Mets, and St. Louis Cardinals. Only a year before Garner was hired in Houston, Jack McKeon, at age 72, had come out of retirement to lead the Florida Marlins to the World Series title over Roger Clemens, Andy Pettitte, and Torre's Yankees—a goal that had eluded him at the previous four managerial jobs where he had been fired.

Much like Torre and McKeon, Garner proved that his poor marks with the Milwaukee Brewers from 1992 to 1999 and with the Tigers from 2000 to April 2002 were not indicative of his ability to manage.

"I never had the caliber of pitchers like Roger Clemens, Andy Pettitte, or Roy Oswalt," Garner said at his introductory press conference with the Astros. "This is a wonderful challenge."

Even now, Garner often jokes that he became much smarter with guys like Clemens, Pettitte, and Oswalt playing for him, but he obviously provided the steady leadership that had been missing. He literally pushed all of the right buttons, challenging veterans and youngsters to produce or land on the bench. Even his own players were left wondering from time to time about his moves, but his moves usually paid off.

"Yeah, I'd be lying if I didn't say, sometimes you scratch your head and say why [is Garner doing that]," Andy Pettitte admitted before Game 1 of the 2005 National League Championship Series. "You do that, I think no matter who the manager is. Even in New York, like I said, I've done that. But I think [Garner is] kind of—he goes with his gut and that's something that I know Joe [Torre] did a lot, just goes with his gut feeling. You live with the consequences of that. You're the manager, and you're the one that has to do it. He's in that position, and I think that's the best way to manage, to tell you the truth. You just go with your gut feeling and do what you feel is right at that time."

Garner doesn't apologize for his moves. He understands he will be criticized if his moves backfire, and at least one pocket of fans grew critical of him after the Astros finished within a game of the World Series in 2004. Considering how lousy the Astros played before Garner helped spur them to the postseason in 2004, it seems like nitpicking to quibble with Garner's maneuvering.

Garner guarded against self-doubt by refusing to read the newspaper during the playoffs. He guards from self-doubt during the regular season by ending any debate once he already has made up his mind. Once he gives a coach an order, he has little use for an opposing view from that coach.

"You guys [in the media], this is not a criticism, but this is the way things are. You're going to analyze things to death, and if it doesn't work I'm open for criticism," said Garner, who has become a media darling because he is willing to fight his point with the media without taking offense or acting as though he is above being questioned about his moves. "And I don't want to taint what I'm going through. I'm going to do what I'm going to do, and I don't want any outside efforts. If it doesn't work and you guys write when it's over that Garner blew it because he did this and did that, I'm fine. But I don't want to second-guess myself going into it. I don't want to have doubts going into that. I'll do it with my coaching staff sometimes. If I got my mind made up and somebody would say, 'How about this or how about that,' I'll say, 'Don't say a word to me. Just do what I'm asking you to do.' When I've got my mind made up, I'm going to do that. I don't mean that personal."

It's that self-confidence and determination that made it easy for the Astros to believe in Garner and themselves when few outside their own clubhouse believed in them. That's not to say Garner doesn't receive a healthy dose of teasing for his intense nature. Needing only one victory to reach the 2005 World Series, Jeff Bagwell and Lance Berkman noticed that their skipper seemed a bit tight. Shortly after Garner left his office for a pregame press conference before Game 5 of the National League Championship Series against the St. Louis Cardinals, Bagwell and Berkman grinned from ear to ear as they tiptoed through the hallway in the home clubhouse leading up to the manager's office at Minute Maid Park. Noticing that all was clear, Bagwell and Berkman placed a container of Vaseline petroleum jelly on Garner's desk. The message was clear: Loosen up. Bagwell and Berkman had just left Garner's office when they saw him walking back. Like a pair of 12 year olds playing a prank on their unsuspecting older sister, Bagwell and Berkman stifled their laughter long enough to tiptoe close to Garner's office.

Once Garner noticed the container of Vaseline, he broke into a hearty laughter that echoed into the clubhouse. He walked out of his office and was greeted by Berkman and Bagwell, who took credit for their handiwork.

"You're right," Garner screamed, "my ass is tight."

It's doubtful Bagwell and Berkman would have felt comfortable enough to play such a prank on Williams, who once fined Berkman for not standing for "God Bless America" at Shea Stadium during one of Berkman's countless episodes of spacing out. Whether it was because of his past with the Astros as a player and coach, his résumé as a former major league player, or his sheer leadership ability, Garner had earned the respect of his players. He bristled at any notion that the Astros were working to rebuild in 2005 after losing Carlos Beltran and Jeff Kent after the 2004 season, often saying the McLane's orders were to win a championship, not groom players for the future.

8

Regrets

As the stunned baseball world looked on, Darryl Kile's former teammates traveled to St. Louis's Busch Stadium to pay their respects at a memorial service held on June 26, 2002, four days after the right-hander died of heart failure in a Chicago hotel. Worried St. Louis Cardinals officials had alerted the Westin Hotel after Kile had failed to arrive at Wrigley Field for the Cardinals' game against the Cubs on June 22. Everyone's worst fears were realized when Kile was found dead in his room.

Kile, a product of the Astros farm system, had been forced to flee Houston for Colorado when Drayton McLane didn't meet his price after the 1997 season. Just five years later, at the tender age of 33, the six-foot-five, 212-pound right-hander had left his widow, Flynn; their six-year-old twins, Kannon and Sierra; their one-year-old, Ryker; and a legion of friends and family throughout the baseball world behind. Darryl and Flynn Kile had spoken on the phone at least three times a day for years, and they had spoken twice June 21 before the final call at 11 p.m.

Flynn, who was setting up the family's new home in San Diego, California, told Darryl she had to get off the phone to unpack. He responded by saying he didn't want to get off the phone.

"Darryl would stay on the phone all night," she said. "I look back at that call, and I wish I'd stayed on the phone, not that it would have made a difference. He said, 'All right, I know you have work to do. I'll call you after the game.' I said, 'I love you.' And he said, 'I love you, too.'"

Flynn found it odd that Darryl did not call early the next morning, as he normally did. Not too concerned, though, she prepared to leave the house in search of new furniture. Darryl Kile was always one of the first players at the clubhouse, a trait he shared with his good friend and former Astros teammate Jeff Bagwell. The Cardinals had grown accustomed to seeing Kile arrive in the clubhouse before most of his teammates. So at

Wrigley Field that morning, several Cardinals players worried when their teammate hadn't arrived.

Kile would never arrive at the clubhouse. He was dead. An autopsy revealed an 80 to 90 percent narrowing of his coronary arteries, and that his heart was nearly 25 percent larger than normal, said Dr. Edmund Donoghue, the Cook County medical examiner. The scheduled June 22 game between the Cardinals and Cubs was postponed.

The team called Flynn to convey the terrible news, but at first she wasn't sure she believed what she had been told.

"I think it was just disbelief because I wasn't there to see him," she said. "I thought I was not being told right. Maybe he was just hurt and they weren't conveying it to me properly. Maybe he just accidentally passed out. I said, 'Where do I need to go? What hospital?' They were saying, 'No, he's been gone now for eight hours.' Oh, my God. It was just a shock because I had just talked to him the night before.

"I hoped it was some lie or some joke because Darryl missed me so much and would love for me to come to Chicago.... I thought, 'Boy, there's no way he could do something this unkind just to get me to fly out there.' You kind of think that at first, but it didn't seem realistic that he passed away. He seemed pretty healthy, and he had a physical every year. I'm probably still a bit in shock. It doesn't seem quite real that he could be gone."

The reality of the situation was sickening, sending Flynn and the baseball world into mourning. After word of the death got to Houston, the Astros shut the clubhouse before their June 22nd game against the Mariners to let the team mourn privately. Bagwell, Craig Biggio, and Brad Ausmus asked out of the starting lineup after learning of Kile's death. They hung Kile's old No. 57 Astros jersey in the dugout to honor him. Even through the 2005 World Series, a red St. Louis Cardinals hat with Kile's No. 57 stitched on it hangs in Bagwell's locker stall at Minute Maid Park.

As fate would have it, the Astros' game on June 22, 2002, went 12 innings, forcing manager Jimy Williams to use Bagwell, Biggio, and Ausmus. Bagwell ended the contest with a game-winning single. As teammates mobbed Bagwell at first base, their joyous celebration turned into a somber march as they embraced Bagwell while he walked off the field weeping.

Bagwell and Kile came up together as rookies in 1991 with the Astros. They had been roommates early in their careers, sharing a bond as deep as any shared between two brothers. They were brothers. They embraced each other's families and even shared an agent, Barry Axelrod.

Although Kile had not played for the Astros since 1997, Flynn remains steadfast in her declaration that the Astros were the team the Kiles felt more kinship with than any other. Taking time out of their schedules, 26 players from around the majors, most of them former Astros, flew to St. Louis and joined the Cardinals on June 26 for Kile's memorial tribute at Busch Stadium.

"We cannot possibly understand why we are here today," Cardinals pitcher Woody Williams, a native of Houston, said at the memorial. "Thank you, Lord, for the time we had with Darryl."

More than 5,000 fans attended the memorial, watching as a few of Kile's friends told stories about him. Bagwell was so overcome with grief that he declined a request to speak at the memorial. Astros owner Drayton McLane chartered a plane to St. Louis, leading a Houston contingent that included Bagwell and his wife, Ericka; Biggio and his wife, Patty; Shane Reynolds; and Brad Ausmus.

While offering condolences, McLane brought a smile to Flynn's face when he told her how much regret he had for not re-signing Darryl after the 1997 season. Kile had reached the majors in 1991 with the Astros, and he proposed to Flynn on the Astros' first trip to Los Angeles to play the Dodgers in May of that year. Flynn was 19, about to turn 20. He was 22. They were young and in love, and they were married January 11, 1992.

Despite a detour to Class AAA Tucson in 1992, Kile's career steadily blossomed after the couple's marriage. He was never better than when he pitched a no-hitter against the New York Mets on September 8, 1993. The no-hitter was a bittersweet moment. Although thrilled about the defining moment of his career, Kile regretted that his father wasn't there to see it. Eight months earlier, David Kile had suffered a deadly stroke at his doughnut shop in Friday Harbor, Washington.

"I don't think I'll ever get over it, because my father was my best friend," Kile told the *Houston Chronicle* in 1993. "But in order to be a man, you've got to separate your personal life from your work life. It may sound cold, but I've got work to do. I'll never forget my father, but I'm sure he'd want me to keep on working and try to do the best I can do."

In 1996, Kile had a 12-11 record with a 4.19 ERA and a career-high 219 strikeouts. In 1997, he won 19 games, was picked for his second All-Star Game, and finished fifth in the National League Cy Young Award balloting. But Kile left the Astros as a free agent and signed with the Colorado Rockies, accepting Colorado's three-year, $24 million offer over the Astros' three-year, $21 million offer.

Kile's decision to leave the Astros stunned Bagwell, and their friendship soured a bit for a few years as Bagwell struggled to forgive Kile for not giving him a last-ditch opportunity to lobby him to stay. For Kile, however, it was a matter of being appreciated. The Rockies made him feel wanted. McLane, many of Kile's fans believed, simply wanted to make an offer just good enough to finish second in the running to retain Kile. Kile struggled with the Rockies in 1998 and won only eight games in 1999 before he was traded to St. Louis on November 16, 1999.

After Kile's departure, the Astros were the hottest team in baseball and surprised the baseball world when Astros president of baseball operations Tal Smith and general manager Gerry Hunsicker pulled off a trade to land Randy Johnson from the Seattle Mariners at the July 31 trading deadline.

The 1998 Astros set a franchise record with 102 victories while claiming their second consecutive National League Central crown. Like the 1980, 1981, 1986, and 1997 Astros, however, the Astros couldn't win a postseason series. Johnson, "The Big Unit," gave up only five runs over 14 innings, losing both starts as Kevin Brown led the San Diego Padres to win the best-of-five series, three games to one. McLane made a run at Johnson in the offseason, but the Astros finished second again. Johnson signed with the Arizona Diamondbacks after the 1998 season and helped Arizona win the World Series over the Yankees in 2001. In Johnson's case, the Astros lost out on him more because of his desire to play and live in Arizona.

A year before Johnson led the Diamondbacks to the World Series another former Astro led a team to the World Series. Left-hander Mike Hampton, who was a year away from free agency, was traded from the Astros to the New York Mets on December 23, 1999. Hampton, who won 22 games in 1999 with the Astros while finishing second to Johnson for the National League Cy Young that year, joined the Mets and became the Most Valuable Player of the National League Championship Series against Kile's Cardinals in 2000.

It was almost a running joke in Houston for Astros fans to follow the playoffs by picking the team with the most Astros. The Astros lost free agents or expensive players on an almost yearly basis. Kile after the 1997 season, Johnson after 1998, Carl Everett and Hampton after the 1999 season, and popular slugger Moises Alou after the 2001 season.

Bagwell had grumbled publicly a few times, but he generally kept his complaints to himself. Biggio also played the role of a loyal employee, but the sports radio guys were always fielding calls from angry Astros fans. After consecutive seasons of finishing out of the playoff hunt, frustrations boiled over for left-handed closer Billy Wagner before the final game of the 2003 season. Wagner, who says Hunsicker told him a few days before the end of the season that he would be the next high-priced player to be traded, went off on McLane for not signing St. Louis right-handed pitcher Woody Williams, a Houston native, before the 2003 season. Short of cursing his boss, Wagner ridiculed McLane and claimed McLane was more interested in competing than winning.

McLane has the ultimate open-door policy—with fans, players, and media. If you have a problem or concern, he's just a phone call away. That access has endeared him with many of his fans and players. It also has left him an easy target for some of his critics because he doesn't hide behind spokesmen. He prides himself on leadership, and being accountable is a major leadership trait. His father taught him that good leaders accept the blame and share the glory with everybody else.

McLane has won over a majority of his critics because time and again he has put up the money and raised the payroll whenever an "extra" player was needed down the stretch. In 1998, he got the biggest guy on the trade market, hard-throwing Seattle Mariners left-hander Randy Johnson. In 2004, he also got the biggest guy on the trade market, Kansas City Royals center fielder Carlos Beltran, a month before the trading deadline and when nobody expected the Astros to even contend for Beltran's services. After the 2003 season, McLane likely secured his legacy by landing the premier free-agent left-handed starting pitcher on the market, Andy Pettitte, and the Hall of Famer everybody assumed was unavailable, Roger Clemens. From the mighty New York Yankees, no less.

Without the benefit of time to cool off or an ability to predict the future without him in Houston, Wagner took aim at his boss. McLane, who even approached Wagner in the clubhouse on the day of the rant to see if he wanted to talk, was stunned by the verbal jabs.

"Why did he do that? Why would he say such things?" McLane kept asking.

Three weeks after Wagner ridiculed McLane, the Astros owner sat down for breakfast in Chicago before Game 6 of the National League Championship Series between former Astros outfielder Moises Alou's Chicago Cubs and the Florida Marlins. The Cubs, McLane kept reminding himself, only beat the Astros by one game in the National League Central that year. The Astros players, not McLane, blew a 1½-game lead over the Cubs by dropping six of their last nine games, including two of the last four against the lowly Milwaukee Brewers.

Wagner, who collected an Astros-record 225 saves while consistently throwing 100-mph fastballs, simply said publicly what many of his teammates had whispered in private and what all of the radio call-in hosts and even some of the *Houston Chronicle's* highly respected columnists had repeated numerous times. Yet, McLane was stunned. The Astros were eliminated from playoff contention by losing the penultimate game of the season, and Wagner arrived at Minute Maid Park the next day knowing he would wear an Astros uniform for the last time. He claimed Hunsicker told him he would be traded after the 2003 season. Hunsicker denied it. Whatever the case, the trade was expected so that the Astros could dump his $8 million salary for 2004.

The surprising part was the shotgun Wagner took to McLane's reputation, saying McLane was more interested in competing than winning. Wagner also bashed McLane for his history of not keeping free agents.

"We'll be looking at a tape job and fill-ins and no marquee additions in the offseason," said Wagner, who was traded to the Phillies on November 3 for Brandon Duckworth, Taylor Buchholz, and Ezequiel Astacio.

Wagner had waited by his phone until nearly midnight on November 3, hoping to hear about the trade from Hunsicker or McLane themselves. After 10 years of loyal, record-breaking service, Wagner deemed himself at least worthy of a phone call. That call didn't come.

"There's no hard feelings about being traded, because I knew it was coming," Wagner said. "I just don't see the respect. If you're going to try to show me up, that's just disrespectful. I never said anything negative about them. I just said what I thought we should do to win."

The backlash regarding Wagner's trade was deafening. In calls to sports radio stations, messages on popular fan board sites such as Astrosdaily.com, and emails to the *Houston Chronicle*, many fans vowed to never attend Minute Maid Park again. Without trading Wagner, however, the Astros' budget likely would never have let them sign Pettitte, whose signing eventually lured Clemens out of retirement. The romantic notion is that Wagner was traded to clear up funds for Pettitte. Wagner's supporters would argue that the trade was part of a plan to cut payroll to about $65 million in 2004.

Whichever case, the reality is that dumping Wagner's salary helped the Astros get the salary flexibility to begin the trickle-down effect that landed Pettitte, Clemens, the eventual National League Championship Series berth in 2004, and the franchise's first World Series berth the next season.

In Philadelphia, Wagner became a media darling with his brutal honesty. He feuded with then-general manager Ed Wade. He ridiculed the cozy confines at Citizens Bank Park, speaking for all the Phillies' pitchers who didn't have the security to speak up. On the last day of the 2003 season, Wagner had said he only hoped the Astros wouldn't trade him to the Philadelphia Phillies or the New York Mets. He wanted to avoid Philadelphia because he didn't want to play for the temperamental Larry Bowa, who was fired with two games remaining in the 2004 season.

Wagner wanted to avoid the circus in New York, which actually is easier on professional athletes than the negativity and bitterness that is present in a city famous for booing Santa Claus. Some would say that Philadelphia has such an inferiority complex to its much bigger and brighter brother up North that the fans and media in the city of Brotherly Love overcompensate while trying to prove they can be tougher than the folks in New York. After two years of dealing with the madness in Philadelphia, Wagner was no longer intimidated about playing in New York.

When charismatic Mets general manager Omar Minaya courted Wagner and his family after the 2005 season, Wagner accepted a four-year, $43 million contract to pitch for the Mets. The tape job he predicted in Houston never materialized, and his Phillies lost 12 consecutive games against the Astros after he landed in Philadelphia.

The 2005 Phillies finished a game behind the Astros in the National League wild card race, and Wagner could only lament his new team's struggles against his old one. Nobody had to remind him that he suffered the losses on September 6 and September 7 against the Astros in the last two games of the series. It cannot be said, however, that Wagner criticizes others more harshly than he criticizes himself. Sincere to a fault, Wagner always saves his best jabs for himself.

"We haven't beaten them since I've been here, and they got to the second round since I left," Wagner said after suffering the 2–1 loss against the Astros on September 6 at Citizens Bank Park. "I'm probably no good to anybody."

Indeed, regrets.

9

The Real Kings of Texas

As sweat trickled off Roger Clemens's brow during a bullpen session in his first spring training with the Astros, Hall of Famer Nolan Ryan was one of the few men in the world who truly understood the task ahead for his good friend. At 41, Clemens started the season at the same age Ryan was during his final season with the Astros in 1988.

Contrary to Dr. John McMullen's prediction, 1988 wasn't the end of Ryan's career. It was only the end of Ryan's stay in Houston. He merely moved the Ryan Express north up Interstate 45. Ryan was pushed out of Houston in one of the franchise's most infamous decisions. Despite his age, Ryan kept playing. He spent five more seasons in the majors after McMullen pushed him right into the Texas Rangers' appreciative grasp on December 7, 1988, sending him all the way to Cooperstown in a Rangers cap with 324 career victories.

Until January 2004 when he was re-signed by the Astros, Clemens was 14 victories away from tying Ryan for 12th on the all-time list with 324.

"Nolan told me, 'It doesn't get any easier, does it?'" Clemens said. "I told him, 'It doesn't.' He knows the amount of work that I put in before I even came here, once I committed to play again. You want it to happen so fast. You want your body to bounce back so fast. You just have to give it time. He knows that. He knows that at this stage in my career, you're really going to have to battle to win games and be effective and be smart when you're out there. He knows it. He's lived it, and I've lived it."

Ryan and Clemens, both hard-throwing right-handers who grew up in the Houston area, can relate to each other. Like Ryan, Clemens leaned heavily on his mid-90s fastball on the road to his first 310 victories in the American League and the next 31 in the National League throughout the 2005 season with the Astros. Also like Ryan, Clemens is an intimidating presence. The six-foot-four, 235-pound Clemens is a tad bigger and broader around the shoulders than Ryan, who played at 195 pounds on his six-foot-two frame. They both intimidated hitters with fastballs and a commanding mound presence that cried out, "I'm in control now. I will beat you or hurt you or both." Ryan sits comfortably atop the list with 5,714 strikeouts. Hall of Fame left-hander Steve Carlton was second with 4,136 heading into the 2004 season, and Clemens entered that season third with 4,099. By May 5, 2004, Clemens finally passed Carlton and moved into second place behind Ryan. Yankees left-hander Randy Johnson, who like Clemens and Ryan once wore an Astros jersey, has also surpassed Carlton on the all-time strikeouts list.

Clemens prides himself on narrowing his field of vision, focusing only on his catcher and the opposing hitter. But even he had to alter his view a bit the night of May 5 to a larger scope, to a historical perspective after passing Carlton. After Pittsburgh Pirates right fielder Raul Mondesi swung through Clemens's 89-mph splitter in the fifth inning, giving The Rocket his sixth strikeout of the evening and 4,137th of his career, Clemens pumped his fist triumphantly and took a few steps off the mound after passing Carlton's 4,136 mark.

Meanwhile, catcher Brad Ausmus tossed the record-breaking ball toward the Astros dugout as Clemens prepared to get back to work for the eventual 6–2 victory that would run his perfect start to 6–0. But the crowd of 35,883 at Minute Maid Park made Clemens wait, giving him a rousing 50-second standing ovation that he acknowledged with a tip of one of the five caps he wore in the contest. After the outing, Clemens handed one cap to Astros owner Drayton McLane and two others to his two eldest sons, Koby and Kory. He also gave his wife, Debbie, the ball he struck out Mondesi with. He saved the ball that tied the record for his mother, Bess.

"I got back up on the mound and the next Pirates hitter [Rob Mackowiak] stayed out of the box," Clemens said after giving up five hits and two runs with three walks and nine strikeouts for his 316th victory. "I appreciate [Mackowiak] giving me that opportunity to acknowledge the crowd. It's hard not to get caught up in that moment. I've been lucky enough to have a few of those moments. It's amazing [Ryan] did it in... 27 years—unbelievable. I won't make it that long. Right now I'm mentally drained from the game just behind us. They get tougher and tougher."

According to Ausmus, however, Clemens was successful because he wasn't focused on getting the strikeouts.

"To me, Roger pitched the game to win and not to break a strikeout mark," Ausmus said. "That's a testament to him, to see him place the greatest importance on a win instead of the immediate passing of Steve Carlton."

"You knew it was going to happen, barring a catastrophic injury," Berkman said of Clemens's mark. "It was great that it was here. It was great that the fans acknowledged the achievement the way they did. It was a special moment. It was one of those deals where you'll remember as a player being on the field when it happened."

Clemens remains adamant that he won't catch Ryan. But when Ryan surveys the major league landscape, he modestly hesitates to say his spot atop the all-time major league strikeouts list is safe. When thinking of potential threats to his record, the Hall of Fame right-hander mentions two pitchers he has mentored: Yankees left-hander Randy Johnson and Cubs right-hander Kerry Wood. Then there's a guy named Roger, the 43-year-old right-hander who grew up in the Houston area watching Ryan pitch at the Astrodome for their hometown Astros.

"That's a lot of innings," said Clemens, who finished the 2005 season with 4,502 career strikeouts. "That's a lot of going out there and getting the work done and putting your time in. It's just a long time. It means you've been at it a long time, and hopefully for the better part of those years they've been quality years. That's how you catch and pass some of these guys with big names."

Clemens would need a few more seasons before reaching the 5,714 strikeouts Ryan had in a 27-year career that included nine seasons with the Astros.

"I think we all had longevity," Ryan said of himself, Carlton, and Clemens. "To be able to pitch that many innings and accumulate that many strikeouts, you have to have longevity and you also have to be able to maintain your style of pitching. It's been real interesting to see how Roger's gotten off to such a strong start with the stuff that he's maintained and how he's throwing. To surpass Steve Carlton reflects that he's been able to maintain his stuff his entire career. Much like in my career, due to the aging process you lose some of your natural ability. Whereas I developed a change-up that made my fastball better, he's developed the split finger. The adjustments that he's been able to make have allowed him to continue to pitch on the level that we're accustomed to seeing him pitch on."

Like Ryan and Carlton, Clemens and Johnson are contemporaries who have filled their résumés with strikeouts.

"It's very possible if they pitch enough innings and are able to maintain the style of pitching to be a strikeout pitcher, but it's hard to say," Ryan said in 2004. "If you look at Randy Johnson and his strikeout ratio this year, [he has] to stay away from injuries so that he doesn't have an off-year like he had [in 2003]."

Kerry Wood is from the younger generation of strikeout pitchers, but Astros fans know he's cut from of the same cloth as Ryan and Clemens.

Wood became the quickest man in major league history to get 1,000 strikeouts—in terms of innings and games—when he accomplished the feat in August 2003 against the Astros by striking out Jeff Kent. It was fitting perhaps that Wood accomplished the milestone against the Astros, the team he dominated when he tied Clemens's single-game record with 20 strikeouts as a rookie on May 6, 1998. Clemens set the record on April 29, 1986, against the Seattle Mariners.

"You know it's hard to make any type of predictions of a Kerry Wood or somebody of that nature," Ryan said. "They certainly have the ability, and it comes down to longevity and being able to maintain that style of pitching."

With a renowned work ethic, Clemens sustained his status as a strikeout pitcher while collecting his record seven Cy Young Awards, one for each no-hitter the legendary Ryan Express collected in the majors. Interestingly enough, Clemens has yet to throw a no-hitter and Ryan never won a Cy Young. Clemens also collected his first 4,099 strikeouts in the American League with the Red Sox (2,590), Toronto Blue Jays (563), and New York Yankees (946). He struck out 218 in his first season with the Astros for his 12th season with at least 200 strikeouts. He added 185 strikeouts in 2005 over 32 starts.

Equally important for both men, Clemens is passing down some of the lessons he learned from Ryan—and not just to Astros pitchers. Clemens is now to Texan Josh Beckett, the 2003 World Series MVP, what Ryan was to Clemens.

"Yeah, I idolized him," Beckett said of Clemens during one of his press conferences at the 2003 World Series. "I don't know that my mechanics are that much like him. I know when I was younger, I used to try to pitch like him and stuff."

Playing home run derby on the street as a child in the Houston suburb of Spring, Beckett pretended he was Clemens. Beckett, now 25, wasn't even born when Clemens used to watch Ryan work out. As Clemens ascended into stardom, Ryan offered encouragement and praise whenever their paths crossed. Their paths will cross more often now that Ryan has signed a five-year personal services contract with the Astros after a 15-year working relationship with the Rangers.

"I can just only imagine what some of these young kids [feel] in this minor league complex and even some of the young pitchers here [in the majors]," Clemens said. "They're not going to get to watch Nolan work,

Roger Clemens's determination when paired with his talent has made him perhaps the most dominant pitcher of his era. This was exemplified during the 2005 season when he pitched and won a game 15 hours after his mother's passing.

but when I had the opportunity to watch him work, I learned from it. When we had an opportunity via golf tournaments or when he'd call me out on the field after he had done his work there at the old Ranger stadium, those were just great talks that we had.

"I even look back to when I was in high school and they had a work stoppage and they came out to work out. Those are just things that leave an impression. It left an impression on me, obviously. Those are things that once I do set my glove down if I walk away and I hear a comment from a [Curt] Schilling, a Josh Beckett, or a Kerry Wood, then I feel like I passed the baton on down."

Although Ryan doesn't live in the Houston area anymore, he appreciates the excitement Clemens and Pettitte brought to the city. Born in Refugio and raised in Alvin, Ryan knows what it felt like for Pettitte and Clemens to pitch near their homes.

"I'm going to get a lot of enjoyment out of watching Roger this year and seeing how much he enjoys being an Astro," Ryan said in 2004. "I think it's going to be very special to him. He and Andy both. I'm looking forward to that, and I think it's going to have a very positive effect on the seasons that they have. I'm going to be watching it with great interest. I think for a young pitching staff, having their presence on a day-to-day basis [is] going to have a big impact. It's going to have a big impact on the entire pitching staff of the Houston Astros' major league ball club and then also on the minor league ball club. Because it's going to give some of these young, aspiring pitchers an opportunity to see how those guys work and see what they do even though they've reached the level and status that they have and how they go about their work and the dedication they have."

Few men pitch inside with the authority that Ryan did during his 27-year career. Clemens is one of those men, and Ryan hopes other Astros pitchers embrace such an aggressive pitching style.

"With Roger being here, he'll establish that he will pitch inside and [to] both sides of the plate," Ryan said. "That's kind of a lost art that [disappeared] over the last 10 to 15 years on the major league level and throughout baseball and with aluminum bats [that high schools and colleges use] and all the things that have happened over the years.

"I think that having Roger here and the style of pitcher he is will probably resurrect that style of pitching to some degree."

10

Finishing 36-10 Without Pettitte

Reaching the playoffs hasn't been a problem for the Astros in the Jeff Bagwell–Craig Biggio era. Like the Astros before them, however, winning a postseason series had been a task. The 2004 season appeared different. Roger Clemens and Andy Pettitte brought a different confidence level home. They expected to win. They were accustomed to winning. More importantly, they were premier pitchers in a sport in which pitching trumps everything else.

With Pettitte and Clemens on board, the outlook for the Houston ball club seemed much brighter heading into the 2004 season.

"I embrace the challenge to be able to be great and to try to take this team to the next level," Pettitte said during his first spring training. "We're not going to be able to do it alone. We're going to have to have a lot of help, but I'm looking forward to try to help this team be great."

Unfortunately for the Astros, Pettitte was not available for the 2004 postseason. After landing on the disabled list with elbow problems for the third time in the 2004 season on August 18, Pettitte and the Astros decided it would be best for him to have surgery on his left elbow. His best fastball never got above the mid-80s at Shea Stadium on August 12, when each pitch sent a throbbing pain through his left elbow. Looking at his good friend in the tunnel between innings, Clemens cringed at the pain Pettitte was trying to pitch through. Despite the pain, Pettitte held the Mets to one run, four walks, and four hits with five strikeouts over 5²⁄₃ innings. He exited with the score tied 1-1 and the bases loaded in the sixth inning. Leaving Shea Stadium that evening, Pettitte tried to be optimistic as he headed back to Houston to meet with Astros team physicians Tom Mehlhoff and David Lintner while his teammates headed to Montreal to continue the trip. He assumed he'd undergo an MRI and be told that his elbow looked well enough for him to continue pitching through the pain. After the MRI in Houston, Pettitte sought a second opinion from famed orthopaedic surgeon James Andrews.

"I just started having a lot of problems during the course of the game," he said. "Other parts of my arm were breaking down. My arm, I pushed it. I didn't want to face the reality of it."

Pettitte was relieved on August 12 by right-hander David Weathers, who had been acquired from the Mets in exchange for outfielder Richard Hidalgo.

Weathers escaped Pettitte's bases-loaded jam in the sixth. Weathers wasn't nearly as effective in the seventh, which Danny Garcia led off with a double to left. Weathers retired the next two Mets, but Joe McEwing broke the tie with a single to left field.

Hidalgo, a popular figure in the Astros clubhouse, had fallen out of favor with then-manager Jimy Williams and general manager Gerry Hunsicker in May and landed in the proverbial doghouse. Once he was traded to the Mets that June 17, he made his disdain for Williams quite clear. Bagwell was only one of the few Astros who publicly supported Hidalgo, saying that Hidalgo would hit his way out of his slump if Astros management—Williams and Hunsicker—would merely quit messing with the outfielder's head. Although Williams had already been fired by the time the Astros visited Shea Stadium in August, Hidalgo wanted to prove Williams wrong. He responded by going four for 11 with one run batted in, three walks, and two doubles in the series. He was also two for four and scored the only run Pettitte gave up on August 12.

"I felt happy to see them," Hidalgo said. "They know what I can do, and I know what I can do."

Hidalgo was the least of the Astros' concerns at that point. By dropping two of three against the lowly Mets, the Astros fell to 56-58. They left New York and dropped the first two games against the Montreal Expos at Olympic Stadium, falling to 56-60, 19½ games behind the St. Louis Cardinals and seven games behind the wild card lead with a little over seven weeks to play. Until then, the Astros had not won a game that they trailed after the eighth inning in the 2004 regular season.

Moreover, they had lost six of seven games heading into the finale of the three-game series that would be the Astros' last in Montreal.

Trailing 4-2 on August 15 at Olympic Stadium, Lance Berkman flied out to right field to start the top of the ninth. Expos right-hander Livan Hernandez's quest for a complete game ended after Jeff Kent and Mike Lamb hit consecutive singles. Expos manager Frank Robinson relieved Hernandez with right-hander Luis Ayala even though Jason Lane, who was zero for three against Hernandez, was now at the plate. The Astros capitalized against Ayala. Lane cut the deficit to 4-3 with an RBI single.

Manager Phil Garner responded with pinch hitter Jose Vizcaino, who tied the score 4-4 with a ground out into the hole at short. Orlando Palmeiro drove in the game-winning run with a blooper over the shortstop's head in shallow left field.

"Our guys did a fantastic job," Brad Lidge, who pitched a scoreless ninth inning for his 13th save of that season, told the *Houston Chronicle*'s Brian McTaggart. "We came back for this one, and now we have a little bit of momentum going into Philadelphia. This was a huge win for us, and this proves to us we can do it."

Nobody could have imagined just how prophetic Lidge's comments were that afternoon. With 7⅔ scoreless innings from Roy Oswalt, the Astros opened their first three-game series at brand new Citizens Bank Park with a 5-0 victory over the Philadelphia Phillies. The Astros' biggest scare that evening was in the stands when Garner's wife, Carol, was hit on the right wrist when one of the Phillies lost control of his bat and sent it flying over the visitors' dugout.

"They can't hit the Astros, so they'll hit the manager's wife," Carol Garner joked.

The two-game winning streak wasn't nearly enough to convince Garner, Hunsicker, or the Astros players that the 2004 season wasn't a lost cause. Only one man in the Astros clubhouse put on a straight face and declared that the season wasn't lost: Mr. Pettitte.

Pettitte was adamant in his prediction that his teammates could still reach the 2004 postseason, but it seemed less likely on August 18 when he and the Astros announced that he would undergo season-ending left elbow surgery to repair a torn flexor tendon. The Astros already were playing without starting shortstop Adam Everett, who didn't return until September 29 from the fractured left ulna he suffered when Expos right-hander Claudio Vargas hit him with a pitch on August 6 at Minute Maid Park. Starting right-hander Wade Miller, who had been the Astros' No. 2 starter the previous two seasons, also was done for the season with right shoulder problems.

"Brutal the way it ended," Pettitte said. "I didn't expect this to happen. I just can't go anymore. It's brutal."

Although there had been whispers about Pettitte's left elbow problems, the Astros had given Pettitte a three-year, $31.5 million contract after checking his medical files. Nothing in Pettitte's 2003 season would have given the Astros concern. He threw 208 innings in 2003, going 21-8 with a 4.02 ERA while making 33 starts without ever having to be skipped a turn because of injury. He also made five starts in the 2003 postseason, going 3-1 over 34⅓ innings.

The torn flexor tendon had not cost Pettitte any starts in 2003, but the injury bit him early and often in 2004. A checked swing in his first start as an Astro on April 6 put him out until April 29. By August 18, he had been on the disabled list twice already, missing a total of eight starts in the process while going 6-4 with a 3.90 ERA over 83 innings and 15 starts.

Two weeks before his last start of the season, Pettitte had been scratched from his scheduled start on July 31 with the elbow problems, which often were announced as forearm injuries to the media. By August 18, Pettitte's elbow wasn't the Astros' only concern. Watching Pettitte pitch through throbbing elbow pain, Garner was certain that Pettitte would have done damage to his left shoulder if he were allowed to make his remaining nine starts and throw the 800 or 900 pitches he would have accumulated over that span.

"Obviously you want to be known as a gamer or competitor," said Pettitte, who had grown tired of his teammates having to worry about him. "I came here to try to help this team get to the playoffs and then try to get past the first round. I'm just very disappointed that I wasn't able to give this team what I wanted to give this team this year."

With that said, Pettitte cautioned against counting the 2004 Astros out of the postseason. The Astros responded to Pettitte's news with a 9-8 comeback victory over the Phillies on a night Clemens exited early with a right calf strain he suffered running to first base on his two-run single to right field. Clemens lasted only three innings, and Garner needed six relievers to pitch the final six innings. One of those relievers, Dan Miceli, pitched with a severe case of pink eye in both eyes and could hardly see the plate.

With the score tied 1-1, the Phillies jumped on Clemens by sending eight batters to the plate while scoring three runs in the third inning. Clemens's teammates erased the 4-1 deficit right away with a six-run rally in the fourth. The Astros got within 4-3 on RBI singles by Kent and Vizcaino. With two men on, one out, and Clemens on-deck, Philadelphia's Cory Lidle loaded the bases with a walk to Brad Ausmus. As Lidle's control problems continued, Clemens showed the patience of a veteran by refusing to chase pitches out of the strike zone as he worked the count to 3-0. After Garner ordered Clemens to take the next pitch, Lidle ripped a 3-0 fastball in for a called strike. Lidle tried to put that pitch over again for a strike. Although Garner still had the take sign on, Clemens pounced and sent Lidle's fastball to right field for a two-run single and a 5-4 lead. Clemens limped on his way to first base, prompting Garner and athletic trainer Dave Labossiere to rush out after him. After a brief chat, Clemens hobbled out of the game.

"I was just disappointed I couldn't continue," Clemens said. "When I got down to first base, that was my first concern. Then, not just jeopardizing the team and the way the situation—to have the opportunity to win the game—was obviously more important than me trying to continue. Running was going to be difficult. Maybe pitching not as difficult, but I wasn't going to be able to find out."

Once Clemens exited the field, the Astros continued the rally with Biggio's RBI double to left field and Carlos Beltran's sacrifice fly to left. Weathers gave one of the runs back in the bottom of the inning by giving up Marlon Byrd's home run to left field. The Phillies jumped on relievers Chad Qualls, Mike Gallo, and Chad Harville to take an 8-7 lead with three runs in the seventh. Beltran countered in the eighth with a two-run double off left-hander Rheal Cormier. Miceli retired the Phillies in order in the bottom of the eighth, and Lidge collected the save despite loading the bases after retiring the first two batters in the inning. The pitching staff wasn't very impressive again the next day against the Phillies, but a seven-run rally in the seventh inning, a two-run rally in the eighth, and home runs by Biggio, Berkman, and Eric Bruntlett pushed the Astros to a 12-10 victory. With that victory, the Astros reached the .500 mark again for the first time since August 7.

The Astros returned to Minute Maid Park feeling good about themselves after salvaging a 5-4 mark on a three-city, 10-day trip through New York, Montreal, and Philadelphia after they lost four of their first five. The Chicago Cubs put the Astros back under .500 with a 9-2 victory over Pete Munro on August 20. The Astros responded with a 4-3 victory the next day, setting up a turbulent series finale on Sunday afternoon with Oswalt on the mound against Kerry Wood.

Oswalt's control problems that day were evident when he issued a leadoff walk to Wood on five pitches in the third inning. Oswalt got the first out when Corey Patterson dropped a poor sacrifice bunt attempt in front of the plate. Once Wood was forced out at second on Patterson's fielder's choice, Oswalt struck out Derrek Lee. Oswalt would have been out of the inning if Patterson had not knocked the ball out of second baseman Jeff Kent's glove while stealing second. If Kent had held on to the ball, the Astros would have been celebrating catcher Raul Chavez's strong throw to second. Instead, Patterson was at second, and Todd Walker was at the plate. Walker tied the score 1-1 with a ground-rule double to right field. Former Astro Moises Alou, Bagwell's best friend and still a popular figure in the Astros clubhouse, followed with a walk.

With two men on, Oswalt induced the routine one-hopper he needed from Sammy Sosa. Mike Lamb couldn't make the play at third, however, and Walker gave the Cubs a 2-1 lead on Lamb's error. Oswalt's frustrations continued when Cubs third baseman Aramis Ramirez ripped a three-run home run over the wall in left-center field. Oswalt's next pitch found Cubs catcher Michael Barrett's ribs. Plate umpire Bill Hohn responded immediately by tossing Oswalt, who put his head down and began walking toward the Astros dugout. When Oswalt lifted his head, he noticed Barrett walking toward him with a few choice words.

In that instance, Barrett prompted both benches and bullpens to empty and meet in front of home plate. Some of the Cubs were still celebrating Ramirez's three-run home run when they changed course and rushed out of the dugout and bullpen toward Barrett and Oswalt. The Astros dugout and bullpen also emptied. No punches were thrown, but the Astros' march toward the National League wild card had been lit at the moment Barrett stepped toward Oswalt to begin a feud that would heat up five days later at Wrigley Field.

The Cubs cruised to an easy 11-6 victory while also hitting the Astros' top two offensive players, Kent and Beltran, after Barrett had been hit. Wood also had hit Jason Lane with a fastball in the second inning after Lamb's home run. Wood actually hit Beltran in the bottom of the third inning with a slider, but Hohn didn't eject him even though some would argue that Wood knew what he was doing with that breaking pitch. Wood, who broke shortstop Julio Lugo's forearm with a pitch during a game against the Astros in 2002, finally got tossed along with manager Dusty Baker when he wasted a pitch on Kent's body while leading 10-2 in the fifth inning. Oswalt has steadfastly denied hitting Barrett on purpose.

"There wasn't even a warning," Oswalt said. "Our guy [Lane] right after a home run gets hit with the next pitch, and there's no warning to [Wood]. And I throw and hit a guy, too, and I don't get a warning. I get thrown out. I don't know. A lot of people say, 'Well, you're not as wild.' It doesn't make sense. If you miss toward the hitter, you miss toward the hitter."

The Cubs weren't the only ones who backed Hohn's assessment of the situation.

"I would have thrown Roy out, too," said Bagwell, the Astros' unquestioned leader. "It looked as blatant as it can be."

Inside the visitors' clubhouse, Oswalt had even fewer supporters.

Wood accused Oswalt of hitting Barrett after getting upset at giving up five runs. Of course, Wood had a convenient excuse for hitting three batters, claiming that his hitting Lane, Beltran, and Kent merely was a byproduct of pitching inside with his two-seam fastball, as though somehow Wood is entitled to the inside part of the plate and Oswalt isn't. Barrett accused Oswalt of being frustrated more than anything. Berkman discounted the controversy as part of baseball. He went a step further by reminding the media that the Cubs were involved in a similar benches-clearing meeting at the plate earlier in the season with the St. Louis Cardinals.

"Baseball is a game of emotion, and things like that happen," Berkman said. "It's been happening for 100 years. The Cubs had a similar incident with the Cardinals earlier this year, so it's nothing unusual or nothing new. I'm sure it's a situation that will be addressed on the field at a later date."

Oswalt had already left Minute Maid Park when he learned of Bagwell's assessment. He was saddened by the comments, feeling a tinge of betrayal. Oswalt didn't back down, though. Hitters and pitchers usually view things differently, and the reactions on August 22 were perfect examples. Actually, Oswalt had endured some snide comments and some backbiting from his teammates for two weeks because he had refused to retaliate against the Montreal Expos on August 6. To understand what happened August 22 and August 27 with Oswalt and Barrett, it makes sense to dissect Oswalt's 4-0 victory over the Expos on August 6. That was the evening Expos reliever Claudio Vargas drilled Adam Everett with a fastball up and inside, fracturing the ulna bone in the slick-fielding shortstop's left wrist and forearm. Everett, one of four Astros batters hit that day by the Expos, fell to the Minute Maid Park dirt in agony almost immediately as Labossiere and Garner rushed to his side. Everett knew he had received more than a glancing blow once Labossiere started applying pressure to the forearm and wrist.

Oswalt threw the third shutout of his career that evening, needing 133 pitches to give the Astros' tired bullpen a rest. He held the Expos to five hits and one walk while collecting eight strikeouts. Afterward, however, one of the veteran Astros—not Bagwell or Kent—began badgering Oswalt for not hitting any of the Expos. That veteran even pleaded with a reporter to go ask Oswalt why he didn't protect his teammates. Actually, Oswalt wanted to retaliate. He was set to hit one of the Expos. After watching starter Rocky Biddle hit Biggio in the left hand, Vargas hit Everett, and reliever Sunny Kim hit Berkman and Bagwell in the seventh inning, Oswalt asked Garner if Garner wanted him to retaliate. Garner told Oswalt that it wasn't appropriate, and Oswalt agreed.

"None of them [was] intentional, the way I saw it," Oswalt told the *Houston Chronicle*'s Brian McTaggart. "None of those guys would like to hit anybody intentionally, and the guy that did hit [Everett] was pretty much wild all night. It just seems like he couldn't find the feel of the ball, and he walked me on four pitches [in the fourth]. There's a time and a place to do it."

Even though Oswalt had protected his teammates on many occasions, his explanation did not sit well with some of his teammates. Other than Everett, though, every Astro who got hit could have protected his own honor by charging the mound if he had been so inclined. Instead of whining about Oswalt not hitting an Expo, any of Oswalt's teammates could have taken his argument to the mound and confronted the opposing pitcher.

Oswalt at least asked permission to retaliate.

Sixteen days later, Oswalt actually accomplished what his teammates had wanted. Wood had hit Oswalt's good friend, Lane, with a pitch after a home run in the second inning. Oswalt hit Barrett after a home run one inning later, even if it was unintentional. Whatever the case, the score stood at one hit batsman on each side until Wood increased the tally with Beltran and Kent.

A day after the Cubs left Houston after that tension-filled Sunday afternoon, Garner brought Bagwell and Oswalt into the manager's office to quell any animosity before it festered and divided the clubhouse. Bagwell and Oswalt also met separately. Oswalt, who has tremendous respect for Bagwell, moved on by declaring that he knows people have likely said worse things about him, but that he can move on without animosity because he is not the type of person who holds grudges. Oswalt got in his teammates' good graces two days after the Barrett incident with an inning of relief to claim the decision in a 4-2 victory over the Philadelphia Phillies.

Two days after throwing only 57 pitches over 2⅔ innings, Oswalt took the mound in the eighth inning against the heart of the Phillies' order for his first relief appearance since July 7, 2002. He kept the score tied 2-2 by striking out Placido Polanco and Bobby Abreu and inducing a ground out from Jim Thome. He was rewarded in the bottom of the inning as the Astros took the 4-2 lead on RBI singles from Berkman and Lamb. The Astros completed the three-game sweep the next night with a 7-4 victory, completing the six-game season sweep against Philadelphia. It was only the second time the Astros had swept a season series of at least six games against an opponent. (They pulled off the trick again in 2005 against the Phillies, collecting consecutive season series sweeps against the same team for the first time in franchise history.)

After the three-game sweep over the Phillies at Minute Maid Park, the Astros flew to Chicago, where all the focus was on the Oswalt–Barrett feud before the crucial four-game series. Oswalt tried to diffuse the situation by saying he had put the issue behind him. Unlike many of his teammates, though, he didn't waste any time lounging around the batting cages with the Cubs before the first game of the series. As if the Cubs weren't upset enough already, Baker grew furious when he learned that Major League Baseball had decided to fine Oswalt instead of suspending him for hitting Barrett.

The Cubs opened the series with an 8-3 rout against Brandon Backe, who didn't get much support, as his teammates went one for 13 with runners in scoring position and stranded 12 runners. Oswalt, Wood, and Barrett went at it the next day. With the wind blowing out and the knowledge that they'd likely be tossed if they hit a batter by pitching too inside on this hot and humid afternoon, Oswalt and Wood understood their ERAs, if nothing else, would take a beating in the second game of the series. Behind the plate, umpire C.B. Bucknor was told to be vigilant five days after Barrett and Oswalt had prompted the benches to clear.

The Astros took advantage of the wind in the first inning on Beltran's home run to right-center. With that shot, Beltran tied the Astros' record with home runs in five consecutive games. Wood walked Bagwell and then hit Berkman with a pitch, putting Wood up 4-1 over Oswalt in the hit batsmen category over the two games. Berkman also was the 12th Astros player that Wood had hit up to that point since reaching the majors in 1998. Kent followed with an RBI single to left, and Morgan Ensberg drove in two more runs with a double to right field to give Oswalt a 4-0 lead.

The Cubs countered with two runs in the bottom of the inning on Nomar Garciaparra's RBI single to left field and Alou's sacrifice fly to left. Barrett was waiting for Oswalt at the plate quickly after Sosa was called out on strikes to end the first inning. Barrett berated Oswalt as Oswalt walked toward the plate from the dugout, and he got in Oswalt's face as soon as Oswalt reached the plate.

Oswalt had been walking to the plate with his head down. When he lifted his head, he saw Barrett in his face.

Oswalt, who initially thought Bucknor was in front of him, looked at Barrett, smiled, and calmly said, "If you're going to do something, do it."

Barrett proved all talk and moved away after Bucknor got between the two. Bagwell was Oswalt's first teammate toward the confrontation, and the entire team joined him out of the dugout in a split second. Bucknor diffused the situation after there was nothing more than a few curse words thrown between the clubs. Barrett wouldn't let it go, though. He chased Oswalt up the first-base line, backing up the play as he should have on Oswalt's ground out to short. He crossed the line, however, by following Oswalt and yelling at him up the line after the out had been recorded. With the entire Astros bench standing at the steps of the dugout, Oswalt's teammates responded by shouting at Barrett with a few choice words of their own.

Heading into the sixth inning, everybody except Barrett had behaved well on both sides as the Astros marched toward a 15-7 rout with their most runs of the season. With Wood already icing his shoulder, reliever Kent Mercker hit Oswalt with a pitch. Not one person among the crowd of 39,038 could have possibly believed Mercker didn't hit Oswalt on purpose. Oswalt took his base without saying a word or even wasting a nasty stare at Mercker's direction.

Oswalt retaliated with his composure on an afternoon when the pitching line could not be judged other than by who won and lost. Oswalt went eight innings, allowing six runs on seven hits and one walk with four strikeouts. Oswalt even played a part in one of the imploding Cubs' many controversies that season.

The Cubs had been feuding with their broadcasters, Chip Caray and Steve Stone, most of the year. For some of the Cubs, Caray and Stone weren't homers enough. Considering all of the elements involved—hot weather, wind blowing out, the tight wild card race, the Barrett feud—Caray praised Oswalt for having a strong outing. Sitting in the cozy home clubhouse at Wrigley Field, Mercker was incensed by Caray's positive commentary. Mercker called the press box to complain about Caray's decision to praise Oswalt. As if the 2004 Cubs didn't have enough issues, Mercker wanted Caray added to Oswalt, the Cardinals, and Stone on the Cubs' hit list.

The Cubs didn't make many friends on the other side, either. The normally quiet Beltran, who invokes God's name often in his sentences and doesn't curse, admitted a desire to kill after watching Barrett confront Oswalt. Beltran settled for his fourth multi-home run game of the season and a four-for-five performance that included the three-run blast that sparked the Astros' six-run rally in the ninth.

"I think Roy was very professional today," Beltran said. "When something like that happens, you want to back up your players. That gave us a little pump to go out there. We wanted to kill. We wanted to kill the opposing pitcher."

Bagwell downplayed any thought of the Astros using Barrett's taunts as a rallying cry, saying a quality pitcher in baseball puts an end to rallying cries. With the victory, the Astros snapped the Cubs' five-game winning streak and moved Houston within five games of Chicago, which was in second place in the NL Central, but first in the NL wild card race.

The victory was Houston's ninth over its last 12 games. More impressively, it also was the start of the Astros' 12-game winning streak. Clearly, the Cubs shook the Astros out of their slumber. Challenged to a fight, the

Astros responded with a genuine ass-kicking over Baker's undisciplined group.

"They had said some things that didn't need to be said, but our boys answered the challenge, and that's exactly the way it should have been," Garner said.

Clemens won the next day 7-6, tying former Astro Nolan Ryan and Don Sutton for 12th on the all-time victories list with his 324th victory. The Astros closed the series with a 10-3 victory, cutting the Cubs' lead in the wild card race to four games as Chicago fell into a tie with the San Francisco Giants and San Diego Padres. Tension built during the Astros' five-run eighth inning when Ryan Dempster hit Beltran on the left knee, knocking the All-Star center fielder out of the game.

Later that inning, Mike Remlinger ripped his fastball near Berkman's head. The ball hit Berkman's bat and not his head, but Berkman fell and squirmed as though he had been shot. Unimpressed, Baker claimed Berkman's performance was worthy of an Oscar.

"I find out he was faking it," Remlinger said. "That's pretty poor. I thought it hit him right in the head [by] the way he was rolling around in the dirt. And he was a guy I had a little respect for. That's pretty poor."

Berkman and his teammates weren't worried about the Cubs' feelings. Dan Wheeler, who had joined the Astros the day after he was acquired from the Mets, made his debut with the Astros by hitting Derrek Lee in the ninth inning. Once again, it was clear the Astros had retaliated even though everybody denied it. The Astros didn't lose again until September 9 against the Pittsburgh Pirates.

The Astros dropped three of their first four in a five-game series against the Pirates, stalling their ride to the wild card a bit. But they won the series finale at PNC Park 5-4 in 10 innings to begin a streak in which they won six of their next seven heading into an important three-game series against the Giants in San Francisco. Carlos Hernandez was clobbered 9-2 in the first game of the series, and Oswalt suffered a 5-1 loss in the second game as the Giants took a four-game lead over the Astros in the wild card race with 10 games to play.

The Astros salvaged a come-from-behind 7-3 victory in the series finale with a five-run rally in the top of the ninth, three of those runs coming on Berkman's home run off of Dustin Hermanson. In avoiding what would have been a disastrous sweep, the Astros knocked the Giants from the top spot in the National League wild card race.

"This has been a crazy season," Berkman told Brian McTaggart. "It seems like every time we're on the brink of destruction or elimination something happens. We have a 12-game win streak, or we have a big inning against a great ball club."

There was little reason to believe the Astros would win. They had only two hits—a triple and a single by Beltran—heading into the seventh inning against hard-throwing right-hander Jason Schmidt. They got within 3-1 when Beltran walked, stole second and third base, and scored on Berkman's single to right field in the seventh inning. Morgan Ensberg's RBI ground out to first cut the Giants' lead to 3-2 in the eighth. It was approaching midnight in Houston, and many Astros fans likely turned off the telecast from San Francisco before Berkman hit his three-run home run over the right field wall to put the Astros ahead 5-3.

The Astros had asked the Giants if they would change the start time for the series' finale to make it an afternoon game instead of a night game. The Giants denied the request, and the Astros finished off the 7-3 victory and rushed to their charter for an overnight flight to Milwaukee. Sleep-deprived, they won the first game against the Brewers 1-0 in 10 innings. The lack of sleep, quality pitching, and quality at-bats caught up with them the next afternoon when the Brewers crushed Pete Munro 8-0. Fortunately for the Astros, the wild card-leading Chicago Cubs also lost that afternoon. With the Cubs' loss against the Mets, the Astros were still 2½ games behind Chicago with a week remaining in the regular season.

The Astros responded by winning their final seven games. They won the series finale against the Brewers 11-7 and returned to Minute Maid Park for a pair of three-game series. They swept three from the runaway NL Central champion St. Louis Cardinals, who were already resting some key players in anticipation of the division series. They won the last game of that series 6-4 to take a half-game lead over the Cubs and Giants in the wild card race.

The Astros received another boost on their day off when the Cincinnati Reds beat the Cubs 2-1 in 12 innings on September 30, putting the Astros a game ahead of Chicago with three games to play. Eight days earlier, the Astros had been 3½ games behind the Cubs and three behind the Giants. Now they entered the final three games of the season tied with the Giants and one game ahead of the Cubs.

Garner called on his bullpen early on October 1 to start the season-ending series against the Colorado Rockies, yanking the floundering Munro, who had given up six hits and walked two in only 2⅔ innings. Six relievers later, the Astros won 4-2 behind Bagwell's two-run home run in the three-run third inning. Gallo, who took over for Munro with two men on and two out in the third, was awarded the victory after throwing one-third of an inning. The Giants remained tied with the Astros after a victory over the Dodgers at Dodger Stadium.

The Astros backed Oswalt with six home runs, a pair of them from Kent, and took the wild card lead for good the next afternoon when Oswalt beat the Rockies 9-3 before a sellout crowd of 43,279. Former Astros outfielder Steve Finley's grand slam in the ninth inning gave the Dodgers the victory over the Giants, putting Houston a game ahead of San Francisco. At Wrigley Field, the Cubs were finally eliminated after losing to the Atlanta Braves.

In a game Oswalt considers one of the most memorable of his career, he held the Rockies to one run on five hits with six strikeouts over seven innings while becoming the only 20-game winner in the National League that season.

"That game was good in two aspects," said Oswalt, who pitched his final game of the 2004 season and that entire postseason while receiving pain-numbing injections on his right side. "It was big because it was for my first 20-win season, and it also counted to get us into the playoffs."

It was assumed that Clemens would start the season finale for the Astros, who knew that if they finished tied with the Giants in the standings, they'd board a plane to play a one-game playoff at San Francisco the next afternoon. Clemens would have started on three days' rest instead of the usual four between starts, but he was scratched with what Astros officials described as a stomach virus.

Galveston Ball High graduate Brandon Backe had just showered late that Sunday morning and was still sitting with his towel wrapped around his waist when pitching coach Jim Hickey stopped by his locker stall with instructions.

"Really?" Backe asked Hickey.

Backe put his shorts on and headed to the trainer's room to check on Clemens.

"Go out there and just do what you've been able to do," Backe remembered Clemens telling him. "Everything will just fall in place."

Everything definitely fell into place for Backe and the Astros. Backe led on the mound and at the plate, taking a 2-0 lead on his two-run single off Colorado left-hander Jamey Wright. Berkman and Kent gave the Astros a 4-0 lead in the third with an RBI double to right field and RBI single to left field, respectively. That was enough for Backe, who held Colorado to five hits and two runs over five innings. Harville, Gallo, Qualls, Russ Springer, Miceli, and Lidge combined on the final four innings as the Astros became the first team in the majors to finish the season with a 36-10 run since the 1951 New York Giants finished with a 35-8 kick. The victory was also the Astros' 18th in a row at home, a new franchise record.

"When I came in today and I found out Roger wasn't going to pitch, I was a little disappointed," Astros owner Drayton McLane said. "Then I said, 'Nothing has gone the way it was supposed to this year, so why should the last day be any different?'"

11

Finally Winning a Postseason Series

T he Astros have a long, melodramatic flirtation with the postseason. The Astros came close in 1980 against the Philadelphia Phillies, who won the decisive Game 5 of the National League Championship Series 12-7 in 10 innings.

There was plenty of reason for optimism in Houston in 1981. Nolan Ryan's Astros had won the "second half" of the season in the NL West Division with a 33-20 record. Ryan threw his record fifth of seven no-hitters on September 26—against the Dodgers. He also led the league with a 1.69 ERA.

Ryan gave more reason for optimism in Game 1 against Fernando Valenzuela, the 1981 NL Rookie of the Year and Cy Young Award winner, in the West Division Series. Ryan gave up only two hits and one run in a complete-game 3-1 victory against Valenzuela, who didn't get a decision after giving up only one run and six hits over eight innings. Dodgers manager Tommy Lasorda called on Dave Stewart in the ninth, and the Astros took advantage with a two-run home run by catcher Alan Ashby. The Astros won the next game 1-0 in 11 innings, winning on a night Jerry Reuss pitched nine scoreless innings for the Dodgers. Knuckleballer Joe Niekro pitched eight scoreless innings for the Astros, Dave Smith added two more scoreless innings, and Joe Sambito gave up only one hit in the 11th to claim the victory. Again, Stewart took the loss as Denny Walling hit the game-winning pinch-hit, bases-loaded single off of Tom Niedenfuer. Burt Hooton, who eventually served as the Astros' pitching coach from 2000 to July 14, 2004, pitched seven strong innings, giving up only one run on three hits to beat Bob Knepper 9-1 in Game 3. Valenzuela returned for Game 4. Lasorda didn't make the same mistake twice with his rookie.

Valenzuela gave up only four hits and one run in the complete game to beat Vern Ruhle 2-1. Ryan returned to the mound for Game 5, giving up four hits and three runs (two earned) over six solid innings. That wasn't nearly enough against Reuss, who threw a 4-0 shutout as the Dodgers marched toward their eventual World Series title.

In 1986, the Astros had the scariest pitcher in baseball going for them. Like Ryan in 1981, however, Mike Scott wasn't enough. Scott, who Astros teammates privately admit was scuffing the ball throughout the year en route to 18 victories, had a league-best 2.22 ERA and 306 strikeouts. That season he became the first Astro to win the Cy Young. He won Game 1 against the Mets with a 1-0 shutout. Ryan lost Game 2 5-1. Dave Smith lost Game 3 against the Mets 6-5, giving up a two-run home run to Lenny Dykstra in the ninth to blow a 5-4 lead. Scott tied the series at two games apiece with another complete game, winning 3-1. Ryan was amazing in Game 5, giving up only two hits and one run in nine innings, but Dwight Gooden was even better while limiting the Astros to one run on nine hits in 10 innings. Jesse Orosco provided two scoreless innings of relief, which were enough because Gary Carter's RBI single in the 12th inning off of Charlie Kerfeld sent everybody home. Game 6 was a classic, which is why author Jerry Izenberg, the famous columnist from *The Newark Star-Ledger,* billed it as the "Greatest Game Ever Played" in his book on the game. The teams played 16 innings in Game 6, and the Mets knew they had to end the series there, because Scott would take the mound for the Astros in Game 7. The Mets won Game 6 7-6.

(Game 6 of the 1986 National League Championship Series stood as the longest game in postseason history until the Astros and Atlanta Braves played 18 innings at Minute Maid Park in Game 4 of the 2005 division series. Adding the 14-inning affair in Game 3 of the 2005 World Series against the Chicago White Sox at Minute Maid Park, the Astros have the record for the longest games in division series, NLCS, and World Series history. They share the World Series record in terms of innings, but they own the record outright in terms of time elapsed in a World Series game.)

The Astros didn't return to the playoffs again until 1997, and they were crushed as the Atlanta Braves swept the best-of-five series. Darryl Kile pitched well in Game 1, giving up only two runs over seven innings. Greg Maddux of the Braves was much better while giving up only one run through nine innings for the 2-1 victory. The Braves knocked left-hander Mike Hampton out in the fifth inning in Game 2 and completed the rout 13-3 with Tom Glavine on the mound. John Smoltz finished the sweep with a complete-game 4-1 victory.

The 1998 Astros seemed the best bet to win it all, entering that post-season with a franchise-record 102 victories in the regular season and a vaunted starting rotation and hefty offense. Randy Johnson had been acquired from the Seattle Mariners at the trading deadline, and he went 10-1 with a 1.28 ERA in 11 starts after the trade. He got the start in Game 1 for the Astros against the San Diego Padres, but right-hander Kevin Brown won the pitchers duel 2-1. Johnson gave up nine hits and two runs over eight innings in defeat on September 29. The Astros tied the best-of-five series two days later by winning Game 2 5-4. Because of the unusual day off between Games 1 and 2, the quirk in the schedule helped the Padres line up Brown on short rest for Game 3 because of the usual day off for traveling between Games 2 and 3. Brown stalled the Astros' offense again in Game 3. Dan Miceli collected the victory with $1\frac{1}{3}$ innings of relief. Scott Elarton suffered the loss by giving up a run in two innings of relief. With Johnson on the mound hoping to stave off elimination in Game 4, he gave up three hits and two runs (one earned) over six innings in Game 4. Left-hander Sterling Hitchcock gave up only three hits and one run to earn the victory 4-1.

Those San Diego Padres won the National League pennant, but Andy Pettitte's New York Yankees had no trouble with them in the World Series.

The 1999 Astros won the franchise's third consecutive National League Central title. They were bounced in the best-of-five division series, three games to one, by the Braves.

The 2001 Astros also received the Braves as a prize for winning the National League Central, and they were swept in that series, 3-0, costing the franchise's winningest manager, Larry Dierker, his job.

Jimy Williams replaced Dierker with the expectations that he'd lead the Astros to the postseason. Drayton McLane introduced Williams by mentioning Williams's close ties to Bobby Cox, the successful manager of the Braves. Williams had coached under Cox in Atlanta, but the Astros didn't reach the playoffs in Williams's first two seasons in Houston.

It didn't take long for the Astros' poor postseason history to come up before the Astros opened the 2004 division series against the Braves, the team that had eliminated them in 1997, 1999, and 2001. Asked if having a pitcher of his caliber on the mound for Game 1 of the best-of-five division series gave the Astros reason for optimism, Roger Clemens somewhat shrugged the question off.

Missing the injured Pettitte and Wade Miller from the starting rotation was all of the disappointing history the Astros were worried about at that point. The Astros had finished the season with an amazing 36-10 kick to win the National League wild card. Now it was up to Roy Oswalt and Clemens to carry the burden for the starting rotation while right-handers Brandon Backe and Pete Munro filled the spots that would have belonged to Pettitte and Miller.

"Roy and I know that we're going to have to go out and pitch and we're going to have to find a way to get the job done," Clemens said. "For me, the way things have been the last month and a half, this game is no different. We have to pitch well, and we have to keep our team in the game, and we have to win. I think I answered that earlier when I said that over that time period, we weren't afforded to have a hiccup or stub our toe or have a very poor outing. So that's the way you go into this type of game, into the playoffs. Atlanta is a team that can score runs. They can do a lot of things. So are we. We have some thumpers in the middle of our lineup, guys who are hot right now. It should be very interesting. We're going to try to make the most of it."

The Astros' thumpers finally performed in the postseason, especially All-Star center fielder Carlos Beltran, All-Star second baseman Jeff Kent, and All-Star right fielder Lance Berkman. Astros icons Craig Biggio and Jeff Bagwell, who had been maligned in the past for the team's shortcomings in past postseasons, also provided crucial contributions against the Braves.

Bagwell, a career .297 hitter in the regular season entering the 2004 postseason, entered the 2004 division series against the Braves with a .174 career postseason average and no home runs. Bagwell's postseason average actually received a boost in 2001 when he was three for seven (.429) in the division series against the Braves. Those three singles accounted for half of the hits Bagwell had recorded over 32 at-bats in 11 postseason games against the Braves. Until then, he had 10 strikeouts and no RBI against the Braves in the postseason. He collected his four postseason RBI in 1998 in the division series against the Padres.

Biggio entered the 2004 division series with five hits and six strikeouts in 43 at-bats in the same amount of postseason games Bagwell played against the Braves. He also had not driven in a run in the postseason against Atlanta.

Bagwell and Biggio understood some of their detractors blamed them for the team's failings, but it's ridiculous to put the blame for the Astros' failures only on them.

But manager Phil Garner actually discussed the past problems with the two veterans.

"Actually we don't kind of let those things… lie under the surface, not afraid to address them," Garner said. "I think there have been several questions asked, and I talked to Bagwell and Biggio, and I thought both of them had answered it well and took the good approach. This is a different era. It's a different time. There's a different supporting cast, even though those two are still here. I think perhaps in the past there had been a lot of focus on them, and perhaps way too much got put on their plate. I think now you've got a lot of other players that can stand with them and can do the job also."

The 2004 Astros quickly answered any questions about their offensive might with a 9-3 victory in Game 1 on October 6, setting a franchise postseason record with nine runs and four home runs. Bagwell went two for five with an RBI double, and Biggio was one for five with a run scored and a stolen base. Beltran made his postseason debut with a three-for-three performance and three runs, including the two-run home run that gave the Astros a 6-1 lead. He also stole a base. Berkman went two for five with two RBI, giving the Astros a 4-1 lead with his two-run homer off of Jaret Wright. Brad Ausmus and Jason Lane also homered.

"[Bagwell and Biggio] did a fine job today, and I think they'll continue to do well. I think they'll continue to play well in this series," Garner said. "I don't think the history of not having done anything is going to apply in our case now; I think we're beyond that."

Three of the Astros' homers were hit off Wright, who had given up only 11 home runs in the regular season.

"This can quiet a lot of people down," Bagwell said. "It can relax a lot of people, and that's a good thing. To come out and play like we did and have that good feeling going into tomorrow, it erases [a lot of doubts]. We don't have to sit here and answer so many questions every single day from people saying, 'Well, the Astros can't beat the Braves. You guys are down again.' Now you can't talk about that. That can't help but be a positive."

Clemens showed no ill effects from the stomach virus that forced the Astros to skip him from the final game of the season three days earlier. Pitching on two extra days of rest, Clemens limited the Braves to three runs (two earned) despite walking six on an afternoon in which he struck out seven and gave up six hits. The Braves put at least two men on base in each of the first four innings, but Clemens pitched in and out of those jams and trailed only 1-0 heading into the third.

"I was concerned early on, because he did get behind," Garner, who considered pulling Clemens after five innings, said of Clemens. "When the pitch count starts getting up there a little bit, you're counting on him to get you deep in the ballgame, and I did get a little bit concerned. But he kept, you know, when he needed to do something, he got something done. They chipped away. He gave a little bit here and there, but they didn't get through to him."

Ausmus's homer over the wall in left field tied the score 1–1 to spark a four-run rally in the third inning, which Berkman capped with his two-run homer. In between those two homers, Beltran singled and scored on Bagwell's double.

The 9–3 victory also marked the first time Clemens won a Game 1 in the postseason.

"I think whenever you have a four-run inning like that in the post-season, which if you want to look at the past, that's probably a huge inning for past Astros teams," Berkman said, "I think it does take some pressure off. The past doesn't have any bearing on us. We might not be any good in the postseason, but we might be. But it's not going to be because of the past teams."

Other than the early troubles for Clemens, the Astros' offense put all of the tension out of the contest early. The only scare for Garner's club came in the seventh inning when Atlanta reliever Juan Cruz drilled Beltran in the ribs with a pitch. Beltran angrily tossed his bat, took a few steps forward, stared at Cruz, and asked the Dominican Republic native if the plunking had been intentional. Cruz denied hitting Beltran intentionally, and Beltran took his base peacefully. Beltran scored later in that inning, but he exited in the bottom of the inning with a bruised right rib cage.

Oswalt faced former Astros left-hander Mike Hampton in Game 2, exiting with a 2–1 lead in the seventh. Bagwell hit his first postseason home run in the first inning off of his good friend Hampton. Raul Chavez, who served as Oswalt's personal catcher throughout the 2004 season, put Oswalt ahead 2–0 with a home run in his first postseason at-bat. The shot carried over the left field wall.

Some would argue that Rafael Furcal should not have even been playing in the 2004 division series. On September 10, 2004, Furcal violated his probation when he was arrested for the second time for driving under the influence of alcohol in Georgia. Hours before Game 1 on October 6, Fulton County judge David Darden sentenced Furcal to 21 days in jail and 28 days in a treatment center.

As a slap in the face to the 525 people who would die in alcohol-related traffic deaths in Georgia in 2004 and the 1,642 who would die in such deaths in Texas that year, Darden and the Braves let Furcal play in the division series. Furcal made the most of his time away from jail. In the seventh inning, he drove in Dewayne Wise with a one-out, RBI single up the middle off of Oswalt to cut the Astros' lead to 2–1.

At that point in the game, controversy ensued. Somehow, the phone in the visitors' clubhouse at Turner Field did not work.

With Oswalt on the mound, Braves second baseman Marcus Giles at the plate, and left-handed reliever Mike Gallo and Brad Lidge warming up in the bullpen, Garner trotted out onto the field and right-handed starter Brandon Backe sprinted toward the visitors' bullpen along the left field line. Cox grew furious, believing Garner was using his chat with plate umpire Phil Cuzzi as a way to stall and give his relievers more time to warm up.

"We kept picking the phone up, picking the phone up. It was busy," Garner said afterward. "You can't see the bullpen from there. My first thought was to send a player down there. If you do that, you're running across the field, they're going to think something's going on. I did the only thing I knew what to do. It's happened to us twice this summer, [those were instances where] I went to the umpire. That's why I ran out there. I said, 'Look, I can't get the phone to work. Get somebody down there.' So, finally, it wasn't until—actually, at that point, when one of our players stepped out and was yelling, 'Pick up the phone in the bullpen,' that somebody picked up the phone in the bullpen. It rang back at our place. Evidently, it worked from that point on. We didn't have any problems with it [in Game 1]. We didn't have any problems with it earlier in the game. It was just at that moment."

Lidge relieved Oswalt to face Giles, prompting Cox to file a protest and play the rest of the game under protest. Lidge, pitching for the first time since the final game of the regular season four days earlier, escaped the seventh inning with the 2-1 lead. He labored through the eighth and gave up Adam La Roche's game-tying RBI double off the wall in left-center field. Miceli, who had been one of the Astros' most dependable relievers while going 6-6 with two saves and a 3.59 ERA over 74 appearances in the regular season, retired the Braves in order in the 10th.

After retiring the leadoff batter in the 11th, Miceli gave up Charles Thomas's single to right field. One out later, Miceli hung a split-finger fastball, which Furcal deposited over the wall in right field for a two-run homer, giving the Braves the 4-2 victory and tying the best-of-five series at one game apiece as the teams prepared to resume the series in Houston two days later.

"I don't even know if a protest like that can hold up," Cox said afterward. "But it just seemed strange to our dugout that Lidge normally pitches the ninth, or sometimes the eighth and the ninth, and sometimes in the seventh, I guess. We didn't think he was warmed up. But they could have had some type of communication problem, but the phone was working absolutely, 100 percent. So it's irrelevant now and doesn't matter."

Even a year later, Garner bristled at the belief that he was stalling. When the Astros returned to Turner Field for the division series in 2005, Garner still remained adamant that the bullpen phones were not working in the seventh inning of Game 2 in 2004 against the Braves. As Cox said, though, it ultimately didn't matter, because Furcal's two-run homer gave the Braves the victory that afternoon.

After a day off, the series resumed at Minute Maid Park with Backe, the pride of Galveston, on the mound for the first time since he pitched the final game of the season. Backe literally grew up dreaming of this day. A star quarterback and outfielder-pitcher at Galveston Ball High, Backe was the baseball team's Most Valuable Player at Ball High his final two seasons before graduating in 1996. He enrolled at Galveston Community College, earning third-team All-America honors in 1998. The Tampa Bay Devil Rays, who played their inaugural season in 1998 and participated in the June draft for the first time in 1997, drafted Backe in the 18th round.

He advanced all the way to Class AA Orlando in 2000 as an outfielder, but the Devil Rays ordered him to focus all his energies on pitching later that year. The move paid off rather quickly with the pitching-thin Devil Rays. Less than two years after he converted to a pitcher full-time, he made his major league debut with two scoreless innings of relief against the Toronto Blue Jays on July 19, 2002.

Backe made nine relief appearances that season, finishing with a 6.92 ERA. He split the next season between Class AAA Durham and Tampa Bay, going 1-1 with a 5.44 ERA over 28 relief appearances in the majors that year.

Astros senior director of player personnel Paul Ricciarini, who was the team's coordinator of professional scouting until he was promoted to his current job in June 2004, was impressed with Backe's potential and energy level. On Ricciarini's recommendation, the Astros acquired Backe in exchange for utility infielder Geoff Blum on December 14, 2003, three days after Pettitte had been signed. The trade brought Backe's father, Harold, to tears. Compared to Pettitte's deal three days earlier, however, the Backe trade was a minor story back in Houston.

Harold described the trade as an early Christmas present, but most Astros fans could not have imagined the gem Ricciarini had uncovered for then-general manager Gerry Hunsicker and the Astros.

Ricciarini had seen Backe pitch five times in the two seasons leading to the trade. Since starting his scouting career with the Cincinnati Reds in 1975, Ricciarini has played a part in signing or recommending former major leaguers George Bell, Kelly Gruber, Todd Stottlemyre, and Mark Wohler, according to his biography sketch in the Astros' media guide. He has played crucial scouting roles for the Toronto Blue Jays, Atlanta Braves, and New York Mets. He worked with Hunsicker in New York and followed Hunsicker to Houston in 1998 as the equivalent of a super scout.

Ricciarini prides himself on sitting back and watching with an open mind. Like most great scouts, his ears are as good as his eyes. Watching the 2002 Class AA Orlando Rays with a few Devil Rays scouts, Ricciarini listened intently as some Devil Rays officials raved about shortstop B.J. Upton, the six-foot-three, 180-pound star Tampa Bay selected with the second overall pick in the 2002 draft. Scouts raved about Upton's athleticism, leading to a discussion about the most athletic players in the Devil Rays farm system.

"Our best athlete," Ricciarini remembers hearing a Devil Rays scout say, "might be Backe. He's played six positions for us, and now he's pitching."

Ricciarini, who had not targeted any player in particular on his scouting trip to Orlando that day, made a note of that comment. He stuck around long enough to see Backe start for Orlando, and he left that evening impressed with Backe's curveball, energy level, and mound presence.

"His curve was really tight and hard," Ricciarini recalled. "He didn't have total command of it then, but on two out of four of his curveballs, you were, 'Wow.' If there was one thing that impressed me other than his breaking pitches, it was just the way he competed. He had a feel for all three pitches. You never know how converted guys are going to be with the feel of their pitches. He just competed so well, and his stuff was so good. He was so energetic. A lot of times in the minor leagues he would overthrow."

Before the 2002 and 2003 seasons were over, Ricciarini had seen Backe pitch five times, mostly out of the bullpen. He saw him at Orlando, at Class AAA Durham, and once in the majors. Considering Backe was still transitioning from making the switch from being a position player to a pitcher, Ricciarini wasn't very concerned with the numbers. The Astros looked beyond the 4-6 record and 4.68 ERA Backe had in 2002 with Orlando or the 6.92 ERA he had that season in the majors. The 2-1 record and 4.64 ERA over 16 games (two of them starts) at Durham in 2003 weren't a concern. Neither was the 1-1 mark and 5.44 ERA over 28 games with the Devil Rays in 2003.

It was obvious Backe was committed to the work that would be necessary for him to improve. Ricciarini knew Astros pitching coordinator Dewey Robinson can work magic on players who are committed and talented enough. More importantly, Ricciarini noticed in Backe a trait that went beyond the won–loss record and earned run average. He appeared unafraid on the mound. In that regard, he compared favorably with the likes of Oswalt, Clemens, and Pettitte.

"There's just something you can't quantify statistically," Ricciarini said. "There are guys who have a certain look about them, the way they pull the hat down and go about their business. He's got the look of a winner, the look of a great competitor. And, quite frankly, I think the bigger the game, the more he dials it up. Be it their expression, body language, or their eyes, you can tell they're not afraid to be out there facing the best hitters in the order. Brandon competed one through nine, I could tell you that. There's a look and a definite observation point in the middle of the order, and he had that look. You can look at a bench of 25 people, and he's going to jump out at you just because of his energy and the way he acts."

Without Pettitte and Miller, the Astros desperately needed Backe to bolster the starting rotation behind Clemens and Oswalt. Backe and the left-handed Gallo were the last two players optioned to Class AAA New Orleans on the final day of spring training on April 3, 2004. Backe's life-long dream to pitch for the Astros in a regular-season game was on hold.

Dejected, Backe vowed to return soon. Seven days later, his contract was purchased when Pettitte went on the disabled list for the first time with the Astros. Backe pitched in relief until he was optioned back to New Orleans on June 3, the day right-hander Pete Munro signed as a free agent.

Backe returned to the majors on August 20, two days after Pettitte announced his season-ending left elbow surgery. A day later, Backe made his first major league start with seven scoreless innings against the Chicago Cubs. He also hit a 94-mph fastball up the middle for a two-run single in the second inning off hard-throwing right-hander Mark Prior for his first major league hit one pitch after Prior had brushed him back with a fastball high and inside. The Astros bullpen blew Backe's lead. Miceli took over in the eighth, but he was yanked with two men on and two outs in the inning. Moises Alou greeted Lidge with an RBI single. The Cubs added two more runs in the ninth off Lidge. Michael Barrett tied the score with an RBI triple and gave the Cubs the lead on Ramon Martinez's sacrifice fly. Lane countered in the bottom of the ninth with a game-winning, two-run single to right field.

Backe made eight more starts in the regular season, including the victory on the final game of the season to finish the regular season with a 5-3 record and 4.30 ERA in the majors. His final start of the regular season proved to Astros fans that Backe had the makings of a big-game pitcher. He raised those expectations in Game 3 of the division series.

Pitching like a man with more than nine major league starts in his career, Backe put the Astros within one victory of the National League Championship Series by beating Atlanta 8-5 before a sellout crowd of 43,547 at Minute Maid Park.

"This team, the Astros, has been my No. 1 team ever since I was a young kid," he said. "Just to have the fans realize that I'm from this area, living a dream, and supporting me 100 percent, it's an awesome feeling. I can't ask for more. I'm living a dream, honestly. There's nothing else I can say."

Backe held the Braves to five hits and two runs with five strikeouts and two walks over six innings, extending the Astros' home winning streak to 19 games. Still bothered by the bruised right rib cage Beltran suffered when Cruz hit him in Game 1, the outfielder continued his postseason surge with a two-run home run in the third inning off of reliever Paul Byrd, who took the mound after starter John Thomson strained his oblique muscle on his left side four pitches into the contest.

"It bothers me when I run," Beltran said of his rib cage. "When I swing the bat from the left side, it doesn't bother me at all. But when I swing the bat from the right side, it bothers me a little bit. But when I hit the ball today, I knew I hit it hard. I hit a little bit off the end of the bat. I knew it was going to be a close play. But I really thank God that ball went out and gave us two runs right there and gave us the momentum just to keep going and find a way to score runs."

Backe couldn't hold the 2-0 lead for half an inning. Johnny Estrada tagged him for a home run to left-center in the fourth inning. With two out and a man on second, Backe intentionally walked Thomas to face Byrd. The move backfired when Byrd ripped an RBI single up the middle. The Astros, who scored five of their runs with two outs, countered with two runs in the fifth. They added three more in the sixth on Berkman's RBI single to left and Morgan Ensberg's two-run double off of third baseman Chipper Jones's glove.

Ensberg, who drove in the Astros' first run in the fifth inning, tied the franchise postseason record with three RBI that day, but that record wouldn't last very long with Beltran in prime form that October. The Braves countered with three runs in the eighth off of Russ Springer, but Lidge set Atlanta down in order in the ninth to take a 2-1 lead in the best-of-five series heading into Game 4 with Clemens on the mound on three days' rest instead of the regular four the next day at Minute Maid Park.

"We're going to ask Roger to come back on short time tomorrow, and we'll do everything we can to get that early lead and to hold on to it, and we'll use everybody [in the bullpen if necessary]," Garner said. "So whatever Roger can give us tomorrow will be good, and we'll go from there.... Well, I stated that I'm not a fan of coming back on three days, but I'm a fan of Roger Clemens. This is one of the greatest pitchers in the game today, so I'm very comfortable asking him to do this, and I think he's comfortable trying to do it."

Even on short rest, Clemens outpitched his Atlanta counterpart, Russ Ortiz, before an eager sellout crowd of 43,336 at Minute Maid Park. The Astros pounded Ortiz, sending him to the showers after the right-hander gave up seven hits and five runs with one walk and one strikeout over three innings. Clemens lasted five innings, holding the Braves to two runs on six hits and two walks with five strikeouts.

Clemens gave up his two runs as the Braves took a 2-0 lead in the second inning. Ortiz didn't keep the lead very long. With one out and the bases loaded, Clemens hit a sacrifice fly to center field to cut Atlanta's lead in half. Ortiz thought he had escaped the inning with a 2-1 lead after he caught Biggio's pop fly, but the ball had hit Minute Maid Park's retractable roof and was therefore out of play. Two pitches later, Biggio hit a 3-1 fastball into the Crawford Box seats behind left field for his first postseason home run. The three-run shot put the Astros ahead 4-2. Beltran kept the rally going with a double to right field, and Bagwell drove him in with a single to left field to cap the five-run rally, which set a franchise record for runs in a postseason inning.

Clemens tired and pitched in and out of trouble in the third and fourth innings, tempting Garner to pull him before the fifth. Clemens lobbied Garner to let him pitch the fifth and rewarded his manager's decision with a scoreless frame.

Brought in to protect the 5-2 lead in the sixth, Chad Qualls gave up a majestic, game-tying, three-run home run to Adam La Roche.

Qualls was in trouble from the start of the sixth. Chipper Jones, who was zero for 11 over the first three games of the series, led off the sixth with a single to center field. One out later, Andruw Jones doubled to left field. LaRoche handled the rest, depositing Qualls's hanging first-pitch slider into the second deck behind the wall in right-center field.

"It was a slider that hung up over the plate," Qualls said. "It was a bad pitch, but he hit it really far."

Gallo, Miceli, and Lidge combined for two scoreless innings of relief with two-thirds of an inning each to keep the score tied. Lidge relieved Miceli in the eighth inning after Johnny Estrada hit a two-out double. Not wanting to remove the All-Star Kent's power, Garner made the Lidge-Miceli switch straight up. He also pulled Biggio instead of Kent in the double switch that brought in Gallo and Lane in the seventh, so

Miceli and Lidge were in Biggio's leadoff spot in the order, and Lane was in the ninth spot.

After Smoltz gave up consecutive two-out singles to Ausmus and Lane in the eighth, Garner saw little choice but to pull Lidge in favor of a pinch hitter. Orlando Palmeiro replaced Lidge and grounded out weakly to the right side of the infield.

"You want to be up in that situation, but a move was made," Biggio said. "I don't second-guess anything that happens. You just deal with the hand that you're played. Jason was able to come through with a big knock."

Garner's critics pounced after the Braves jumped on Springer for the winning run in the ninth. Springer retired the first two men he faced in the ninth and was within one strike of escaping the inning. He got in trouble after his 2-2 fastball tailed inside too much and hit Furcal, the Braves' hero in Game 2. After Furcal stole second, and J.D. Drew drove him in with a single to right field. Smoltz entered in the eighth inning after Game 2 starter Mike Hampton threw a rare inning of relief in the seventh.

Bagwell gave the Astros reason for hope with a one-out single to right field in the ninth off of Smoltz. After Garner sent Adam Everett to run for Bagwell, Berkman put runners at the corners with a single through the left side, drawing a roar from the sellout crowd, which stood on its feet as Kent strolled to the plate with the opportunity to tie the score or eliminate the Braves altogether. The threat soured when Kent hit a double-play grounder to short, prompting Smoltz to pump his fist and let out a primal yell as he and his teammates celebrated the 6-5 escape, which snapped the Astros' 19-game home winning streak with Houston's first defeat at Minute Maid Park since August 22.

"Honestly, I try to slow things down when the crowd goes nuts," Smoltz said, acknowledging the energy at Minute Maid Park. "I've been in so many different hostile environments in so many different pivotal games that that helps, but you still have to make a pitch. With Kent I was honestly trying to get a double-play ball, get him to pull an outside pitch. It kind of happened in slow motion, but what I've learned in past experience is just to slow down in my mind and not get too carried away with the next batter or the next out. I'd like to say I'd give up two hits on purpose the inning before to get Lidge out of the game, but that was not decided by any means. And this is one of the loudest places in baseball.

"If there's anything in the beginning of the series that you try to help other players [with, it's to] use the crowd for your advantage. And what I mean by that is when they're super loud, you know, try to get them a little bit calmer and try to get it a little bit duller of a roar. Because guys can get a little bit more anxious when you're at home at times and want to be the guy—drive the ball, swing a little harder. It can work to your advantage if you want it to, but if you play the 'what if' games and 'This is loud, oh, my gosh, he gets a hit, we're tied,' those are the things that go against you. That's where experience probably does help a little bit."

With that 6-5 loss, the Astros fell to 0-6 in franchise history in post-season games in which they could clinch the series with a victory. They headed back to Turner Field for the winner-take-all Game 5 with a disappointing 0-7 record in games in which they faced postseason elimination.

The Braves weren't exactly the most clutch team in baseball history, though. They had only one World Series title to show for their 13 consecutive division titles up to that point. The Braves also had lost their previous two Game 5 contests, falling to the Giants in 2002 and to the Cubs in 2003. They were limited to one run in each of those games.

"We would have loved to have done it here," Garner said after the game. "The crowd was really into it. People were excitable and exciting. The place was rocking. We didn't close it out, but we've been doing things very unusual for the last couple of months. I don't know if it's going to be—it certainly is going to be difficult, but that's what we've been doing, difficult things. Now we have to go to Atlanta. Obviously they're feeling pretty good after this today. They won two ballgames on us, late in the ballgame. We're going to have to tighten up our belt. We're going to have to play a little tougher tomorrow."

Not long after the Astros boarded their plane for Atlanta, former teammate Ken Caminiti, 41, was pronounced dead at New York's Lincoln Memorial Hospital. Later that night, several Astros received telephone calls to their Atlanta hotel rooms informing them that he had died of a heart attack in the Bronx, New York. Caminiti, a former National League Most Valuable Player, had been a fan favorite in Houston and San Diego. His ex-wife, Nancy, is beloved by the older Astros wives, and she was even in the Astros' family section at Minute Maid Park for one of the division series games against the Braves.

It would be a while before it would be verified that Caminiti died of a drug overdose. A day before the division series started, Caminiti had been sentenced to 180 days in jail in Houston for testing positive for cocaine, a violation of the probation he received in 2002 when he pleaded guilty at his trial for a cocaine arrest.

On the same day Atlanta's Furcal was arrested for drunken driving in Atlanta, Caminiti was arrested in Houston for failing his drug test on September 10. A day before Furcal's sentence was suspended in a Fulton County court until after the Braves were eliminated from the playoffs,

Houston District judge William Harmon released Caminiti by giving him credit for time served in jail and at a court-ordered drug treatment center.

Soon after his release, Caminiti landed in the Bronx with a girlfriend. By then, he had already been out of touch with many of his former Astros teammates. Biggio and Bagwell had spent countless hours trying to help Caminiti, one of the first star baseball players to admit to past steroid use. Countless others in Houston had rallied behind Caminiti, hoping to help him kick his drug problem.

Gus Gerard, a former drug addict who now serves as a drug counselor in Houston, was one of Caminiti's many friends who offered the three-time All-Star third baseman help.

"The problem is that the ego of an athlete, especially one like Ken, gets in the way [of recovery]," Gerard told the *Houston Chronicle's* Michael Murphy and Dale Robertson a day after Caminiti died. "A lot of times he'll say, 'Oh, this time I can beat it.' In addiction, you have to surrender to win, and if you don't fully surrender, you're going to struggle. But athletes are taught to never surrender, to fight every last inch of the way. So you continue to put yourself in bad places and high-risk situations, hanging out with the wrong people, and you relapse. That was Ken's problem. I've seen him speak to kids and donate money and time for [various causes], but he also had this other side to him that was just totally dark and diseased."

Caminiti spent the greatest parts of his 15-year career with the Astros and Padres, but he also played a brief time with the Braves. The news of his death hit a segment of both clubhouses hard even though Bagwell had gone a few years without speaking much to Caminiti.

"We're both kind of devastated about it and feel terrible," said Biggio, speaking at the time for himself and Bagwell. "It's something that we played with this guy for a long time—eight, nine years. My wife and his wife are best friends, we know their kids. It's tough…. I guess the best thing we can do today for him is just go out there and play well."

"This is obviously awful news," Bagwell said. "I mean things go bad for people and all that kind of stuff. It just shows you that all this stuff, we're sitting right here, it's great, it's a great game, the game has brought us all together, but it goes far beyond that. To lose another friend and somebody like him, it's tough on all of us."

Biggio and Bagwell hoped Caminiti would be remembered for more than his struggles with chemical dependency. They want fans to remember just how much Caminiti loved and cherished his three daughters—Nicole, Lindsay, and Kendall.

"The way I view people in the world; there's givers and takers," Biggio said. "To me, he was a giver. You looked at him, he looked mean. He played the game mean. Off the field he was a teddy bear even though he had that fu-manchu, looked like a big, nasty guy. If you needed a dollar and he had a dollar in his pocket [and] that was the last dollar he was ever going to make, he'd give it to you and not ask for it back. He had the ultimate respect from his friends, his teammates. He loved his girls, his family. I just think he was probably the greatest third baseman that I ever played with or against. He should be remembered for all the things that he's done on the field. Yeah, he's had some misfortunes the last couple years, but he needs to be remembered for all the charity work he did in Houston and San Diego, all the great things he did out there, brought [the Padres a National League] championship out there. He, to me, is kind of like Baggy, a constant professional."

Bagwell and Biggio displayed their own professionalism with steady performances as the Astros pounded the Braves 12-3 in Game 5 of the division series, winning a postseason series for the first time in franchise history. Biggio was three for five with one RBI and two runs. Bagwell, who got a hit in each of the division series games, was one for four with a home run and two RBI as the Astros collected a franchise postseason-record 17 hits and 12 runs before a disappointed sellout crowd of 54,068 at Turner Field.

Pitching on three days' rest instead of the regular four, Oswalt held the Braves to two runs on seven hits and three walks with four strikeouts to finish the division series with a victory and a 2.38 ERA.

"Today was a tough day," Biggio said. "Emotions were all over the place, and I think Cammy was out there with us."

Wright gave up six hits and four runs over 5⅓ innings for his second loss in the series. Berkman got the Astros' offense started with a leadoff single to right field in the second inning. Kent added a double to left, and Ensberg's ground out to short put the Astros ahead 1-0. Jose Vizcaino's sacrifice fly to left field gave Oswalt a 2-0 cushion. Beltran gave the Astros a 3-0 lead in the third inning with his third home run of the series and the first of two in Game 5.

Furcal cut the Astros' lead to 3-1 in the fifth with a leadoff home run over the wall in right-center. Oswalt gave up another home run two outs later to Estrada, who put his shot over the wall in right field. Oswalt walked Andruw Jones, prompting the crowd to stir in anticipation as Qualls began stretching in the bullpen. LaRoche, whose three-run home run off of Qualls changed the momentum in Game 4, flied out to center field to end the inning. After throwing 111 pitches on short rest while also needing shots to numb the pain on his strained right side, Oswalt turned the game over to Qualls to start the sixth inning. Beltran gave the Astros a 4-2 lead in the sixth when he ripped Wright's 2-2 offering for a home run to right field, collecting the first multi-home run performance by an Astro in the playoffs. Beltran finished the evening four for five with five RBI, a franchise record for a postseason game. His four homers in the division series also set a franchise postseason record.

The Astros added four of their five runs in the seventh inning off of reliever Chris Reitsma. Left-hander Tom Martin gave up the fifth run of the rally. The Astros added three runs in the eighth inning off of Juan Cruz, cruising to a comfortable finish.

Once Dan Wheeler recorded the final out against the Braves, Bagwell, Biggio, Beltran, and the rest of the Astros sprinted toward the Turner Field mound to celebrate. In their 43rd season, the Astros had finally won a postseason series. Nobody could possibly have enjoyed it more than Bagwell and Biggio, the club icons who had been through all the disappointments in 1997, 1998, 1999, and 2001.

"To get to this point, it means a lot to both of us because we've wanted nothing more than to have the opportunity to do this for us, the organization, and for the city," Bagwell said. "We shared hugs a few times. It was in the tunnel at first, outside, and then in here. It's a big thing for Craig and [me]. We've been through a lot. To get this opportunity is what we've played for."

Fittingly, perhaps, the road to the National League Championship Series went through Atlanta.

"We should all take pride in this," Biggio said. "To beat an Atlanta Braves team that has sent us home three times in the past and be able to play well, we should all take pride."

12

Almost There

The 2004 St. Louis Cardinals reached spring training in Jupiter, Florida, without much fanfare. Manager Tony La Russa, long considered one of the best tacticians and motivators in baseball, was blessed early in the year with the benefit of nobody outside his organization picking his team to succeed in the revamped National League Central. The defending National League Central champion Chicago Cubs had been within a victory of the National League pennant in 2003. The core of the team that lost to the Florida Marlins in the 2003 National League Championship Series returned to the North Side of Chicago, including hard-throwing right-handers Mark Prior, Kerry Wood, and Carlos Zambrano, and perennial All-Stars Moises Alou and Sammy Sosa.

The Astros, who finished a game behind the Cubs in the NL Central race in 2003, had upgraded dramatically by signing Roger Clemens and Andy Pettitte. Even with perennial NL MVP candidate Albert Pujols, perennial All-Star Scott Rolen, and perennial All-Star Jim Edmonds fortifying the Cardinals batting order, the so-called experts picked the Cardinals to finish a distant third behind the Cubs and Astros in the division. There definitely was a huge distance between the 2004 Cardinals and the rest of the NL Central, and that was because La Russa's club pulled away in the division race relatively early.

The Cardinals won the 2004 NL Central race by 13 games over the second-place Astros and finished with the best record in baseball at 105-57. After a rough 6-7 start to the season, St. Louis settled in and finished with a 12-11 mark in April, putting them in fourth place in the division while trailing co-division leaders Chicago and Houston by only $1\frac{1}{2}$ games. By June 1, the Cardinals were tied with the Astros and Cubs for second in the division behind the surprise leaders, the Cincinnati Reds. By June 9, the Cardinals had pulled into a tie atop the division with the Reds while the Cubs fell into fourth and the Astros moved into third. At that point, only 1½ games had separated the Astros and Cardinals.

A month later, the Cardinals had a comfortable seven-game lead over the second-place Cubs and a 9½-game lead over the Astros. The Cardinals entered the 2004 All-Star break with a seven-game lead over the Cubs and a 10½-game lead over the Astros.

The Cardinals led the Astros by as much as 20½ games, a lead they took the day Roy Oswalt was ejected for hitting Chicago's Michael Barrett with a pitch. As La Russa gave some of his key players some rest down the stretch and the Astros charged to a franchise-best 36-10 finish, Houston got within 13 games of the Cardinals to win the NL wild card.

Throughout their dominant regular season, the Cardinals lost the season series against only one opponent in 2004: the Houston Astros. St. Louis lost 10 of its 18 games against the Astros in the regular season, giving Phil Garner's club a sense of confidence heading into the National League Championship Series, despite finishing 13 games behind La Russa's club in the regular season.

Unfortunately for the Astros, their starting pitching staff could hardly have been set up any worse for the NLCS. Clemens and Oswalt were unavailable after pitching Games 4 and 5, respectively, in the division series on short rest. Right-hander Brandon Backe, making only his 11th start in the majors, got the nod for Game 1 of the NLCS at Busch Stadium on October 13.

The Astros' offense did its part with two-run homers from Carlos Beltran, Jeff Kent, and Lance Berkman, and another home run by Mike Lamb. That output wasn't enough. Backe lasted only 4⅔ innings, giving up four runs on five hits with two walks and six strikeouts. Each team scored twice in the first inning, but Kent gave the Astros a 4-2 lead in the fourth inning with his two-run home run.

The Cardinals responded with two runs in the bottom of the fifth. Woody Williams, the former University of Houston star who grew up cheering the Astros, got that rally going with a one-out double to right field. Williams, who gave up four hits and four runs over six innings, cut Backe's lead to 4-3 when Larry Walker hit a broken-bat blooper the other way for an RBI double to left field. After walking Pujols on five pitches, Backe gave way to Chad Qualls. Backe was not pleased with Garner's decision, and he didn't feel much better after Rolen tied the score 4-4 with an RBI single through the left side. Until that at-bat, the ailing Rolen had been held hitless in the 2004 postseason.

Qualls's problems continued in the sixth inning when the Cardinals took control with a six-run rally. Edgar Renteria got that inning started with a single up the middle. Reggie Sanders added a broken-bat infield single over the mound. Mike Matheny sacrificed the runners over, and La Russa sent former Astro Roger Cedeño to hit for Williams. Cedeño had extra incentive. While playing for Garner with the Detroit Tigers, Garner suspended him for the final month of the 2001 season after a testy exchange during a workout shortly after the September 11 terrorist attacks.

Cedeño put the Cardinals ahead for good with a ground out to first. In retrospect, Jeff Bagwell could have waited to see if Cedeño's slow roller would go foul before getting to first base. Cedeño has world-class speed, though, and he would have likely reached safely if Bagwell had hesitated too long hoping the ball would roll foul.

"I've had those balls kick fair and go down the line for a double when I tried it one time," Garner said. "You never know what's going to happen with that ball. I wouldn't second-guess Baggy on that."

Whatever the case, the Cardinals led 5-4.

Tony Womack followed with a two-out RBI single up the middle. He stole second and scored when Jose Vizcaino committed an error on his throw to first after fielding Walker's single to short. Pujols added a walk, prompting Garner to yank Qualls. Garner turned the ball over to right-hander Chad Harville, who provided no relief. Harville threw only one strike to the struggling Rolen, who loaded the bases with a walk, and he found too much of the strike zone against Edmonds, who gave St. Louis a 10-4 lead with his three-run double to right field.

The Astros got within four runs when Berkman hit his two-run homer off of Ray King in the eighth. Lamb hit his homer in the ninth. La Russa had seen enough and sent closer Jason Isringhausen to close the victory and take a 1-0 lead in the best-of-seven series.

With Clemens and Oswalt still unavailable, journeyman Pete Munro started Game 2 at Busch Stadium, forcing Garner to call on his bullpen in the fifth inning for the second consecutive night. If not for Major League Baseball's marriage to the Fox network, Game 2 of the NLCS would have been postponed, giving the Astros the break they wanted.

Considering all of the national media attention the 2004 American League Championship Series between the Boston Red Sox and New York Yankees was getting, the 2004 NLCS was derisively referred to as the NIT by many of the media covering the event, equating the ALCS with the more prestigious NCAA basketball tournament.

The Yankees and Red Sox had October 14 off, though, and there was no way Fox wanted to postpone Game 2 of the NLCS and waste that night's primetime broadcast. That was the biggest reason why Game 2 of the NLCS got underway despite consistently strong rain showers that formed puddles in the outfield and made a mess of the mound. The soaked outfield and wet mound definitely put the players at risk of injury, but it was no secret why the Astros would have benefited from a rainout.

If Game 2 had been rained out and played the next day, Munro would have been scratched and replaced by Clemens. Then Oswalt would have started Game 3 at home on regular rest, lining up Clemens for the potential Game 6 at Busch Stadium on regular rest and Oswalt on regular rest for the potential Game 7.

The wet conditions and chilly weather were only bad enough to delay the start by 28 minutes. Heading into the bottom of the fifth inning, it seemed as though the Astros would be glad the game wasn't postponed. Beltran continued his postseason assault with a home run in the first inning off right-hander Matt Morris, putting his home run total at six for the postseason and four over three consecutive games, dating back to Game 5 of the division series. Morris appeared vulnerable in the second and third innings, but the Astros couldn't capitalize. Biggio stranded the bases loaded with a fielder's-choice grounder to second base in the second inning. After Beltran and Bagwell began the third inning with consecutive walks, Berkman flied out to center field. Kent struck out looking, and Bagwell was doubled up at first base by Matheny, setting the tone for a game in which the Astros left 11 men on base while finishing two for 14 with runners in scoring position.

Morgan Ensberg wasn't nearly as forgiving as he led off the fourth inning with a home run over the left field wall, giving Munro a 2-0 lead. The Astros added another run in the fifth inning on Berkman's RBI single to right field.

The Cardinals erased the 3-0 deficit in the bottom of the fifth with four runs. After retiring the first batter in the fifth, Munro walked Marlon Anderson. Munro got the second out of the inning by inducing Womack's fielder's-choice grounder to third, but Walker got the Cardinals within one run by ripping Munro's change-up for a two-run homer to right field. Pujols kept the two-out rally going with a single to center, prompting Garner to call on Harville in a crucial situation for the second night in a row. Once again, the Cardinals capitalized. Rolen put the Cardinals in front 4-3 with a two-run homer over the left field wall. The Astros tied the score 4-4 in the seventh inning when Ensberg drove in Berkman with a single up the middle against the drawn-in infield. Dan Wheeler kept the score tied through seven after his second inning of relief. Right-hander Dan Miceli's postseason nightmare continued in the eighth.

Before Miceli could even settle in, Pujols and Rolen got the bottom off the eighth inning started with consecutive home runs with the first back-to-back home runs ever hit by the St. Louis Cardinals in the post-season.

"I got a couple pitches up," Miceli said, "and they hit them out."

By then, poor Miceli had grown tired of repeating that line.

The Astros left Busch Stadium hoping to join the 1984 San Diego Padres and 1985 Cardinals as the only teams to reach the World Series after dropping the first two games of the NLCS. The other 14 teams to have lost the first two games of the NLCS were eliminated.

"I don't think you celebrate," Rolen said. "I think you look at what's ahead of you. The biggest thing is not to look at what's behind you, so to speak, and not to look too far ahead of you but look at the game at hand, which is the first game. I think Clemens is pitching that game. We're going to have our hands full that night, no doubt we're going to have to play well. I don't know if celebrate is the right word. I think that you look at the game and you feel that you came out and you did your job, and we did what we could at home to head to their home. So now they have home-field advantage with three days, and we're going to do everything we can to play the best we can down there."

The only consolation for the Astros was the knowledge that the series was shifting back to Minute Maid Park with Clemens, Oswalt, and Backe lined up to start Games 3, 4, and, if necessary, 5.

"Those guys have been our horses all year," Garner said of Clemens and Oswalt. "We'll turn to them now and ask them to do what they've been doing all year, and that's win for us."

Biggio, Bagwell, Berkman, Clemens, Astros owner Drayton McLane, and then-general manager Gerry Hunsicker used the day off between Games 2 and 3 to join the 300 mourners at a private memorial service for Ken Caminiti at Houston's Second Baptist Church. The next day, the Astros opened their first home NLCS game since October 15, 1986, by playing a video tribute to Caminiti on the Minute Maid Park big screen.

This time, the Cardinals took the early lead when Walker hit a solo home run over the wall in left-center field in the first inning. The Astros countered with three runs in the bottom of the inning against St. Louis's Jeff Suppan, sending a thunderous roar throughout the sellout crowd of 42,896, which included former president and first lady George and Barbara Bush.

Biggio started the rally with a leadoff single to left, and Beltran followed with a walk. After Bagwell hit into a double play to third, the speedy Beltran tied the score on Berkman's single up the middle. Kent, who fell behind in the count 0-2 before working the count to 3-2, gave the Astros a 3-1 lead with a two-run home run into the short porch in left field.

Edmonds got one of those runs back with a leadoff home run over the right-center field wall in the second inning. The Cardinals couldn't get anything else off of Clemens. Beltran added his seventh home run of the postseason with a leadoff shot to left-center off of Dan Haren in the eighth inning.

"You're seeing what a true talent as a baseball player he is," Garner said of Beltran after the game. "We know him more personally, and he's certainly a wonderful guy. But he is just some kind of talent. You're seeing what he can do. I think if he keeps hitting the wall out there, he's going to cause a little structural damage to the stadium. He's hitting the ball extremely hard, and he's done it now for quite some time."

Berkman capped the scoring one out after Beltran's home run with his own home run into the Crawford Boxes behind left field. Lidge worked the final two innings, giving up one walk and one hit while striking out five to earn the save before an appreciative and boisterous Saturday afternoon crowd of 42,896.

"I mean, the atmosphere is electric here right now," Lidge said after the Astros won at home for the 20th time in 21 games dating back to the regular season. "We've been playing really well. We've been playing with a lot of confidence at home. Yeah, we were down 0-2 [in the series], but I think anytime you come home and you've got Roger and Roy going, you feel pretty good about your chances of getting two. Like I said, we were playing with a lot of confidence here, and it's nice to get back."

There's much to be confident about on days Clemens holds the opposition to a pair of solo home runs and four hits overall with two walks and seven strikeouts over seven innings.

"It's kind of what you expect from him," La Russa said. "I mean he's got a lot of credits on his résumé, and he's earned every one of them. Got the two early runs. I mean, we had a great chance to win it because [Suppan] was outstanding. I kept thinking we'd break through, [but we] could never put anything together. And that's a credit to Clemens and then to Lidge at the end, the last two innings."

Oswalt wasn't nearly as dominant in Game 4 the next day, but he lasted long enough to exit with the score tied 5-5 after six innings. The Cardinals had taken a 3-0 lead in the first inning against Oswalt, who was showing signs of the strain he was trying to pitch through. The Cardinals got their three runs in the first inning on Pujols's two-run homer and John Mabry's RBI single. Bagwell cut St. Louis's lead to 3-1 with an RBI double to left-center field, but Edmonds put the Cardinals ahead 4-1 with a sacrifice fly to right field in the third inning. Berkman cut St. Louis's lead to 4-3 in the bottom of the third. After retiring the first two

Cardinals in the fourth, Oswalt gave up another run when he walked Womack, and gave up a single to Walker and an RBI single to Pujols.

Oswalt settled down and held the Cardinals scoreless in the fifth and sixth before handing it over to Wheeler. Berkman led off the bottom of the sixth inning with a home run into the Crawford Boxes off of reliever Kiko Calero. Vizcaino kept the inning going with a two-out double to left field, and catcher Raul Chavez tied the score 5-5 with a bloop single to center, prompting La Russa to call on left-handed reliever Ray King to get out of the inning.

After Wheeler threw a scoreless seventh inning, Beltran made Tavarez the pitcher of record with his record-tying eighth postseason home run in the bottom of the inning by ripping a 2-2 slider over the right-center field wall.

"Well, I'm seeing the ball [well], but I just have to say that I knew who I was facing," Beltran said. "I was facing Tavarez. He's a guy that has a real good sinker, real good slider, and also has a split. After I took two [sliders] in the back door, I knew that he probably was going to be able to throw another one, so I just told myself, 'Just relax, stay back, and try to put the ball in play.' That's what I did. I saw the ball, and I hit it with the fat part of the bat. When I saw that ball just leaving the ballpark, I just felt great."

Hours later, Tavarez still couldn't believe it.

"I don't know who else can hit that pitch out of the park besides Beltran," Tavarez said. "I went over the tape to see how low it was to the ground. Barry Bonds is the best hitter in baseball. I don't think Barry would have hit that pitch. I don't believe it."

Tavarez had made a seemingly perfect pitch, breaking the slider at Beltran's shoelaces while coming in at 81 mph. Beltran crushed it out anyway, tying the postseason home-run record Bonds set in the 2002 postseason for the San Francisco Giants.

"Superman," Biggio said, "comes through again."

Tavarez did not handle Beltran's home run well. He wasn't even starting to calm down when Bagwell followed to the plate after Beltran's home run. Tavarez's next four pitches were out of the strike zone, and the fourth nearly nailed Bagwell in the head. Almost every person among the sellout crowd of 42,760 had to believe Tavarez tried to take out Bagwell.

Bagwell, who hardly ever shows emotion that would be considered confrontational by opponents, definitely took offense at the high fastball. He shouted at Tavarez before taking first base, prompting plate umpire Mike Winters to issue warnings to both dugouts.

Tavarez bounced his first pitch to Berkman before intentionally walking him. Tavarez got ahead in the count 0-2 against Kent, but he hit him in the left calf with the next pitch to load the bases. Tavarez escaped further damage when Ensberg hit into a double play.

Finally out of the inning, Tavarez stormed off the mound, marched into the visitors' dugout, slapped a water cooler around, and completely pummeled the dugout phone with his left hand. In making a complete ass of himself, Tavarez also suffered multiple fractures in his left hand. The tantrum was shown on the big screen at Minute Maid Park, drawing a nasty response and a backhanded compliment from La Russa after the Astros tied the best-of-seven series at two games apiece heading into Game 5 between Backe and Woody Williams.

"Well, I think, ever since I've been around, since 1996 [with the Cardinals], the Astros are classy organization as anything I've met in the National League," La Russa said. "But even Sinatra clears his throat, and I think that was below their standards, and that was disappointing."

McLane initially didn't see the tantrum displayed on the Minute Maid Park Jumbotron. He vowed to review the situation and offer an apology to the Cardinals if he and his top officials deemed that the Jumbotron operator had been out of line. After less than an hour of discussion, Astros vice president of communications Jay Lucas told the *Chronicle* that he would apologize on behalf of the Astros to La Russa and the St. Louis Cardinals' highly respected general manager, Walt Jocketty.

As if fracturing the fourth ring finger and the fifth metacarpal bones in his left hand didn't make Tavarez look like an idiot enough, he compounded the misery when he tried to rationalize his poor behavior by perpetuating an old stereotype that Latino ballplayers have long fought to dispel.

"I wasn't able to stop it," Tavarez said. "I was upset with myself. I think most Latin guys would have done it. That's how we are. We're so emotional. We care so much about the game."

Never mind that Beltran, a Puerto Rican star, had become the story of the 2004 postseason with a calm, methodical, powerful, and intelligent approach at the plate and in center field. Never mind that St. Louis Cardinals star Albert Pujols saves all his rage for attacking the baseball. Tavarez finally made sense a day after his tantrum, admitting that he was stupid and should have calmed down. Vizcaino, who played with Tavarez in Cleveland, was insulted by his Dominican Republic countryman's decision to use race as a reason for his inability to control his temper. Yankees right-hander Kevin Brown, who is white, broke his hand in a similar tantrum during the 2004 regular season and Vizcaino used that situation to make his own point.

"Is he Latin?" Vizcaino sarcastically asked about Brown.

Seven years before Tavarez was born, the first major assault in Houston on a visitors' dugout phone occurred at the Astrodome on June 12, 1966. Growing angry as the Astros took control for an 8-4 victory, Chicago Cubs manager Leo Durocher ripped the dugout telephone off the wall and tossed it on the floor. The Astros sent Durocher a bill, but the cost obviously didn't deter the fiery manager.

Durocher pulled another telephone off the wall in the visitors' dugout at the Astrodome during another fit of anger on August 26, 1966. Adding a twist, he threw the phone on the field during a pitching change. According to unofficial Astros historian Mike Acosta, after that 7-4 victory over the Cubs, the Astrodome scoreboard read, "Sorry about that, Leo."

Obviously more tolerant than La Russa about taunts, Durocher became manager of the Astros late in the 1972 season. He remained manager through 1973, the year Tavarez was born.

If not for the tantrum, Tavarez would be remembered in Houston as just one of the many pitchers Beltran abused in the 2004 postseason.

"Well, I just feel great," said Beltran, who also set a postseason record with home runs in five consecutive games. "It feels great just to be able to do something that Barry Bonds did. But at the same time, I'm just going out there and trying to do my job. I'm not thinking about hitting home runs, I'm thinking about doing things differently. I'm just thinking about, 'Just put the ball in play, see the ball, hit the ball,' and good things are happening to me right now. I'm seeing the ball [well]. I have a good approach at the plate. I'm not trying to do too much. I'm just relaxed, and being relaxed on the plate, patient, feels good."

With all the talk about Beltran, Berkman was overshadowed even though he had raised his NLCS average to .467 after going two for two with two walks and three RBI in Game 4. With those two switch hitters in the batting order, the Astros had found the ultimate Killer B's.

"When you have guys who are equally as capable of hitting the ball out of the ballpark, equally as capable for hitting on average, driving in runs with base hits, and you can get three or four of them in a row, now you have a tough lineup to keep getting through four times in a ball game," Garner said. "I think that has been, in a large part, the reason for some of our success down the stretch. Because if it hasn't been Beltran or Biggio or Baggy or Berkman, it's been Kent and so on and so forth. That's what makes the lineups extremely difficult."

There wasn't much offense on either side the next day in Game 5 as Backe and Williams provided a quality pitchers duel between right-handers from the Houston area. Backe's backers had made it in from Galveston and League City. Williams, a product of Houston's Cypress Fair

High School and the University of Houston, had distributed 50 tickets to family and friends.

Williams held the Astros to one hit (a single by Bagwell) over seven scoreless innings, needing only 94 pitches. Backe, 11 years and eight months younger than Williams, countered with eight scoreless innings of one-hit ball. Both men walked two, struck out four, and had their Houston-area supporters tuned in to their every move.

"You kind of can't really describe what happened out there," said Backe, who carried a no-hitter for $5^2/_3$ innings before Womack broke it with a single. "We were just both in a rhythm and feeling good about ourselves. You would think that with the lineup that we have and the lineup that they have, there's going to be some runs scored. But I think when you have two guys—I can only speak for myself—when you feel as good as I did out there tonight and felt in the rhythm that I was in, you just feel like nobody can hit you."

After retiring the Cardinals in the eighth inning, Backe headed to the dugout and grabbed his batting gloves and batting helmet as though he believed Garner would let him hit in the bottom of the inning. He knew the score and inning called for a pinch hitter, but he wasn't conceding anything. At least mentally, he wanted Garner and his Astros teammates to understand that he wasn't ready to call it a day. Backe realized his job was done when pinch hitter Orlando Palmeiro headed out to hit for him.

A day after struggling through Game 1 of the NLCS, Backe sat down with Clemens for a chat. Clemens, who channels the fire he displays on the mound and in the dugout on the days he pitches, urged the bouncy Backe to relax and use all his extra energy in a constructive way. All that energy that made Backe stand out to Astros scout Paul Ricciarini at Class AA Orlando in 2002 needed to be harnessed. Clemens implored Backe to channel his energy toward each pitch and focus on catcher Brad Ausmus, who controlled the pace and led Backe through the perform-ance with near perfection. Ausmus also offered a steady hand after Womack broke Backe's no-hitter in the sixth.

"Well, I think Backe gave us a tremendous game, absolutely tremen-dous game," Garner said. "And you know what really concerned me was when I see pitchers—and it doesn't matter if it's young pitchers or veteran pitchers—pitching so well, [who] have a no-hitter going through the middle part of the game [and] then they give up a hit, how many times have you seen it turn into three, four, five runs real quick? I was concerned as we got deeper in the game and the crowd kept getting into it more and more. When he gave up the hit, I was concerned. Sometimes hitting can turn into a frenzy when something like that happens. He got out of that, got us through the eighth inning. I thought that was a terrific job. So you don't need to savor beyond the ninth inning. Brad [Lidge] was good for one inning tonight. It was fortunate that that's all it took."

Lidge retired the Cardinals in order in the ninth, collecting two strikeouts in the process. Isringhausen, who relieved Williams with a scoreless eighth, could not get out of the ninth inning. Kent had grown tired of all of the Killer B's talk. Some fans in the stands were even adding him to the Killer B's by putting a B in front of his last name on posters. "Jeff B-Kent," they wrote on many signs.

Kent wasn't amused. Before going out on the field for Game 5, Kent watched Boston Red Sox first baseman David Ortiz earlier that afternoon celebrate a walkoff home run over the New York Yankees in the American League Championship Series. The kid in Kent longed to feel the jubilation crossing every cell in Ortiz's body at that moment.

Although Kent had hit safely in three of the first four games in the series, he entered the ninth inning of Game 5 with a .214 average (three for 14) in the NLCS after starting that game zero for three. Again, Beltran was the catalyst. Beltran led off the ninth with a single to right field. One out later, Beltran collected his first stolen base of the series to move into scoring position as Berkman took Isringhausen's ball out of the strike zone, evening the count at 2-2. La Russa had already instructed Isringhausen to walk Berkman and go after Kent if Beltran stole second.

Berkman was having one of the best postseason performances in Astros' franchise history. After hitting .409 in the division series, Berkman was hitting .412 in the NLCS heading into the ninth inning of Game 5. So instead of pitching to Berkman with first base open, Isringhausen intentionally walked him after the count got to 2-2. Most of the 43,045 at Minute Maid Park were up in anticipation, stomping their feet and sending an ear-piercing buzz throughout the stadium as Kent walked to the plate.

Of the 30 teams in the majors, only the Astros did not have a walkoff home run during the 2004 regular season. Ironically, the Astros' last walkoff home run had come off Isringhausen in 2003. The man who hit it? Kent. The stakes were much higher on October 18, 2004.

Isringhausen left a cut fastball over the middle of the plate, and Kent hammered it toward the Crawford Boxes behind the left field wall. With that powerful swing, Kent pushed the Astros within one victory of the World Series. Kent even broke out a rare smile before tossing his helmet behind his back a few feet away from the plate, where all his teammates and the coaching staff waited to pound on him and celebrate the 3-0 victory.

"When we were in St. Louis, I watched Albert Pujols hit the game-winning home run against us and saw the excitement in his body

Jeff Kent rounds the bases after his clutch home run in the 2004 NLCS.

language," Kent said. "I wanted to feel like that. I felt pretty down at that time. So this was just a turn of the tables for us tonight in the same situation. But I've played the game a long time. I've struggled with my emotions at times to try to control them while I played this ballgame. I think I've been able to do that better now through the latter of my career. I'm just trying to continue to do that. I let my parents and my kids get overly excited, but I try to keep an even keel.... I took this whole scenario out of the bag of watching Pujols hit his home run and Ortiz hit his home run. I thought you guys knew where that was coming from. But I want to feel like that. Watching those guys do what they're doing, knowing the emotions that they probably are going through, I wanted to be those guys. That's the kid in me that loves to play this game. I want to be the other guy who's having a great time, and that's where that came from. I didn't mean that to show anybody up, I was just trying to have a good time in our last ballgame here before we headed off to St. Louis."

Kent's home run sent the Astros back to Busch Stadium with a 3-2 lead in the best-of-seven series, putting Houston within a victory of the World Series for the second time in franchise history. The 1980 Astros also got within a victory before falling short against the Philadelphia Phillies in what was then a best-of-five NLCS.

"It's very, very important not to take anything for granted," Kent said during the off-day workout between Games 5 and 6. "I think the consensus around here, too, is that we haven't accomplished anything yet. We had a big homestand and a great pitched game. But if we think we've achieved anything, that's flat wrong. I think the guys understand that and know the Cardinals are a very dangerous ball club."

The Cardinals didn't give the Astros anything else to celebrate when the series shifted to Busch Stadium. Instead of going with Clemens on short rest, Garner turned the ball over to Munro.

"You want to make sure you've covered all your bases in the sense that you've considered everything that you feel like is a possible factor," Garner said. "I talked with my staff. I thought about it for quite a bit. The process was a day or two, day and a half, I guess. And then you sit around and you think a little bit more. I think you can overthink it, you can see all kinds of scenarios. There's going to be a lot of people saying to you to do the opposite, start Roger. But what I feel in my gut is what I have to do. If you take all the information that's available to you, all the facts, you assimilate them, and I haven't heard anybody give me anything I haven't thought about. So given all those circumstances, I think this is the best way to go."

Munro gave up eight hits and four runs while lasting only $2\frac{1}{3}$ innings, but the rested bullpen kept the Astros' offense close. The Astros cut St. Louis's lead to 4-3 in the fourth inning on Lamb's leadoff home run to right field. For the second consecutive game, Isringhausen paid for issuing an intentional walk. With Ensberg at second and two outs, Isringhausen intentionally walked Beltran. Bagwell followed with an RBI single to left field, tying the score 4-4.

Lidge retired the Cardinals in the ninth to force extra innings, and he added two more innings to finish with three perfect innings of relief. The Astros bullpen had been spectacular heading into the 12th inning. Harville threw two-thirds of a scoreless inning. Qualls followed with three scoreless innings, and Wheeler added two scoreless innings before turning it over to Lidge. Miceli's march toward Astros infamy continued, though, in the 12th when he gave up Edmonds's walkoff home run over the right field wall.

"Yeah, this is what it's all about," Edmonds said after the game. "I think we all watched TV as kids and we all hear all the stuff you guys say and write and show us. We finally get to play in Game 7. I mean, it's better than going home. So our team has been playing hard, and they've been. Home field advantage has been good to both teams. We'll see what happens tomorrow."

The storyline could hardly have been more appropriate for the Astros to succeed. Clemens, whose January signing raised all of the World Series expectations in Houston, was on the mound for his hometown in a winner-take-all Game 7 against the St. Louis Cardinals. A win on this chilly October 21 night would send Clemens to the World Series against the Boston Red Sox, the team that ushered him into the majors in 1984.

Clemens had pitched with Boston through the 1996 season, leaving via free agency after then-Red Sox general manager Dan Duquette claimed he had nothing left. Eighteen years before his Game 7 appearance in the 2004 NLCS for the Astros, Clemens won Game 7 of the American League championship over the California Angels to send the Red Sox to the 1986 World Series against the New York Mets.

Fans in Houston hoped he'd accomplish the same for the Astros in Game 7 at Busch Stadium.

Biggio, who has hit more leadoff homers in the National League than any player in history and trails only future Hall of Famer Rickey Henderson in that category, led off the evening with a home run to left field.

The Astros' fate in Game 7 was likely sealed in the next inning. Kent got the second inning started with a leadoff walk from Suppan, and Vizcaino hit a one-out single to left field. Ausmus followed Vizcaino with his line drive, and it seemed as though at least one run would score.

Instead of conceding one run to not risk letting the ball go behind him, Edmonds gambled. He sprinted back toward left-center field, dove at the ball, and came away with the acrobatic catch, providing the moment that would haunt Ausmus and the Astros for months.

"I don't want to say it cost us the game, but I think it ultimately turned the game in the Cardinals' favor," Ausmus said. "If that gets over Jimmy's head, you're looking at two runs in and a man on second. It's a 3-0 game. It was a great play, and I think it went a long way toward winning Game 7."

As Edmonds popped back up with the ball, Kent and Vizcaino desperately rushed back to their previous bases to avoid a double play.

"Jimmy, that was probably the game-saving play," La Russa said. "That's going to be two runs, who knows how many more."

Suppan struck out Clemens to end the second inning. Edmonds couldn't deny the Astros in the third inning. After retiring Biggio to start the inning, Suppan walked Beltran on four pitches. Beltran stole second with Bagwell at the plate and advanced to third on Bagwell's fly ball to center. Edmonds rushed his throw to third base and sent the ball past fellow Gold Glove winner Rolen. Beltran sprinted home with the run on the error.

Suppan cut the Astros' lead in half with a perfect suicide squeeze toward first, driving in Womack, who had led off with a double and taken third on Matheny's ground out.

"Well, you see [Clemens was] pitching well, so a man on second with nobody out is one of those situations that are big momentum things," La Russa said. "If they can stop you from scoring, they get the momentum. If you can score, if it happens, it's something good for you. We were at the bottom of the lineup. I thought we weren't going to bunt the man over at third. Mike Matheny did a great job of getting him over. That's a high-risk play. You put it on because if you don't, I don't think Sup is going to hit the ball out of the infield. So sometimes you go ahead and take a shot. Worst thing that can happen is Edgar [Renteria] is leading off the next inning."

The Astros mounted another threat in the fourth. Kent led off with a walk, and Ensberg followed with a single to left field, prompting Cardinals pitching coach Dave Duncan to visit with Suppan on the mound.

Suppan collected the first out on Vizcaino's fielder's-choice grounder to first. He fell behind in the count 3-0 against Ausmus. With the take sign on, Ausmus took Suppan's 3-0 pitch for a strike. Ausmus fouled the next pitch and struck out on a 90-mph fastball. Suppan escaped the fourth in the same way he escaped in the second inning, catching Clemens looking at a called third strike.

Trailing 2-1, the Cardinals responded in the bottom of the sixth. Pinch hitter Cedeño led off the inning with a single to center, guiding the ball just inches away from Kent's diving stab attempt. Cedeño reached second on Renteria's sacrifice and third on Walker's ground out to Clemens, prompting Garner to visit Clemens at the mound.

Garner asked Clemens if he wanted to pitch around Pujols and take his chances with Rolen. Clemens decided to challenge Pujols because Rolen had also been swinging the bat well in the NLCS. It was obvious that Clemens would not pitch around Pujols, who took Clemens's first fastball for a strike. Clemens's next fastball was out of the strike zone. Clemens pumped another fastball at Pujols, who fouled the pitch back. Pujols ripped Clemens's next fastball for an RBI double to left field, tying the score 2-2.

Rolen lined Clemens's next pitch over the left field wall for a two-run home run. The Astros never recovered before the red-clad sellout crowd of 52,140 at Busch Stadium, falling to St. Louis 5–2.

"Well, I just told my players that without question this is one of the greatest runs in the history of the game," Garner said. "We would have liked to have taken it farther, there's no question. I would hope that everybody in our organization, this just makes us more determined, the whole organization, to make that next step and get to the World Series and have a little taste of this now. It was a fantastic run. There's a lot of good things that happened. But I've said it several times, I say it again tonight, that our veteran leadership pulled this ball club up at a time when it looked almost impossible. I described our season from midway on as very improbable. I think that's appropriate. But our veteran leadership definitely took charge, and that was the reason that we played the way we played. We fell one game short of getting to the World Series, but we're very proud of what our players accomplished."

13

Tim Purpura
Steps In

Almost two weeks after losing the National League Championship Series, all of the attention in Houston was on the potential of the Astros' re-signing All-Star center fielder Carlos Beltran, who captivated Astros fans with his historic prowess in the postseason.

For one day, the attention shifted away from Beltran when the Astros announced the stunning resignation of popular general manager Gerry Hunsicker and the promotion of his longtime assistant Tim Purpura. All of the parties involved have maintained that Hunsicker resigned on November 1, 2004, for personal reasons, but it has been speculated that he was forced out even though the Astros reached the postseason in five of the nine years he served as general manager.

"After the extra emotion and demands of this year and all the major issues hanging over this organization," Hunsicker said, "knowing that next year would be my last, the more we talked about it, it made some sense that this might be in the best interests for everybody."

Hunsicker, the 1998 *Sporting News* Executive of the Year, oversaw four National League Central champions (1997, 1998, 1999, and 2001) and the 2004 wild card Astros. Although the franchise had gone 793-665 for a .544 winning percentage during his time in Houston, it was no secret that Hunsicker's relationship with owner Drayton McLane cooled. Still, it was a surprise when Hunsicker walked away from the Astros with a year left on his contract. At the time of the announcement, it was claimed that Hunsicker would serve the final year of his contract—which was worth about $1 million a year—as an adviser to Purpura.

That "adviser's role" consisted of getting out of the way because Purpura and Hunsicker didn't speak throughout the 2005 season and Hunsicker was not at any of the Astros' playoff games in 2005 as the team marched to the franchise's first World Series berth. Hunsicker's supporters—and there were many in Houston—acted as though the

Tim Purpura (right), in his new role as general manager, lifts the "interim" status off of manager Phil Garner's title.

Astros had somehow been left without any competent baseball minds in the front office.

That theory was silly and just plain wrong.

For almost half a decade, Purpura had been known as one of the top assistant general managers in baseball. Purpura was often mentioned as a candidate whenever a general manager's position opened. He had already interviewed for vacant general manager posts with the Cincinnati Reds, Anaheim Angels, and Pittsburgh Pirates. As director of player development, Purpura built the farm system that was ranked as the top in baseball in 2001 by several baseball publications.

Purpura also played well with others in the front office, a quality that McLane desperately wanted in the general manager's role.

More importantly for McLane, the Astros' front-office team was still strong from top to bottom after Hunsicker left. Astros president of baseball operation, Tal Smith, the legendary figure who oversaw the building of the Astrodome and Minute Maid Park, was still in place to guide Purpura and McLane.

"Tal is probably the most experienced baseball executive in all of baseball," McLane said. "He first went to work in baseball in 1958. He worked with the Astros and Yankees. I think he's one of the most knowledgeable and one of the most intellectual people about sports. Tal was here. Tim had been here longer than Gerry.... Gerry was here nine years and Tim had been here 11 years. And Tim had been the person responsible for our player development program. Tim was a highly, highly experienced person."

Smith, who received *Baseball America*'s Lifetime Achievement Award in December 6, 2005, was the general manager for the 1980 Astros that finished one win shy of the World Series. Since receiving his first major league job in the farm system of the Cincinnati Reds in 1958, Smith has become one of the most respected and influential baseball officials in America. His reputation throughout baseball is such that he was offered the commissioner's job.

Smith, who joined the Houston franchise in 1960 as the assistant general manager shortly after Major League Baseball awarded Houston the team, has mentored several of baseball's general managers, including Hunsicker, Pat Gillick, Ed Wade, and Purpura. Perhaps no man has done more for baseball in the city of Houston in the last 45 years than Smith. Hunsicker definitely had the best tenure of any general manager in Astros' franchise history, and it became easy for some of McLane's critics to forget all the key personnel who helped Hunsicker and McLane in their successful run together.

"The thing I would say—and I know people get sick of me saying this—is that organizations win," Purpura said. "All the work the people do in organizations is cumulative. One person may be the person that gets the attention, whether it's the GM or whatever. At the end of the day the general manager and the owner have to make the decision, but it's the work of all the people over the years that gets you to the place you want to be.

"All the people in the organization deserve the credit, whether it's the scouts that scouted Adam Everett or made their voices known for that trade or the guys that put in the extra work with Jason Lane and Morgan Ensberg or our pitching people who worked with Roy Oswalt and Brad Lidge. I don't think any GM would take credit for what the organization achieves. It's ridiculous. You're one person. You have to set the climate so people can do their jobs to have an impact and have their voices heard. The way I was taught in this game, when things go wrong, the GM takes the hit. And when things go well, the GM credits the organization for the things that go well."

Purpura learned his early lessons in baseball from former Angels general managers Mike Port and Bill Bavasi, the son of legendary baseball official Buzzie Bavasi. Purpura received his first internship from Port with the Angels in 1990, when Bavasi served as the Angels' farm director. As the dean of students at the University of California at San Diego in the late 1980s, the Oak Lawn, Illinois, native noticed former Chicago

White Sox general manager Roland Hemond sitting at San Diego's Jack Murphy Stadium during a Padres game.

Purpura, a lifelong White Sox fan, approached Hemond and introduced himself as a fan who remembered Hemond as the general manager of the White Sox. After some small talk, Purpura asked Hemond for advice on breaking into baseball's front offices.

"Go to law school," Hemond said, "because someday lawyers are going to run the game."

Purpura took Hemonds's advice and enrolled at Thomas Jefferson School of Law in San Diego, learning the multitasking and time management skills that served him well during the first tests of his tenure as a rookie general manager. Halfway through law school, Purpura married his wife, Shari. Shortly after graduating from law school in 1992, Purpura joined Port on the inaugural front office staff at the Arizona Fall League, a league where teams throughout the majors send their top major league-ready prospects in October. Two years later, Purpura joined the Astros as an assistant director of minor league operations and as director of player relations. He was promoted to director of player development on October 24, 1997.

Purpura picked up extra duties each year. By 2004, he ran player development and made sure Hunsicker was in tune with all of the rules and waivers. Not surprisingly, Purpura was on a scouting trip in the Dominican Republic in August 2003 when Hunsicker announced that he had reached a free-agent deal with reliever Rick White. At the time of the announcement, White was actually property of the Chicago White Sox. Believing they had reached a deal with White, Hunsicker and manager Jimy Williams informed right-hander Kirk Saarloos that he had been demoted to Class AAA New Orleans on the night of August 6.

The next morning, Hunsicker called Saarloos to tell him to stay because the White Sox had not put White through waivers after designating him for assignment on August 1. Teams have 10 days to trade, put through waivers, or release a player after he is designated for assignment.

"There was a misunderstanding as to the status of the player," Hunsicker said the next day after White Sox general manager Kenny Williams vowed to file a complaint with the commissioner's office. "I certainly thought he was a free agent. It turned out this morning that that wasn't the case. He's still the property of the Chicago White Sox. Therefore, the transaction can't move forward. We're back to where we were pregame [August 6] with Saarloos still on our club and Rick White a member of the White Sox."

It's not unusual for a general manager to not know all the rules or the waiver activity, but it's rare when a general manager claims to have signed a player who belongs to another team. On that day, it was easy to see just one of the ways that Purpura was valuable to Hunsicker and the Astros.

In 2004 Purpura also handled contract administration and some contract and arbitration negotiations and budgets. He was in charge of handling personnel issues and making sure the player's insurance issues were in order. He also oversaw worker's compensation and the foreign baseball academies, making sure wire transfers were made each month so that the Astros' Venezuelan and Dominican academies met their budgets each month. Senior director of baseball operations David Gottfried, known as the chief of staff around the Astros' Union Station offices, absorbed most of those jobs when Purpura was promoted to general manager.

"He's the guy who keeps the team afloat on rules," Purpura said of his most trusted confidant, Gottfried. "A lot of the roles that I used to have in the office, David took over. I know how tough that job is. There are so many things you have to do on a continual basis."

Purpura leaned heavily on Gottfried, who had been one of his key assistants since 1998. Purpura also retained the services of top Hunsicker confidant Paul Ricciarini, the senior director of player personnel. Purpura hired Ricky Bennett away from the Detroit Tigers to serve as assistant general manager. He also brought former Arizona Diamondbacks manager Al Pedrique, a former minor league manager with the Astros, as a special assistant.

Purpura broke down the figurative walls between player development and scouting, urging all voices to be heard equally. He also leaned heavily on longtime scouts Fred Nelson, Gordy McKenzie, and Walt Matthews. He encouraged open communication and challenged each employee to push the organization toward the World Series.

Two days after he took the job, Purpura lifted the interim tag of Phil Garner's manager title. A day later, he delivered his first bout of bad news to Astros fans when he announced that three-time All-Star outfielder Lance Berkman would undergo right knee surgery to repair a torn anterior cruciate ligament. Berkman was coming off a season in which he led the team in average (.316), home runs (30), and games (160). He also led the team in walks, slugging percentage (.566), on-base percentage (.450), and total bases (308) while driving in 106 runs.

If not for Beltran's exploits, Berkman would have been the Astros' star in the postseason. Against the Braves in the division series, Berkman hit .409 with one home run, three RBI, and five runs. In the NLCS he hit .292 with three home runs, nine RBI, seven runs, and five walks. But seven days after the Cardinals eliminated the Astros in Game 7, Berkman made the mistake of playing flag football at Houston's Second Baptist Church.

Although Berkman realized he should not have been anywhere near a flag football game, he had often kept in shape after the season by playing the sport. He had much to lose, because his three-year, $11 million contract ran out after the 2004 season and he was entering his final season of arbitration eligibility. Privately, Purpura was disappointed that Berkman had put himself and the team at risk. Publicly, Purpura said all of the right things. He praised Berkman's honesty. Another person might have lied about the way he got hurt, but Berkman has definitely built a reputation as a forthright and accountable person.

Purpura tried to sound optimistic about having Berkman doing baseball activities four months after the surgery in hopes of hitting the recovery target of five to six months. Berkman refused to concede that he'd miss opening day. At one point, Berkman even claimed he thought he could be ready by opening day in April. Garner called bull on those comments.

If nothing else, Berkman provided the Astros and their fans a good chuckle with another of his lengthy list of wacky antics. Berkman played safety and quarterback on October 28 when he suffered the injury. He was on defense tracking an opponent running down the opposite sideline when he first felt the knee problem. Berkman planted his right foot and immediately heard a "nasty crunch sound." After an "Oh, gosh," he kept playing. Berkman finally quit when he felt more discomfort when he landed after jumping to make a throw.

Berkman's knee injury guaranteed that the 2005 Astros would start without at least one of the 2004 club's All-Star offensive players. On December 7, the Astros decided against offering 2004 RBI leader Jeff Kent salary arbitration, leaving Beltran on the free-agent board. The Astros held a $9 million option on Kent's contract. On the same day Berkman suffered his right knee injury on the other side of town, Hunsicker declined Kent's option and picked up the $3 million option on Craig Biggio's contract.

Kent's signing had pushed Biggio from second base to the outfield in 2003 and 2004, and several Astros officials were ready to put an end to that experiment. Biggio was going to get every opportunity to regain his second base job in spring training against rookie Chris Burke. Nonetheless, the Astros made an effort to re-sign Kent. After opening the negotiations with a one-year, $4.5 million offer, the Astros raised the offer to $6 million on November 11. The Astros made Kent a final offer of $7 million for 2005 with a vesting option for $7 million in 2006 if he made 538 plate appearances in 2005.

Kent spurned the Astros' offer and signed a two-year, $17 million deal with the Los Angeles Dodgers, the team he had cheered as a child.

A few days after Purpura and the Astros landed in Anaheim on December 10, 2004, for the start of Purpura's first winter meetings as a general manager, it became apparent to the other 29 teams that the Astros' main focus that winter would be Beltran and Clemens, but mainly Beltran.

With the temptation to do something, anything, Purpura refused to make a move merely for the sake of making one. He had seen all of the Astros' young stars since the day they were signed. He ushered guys like Burke, Wandy Rodriguez, Ezequiel Astacio, and Chad Qualls through the farm system. He had sat with each one of them every spring training to discuss their futures. He felt more than an investment in their careers. He knew they could contribute even though the Astros entered the season not knowing what they could count on from those rookies.

Although Berkman's knee injury and Kent's departure didn't make Purpura's new role any easier, it wasn't as though Purpura didn't have the work ethic and critical mind to find solutions.

Purpura left his first winter meetings with some good news when Houston-based agents Alan and Randy Hendricks visited with him to say Clemens would accept the Astros' salary arbitration. Although Clemens still wasn't ready to decide whether he'd return for his 22nd season, by accepting arbitration on December 11, 2004, he was automatically put on the Astros' 40-man roster and taken off the free-agent market. Clemens would play for the Astros in 2005 or for nobody else.

Purpura, McLane, and Clemens hoped Clemens's decision to accept arbitration would serve as a positive in the Beltran negotiations.

"Roger has expressed his thoughts as far as Carlos is concerned," Purpura said on December 11, 2004, at the Anaheim Marriott. "Certainly, Carlos has expressed his thoughts in regards to Roger. They fit perfectly for us, and I think it's a good indication, hopefully, to Carlos. If Roger plays, he will play for us. I don't see it being anything but positive on both sides."

Beltran's agent, Scott Boras, also indicated that Clemens's decision couldn't hurt the Astros' talks with Beltran.

"Carlos is very favorably impressed with Roger Clemens," Boras said that day. "He was a great teammate to him and certainly somebody he will always remember that he played with. I'm sure in his considerations about Houston he's very happy that he's returning."

Purpura left the winter meetings hopeful that talks would pick up with Beltran and that ultimately Clemens would decide that he could pitch another season. There were good days and bad ones, frustrating ones and fulfilling ones. He was finally the general manager of the Houston Astros, a post his father, Jim, had started preparing him for since they went to old Comiskey Park decades earlier.

"I think in all those situations you think, 'How do we handle this,'" Purpura said. "What are the best decisions? You try to be analytical, I guess, from the 'How do we get through this' point of view. I reflect to when I went to law school. I went to law school while working full-time. If I made it through that, I [can] make it through anything. That's what fueled me. When you get through that and then have more challenges, you know you can work through it."

14

Chasing Beltran

Preparing for a celebration, Elizabeth McLane baked a chocolate cake after her husband left to his office in Temple, Texas, on January 8, 2005. Drayton McLane has a tremendous sweet tooth, and he loves no dessert more than his wife's chocolate cake.

Elizabeth and Drayton McLane had hoped to celebrate signing Carlos Beltran with that dessert later that afternoon. Until that day, McLane had no doubt he'd land Beltran. He had chased the All-Star like he'd chase no other player. He had enlisted all segments of his organization to help. Rosi Hernandez, the Astros' bright young vice president of market development, recruited some of the top business and political leaders in Houston's Latino community to write letters encouraging Beltran to re-sign with Houston. Vice president of communication Jay Lucas's staff put together a highlight video for Beltran, hoping to remind Beltran how much he moved Astros' fans during his amazing postseason assault.

The Astros even presented Beltran with a framed copy of the *Houston Chronicle*'s October 18 edition sports cover, which had the headlines "The Equalizer, Superman Turns Golfer, Tees off on Tavarez" over a four-column picture of Beltran hitting the game-winning home run off of St. Louis's Julian Tavarez in Game 4 of the 2004 National League Championship Series.

On the field, Beltran is the ultimate five-tool player. He's a switch hitter who can hit for average, run, field, throw, and hit for power. He plays exceptional defense at a premium position, and he stole bases in 2004 with relative impunity. He also displayed the rare intangible of being able to perform up to his talents.

"He's the best player I've ever played with as far as overall ability is concerned," said Astros first baseman Jeff Bagwell, who has likely already assured his own place at the Hall of Fame. "He's got power from both sides of the plate, his speed is unbelievable, and he's a great defensive player. When they talk about a five-tool player, he should be the poster boy."

Off the field, Beltran had developed a reputation as a person of high morals. He doesn't drink beyond the casual glass of wine over dinner with his wife, Jessica. He doesn't smoke or curse. And he rarely discusses any success without thanking the Lord several times. Not one to run the street with the guys, he was usually with his wife on the road. At six feet, one inch and 190 pounds with a ready smile and movie star looks, he quickly built a cult following among the ladies in Houston. His mere talent on the baseball field was enough to lure the men and boys into his corner, littering Minute Maid Park with folks wearing his Astros jersey.

Although Beltran had been with the Astros only since the June 24, 2004, trade that brought him from Kansas City, he had captivated the entire city and franchise with his personality and play. In a city where Spanish is heard as much as English and the Latino community is growing to more prominence each day, McLane wanted Beltran to join Lance Berkman and Roy Oswalt as the future faces of his organization.

By Beltran's third month with the Astros, several of the top Latino business leaders in Houston had been impressed enough to hold a luncheon in his honor at Minute Maid Park's 9 Amigos restaurant. Led by Houston Hispanic Chamber of Commerce president Rick Jaramillo, the HHCC honored Carlos and Jessica Beltran in September 2004 as a gesture to let the Beltrans know that they would have a supportive home if they decided to stay in Houston. Not since Jose Cruz played with the Astros had a classy Latino player been so embraced by the people of Houston. Former Astros pitcher Jose Lima built a cult following with his quirky personality, but Lima could likely never be half as refined as Beltran.

McLane wanted to charter a plane full of his top baseball executives to Puerto Rico to visit Carlos and Jessica Beltran at their home in the small town of Manati. Agent Scott Boras denied the request, so the Astros met with Beltran and Boras at the team's spring training facility in Kissimmee, Florida, on December 22, 2004. Boras and Beltran met a day earlier with Yankees owner George Steinbrenner at the Yankees' training facility in Tampa.

General manager Tim Purpura and Astros president of baseball operations Tal Smith joined McLane at the meeting inside one of the conference rooms at Osceola County Stadium. McLane arrived at the meeting with multiple gifts for Beltran. He gave him a book with 250 emails from fans urging Beltran to stay in Houston. He showed him the highlight video with footage of the hundreds of signs throughout Minute Maid

Park imploring Beltran to stay during the playoffs. Beltran was given the framed *Houston Chronicle*'s "The Equalizer" page. Banco Popular, one of Puerto Rico's top banks with offices in Houston, sent Beltran a Banco Popular leather jacket with the word *Beltran* and a Puerto Rican flag embroidered on the back.

Houston mayor Bill White and councilwoman Carol Alvarado, the mayor pro tem, sent letters with McLane urging Beltran to re-sign. Banco Popular-North America president Roberto Herencia, Jaramillo of the Hispanic chamber, and top Houston restaurateur Michael Cordova also wrote letters for McLane to deliver. Compared to McLane's push for Beltran, the previous winter's full-court recruiting effort on Clemens seemed tame.

McLane is the ultimate salesman. There are literally thousands of Astros fans around the city who have a story about discussing the team personally with McLane at Minute Maid Park. He attends a great majority of the Astros' games, leaving his Diamond Level seats on the front row behind home plate after about two innings to work his way up to the suite level. On his way up, he visits with fans. He'll listen intently after asking many fans what they think must be done to make the Astros champions. Most of the time, he doesn't need to ask.

Since buying the franchise from Dr. John McMullen in 1992, McLane has lured back many of the fans who turned against the Astros when McMullen pushed the legendary Nolan Ryan out the door. McLane gave Astros fans a sense of ownership in the organization. He often can be seen posing for pictures with fans or kissing babies. If you didn't know any better, you'd think he were running for office. The only difference, of course, is that McLane is more than a politician. He has kept his home phone number in Temple, Texas, listed. He'll hand out his business card and answer letters when fans write to him.

He bristles politely when he is referred to as Mr. McLane, urging fans to address him as Drayton. Always ready with a hug, he urges fans during his chats to think of themselves as his partners. As he gets closer to folks, he'll even ask them to think of him as Uncle Drayton. That personality serves McLane well in Houston, which for the most part has managed to maintain a small-town approach to life even though it's the fourth largest city in America.

Houston doesn't have the ego of New York; the spunk of Newark, New Jersey; the laid-back personality of Los Angeles; or the undeserved self-importance of the much smaller Dallas up north. When Houston's Reliant Stadium held Super Bowl XXXVIII in February 2004, billboards around town encouraged residents to 'Smile, company's coming.' Some visitors during Super Bowl Week mocked the city's need to please. But the fact remains that Houston folks actually care about their guests. And nobody was laughing in 2005 when Houston was the first major city in America to open its doors to the victims of Hurricane Katrina. While other major cities wondered what to do to help the people of New Orleans, Houston's leaders were already accepting the first wave of at least 150,000 evacuees who landed in the city. Who can forget the thousands of folks seeking shelter at the Astrodome, the Astros' old home?

McLane hoped Beltran would understand that playing in Houston had value beyond a rich contract and no state taxes in Texas. That's not to say the Astros didn't step up on the financial side. At the end, McLane offered Beltran a franchise-record $108 million contract, a $38 million jump from the opening offer McLane gave Beltran at their meeting in Kissimmee.

Sitting across the table from Beltran and Boras on December 22, McLane slid a paper across the table to Beltran and encouraged the All-Star to open it. Beltran opened the paper and read the five-year, $70 million offer. Without making much of an expression, Beltran folded the paper back up and slid it back to McLane. He turned toward Boras and told McLane that Boras would handle all of the negotiations.

After returning to Houston later that evening, Purpura announced that a substantial offer had been made. McLane's personal touch has worked well with Bagwell, Craig Biggio, Andy Pettitte, Clemens, Berkman, Oswalt, and countless other players. None of those guys, however, is represented by Boras, who has become one of the most powerful agents in baseball by controlling the entire negotiation process. Boras forbid McLane from making contact with Beltran, and McLane never got his chance to make a personal appeal at Carlos and Jessica Beltran's home in Puerto Rico.

Two days after the Astros' meeting with Beltran in Kissimmee, Mets general manager Omar Minaya spent a major portion of his Christmas Eve on the phone collecting scouting reports from people who had dealt with Beltran in the past. On paper, Beltran was impressive enough after hitting .267 with 38 home runs, 104 RBI, and 42 stolen bases in the 2004 regular season. He also wouldn't turn 28 until April 24, 2005.

With Boras crunching the numbers, Beltran's statistics rated favorably in many categories to Barry Bonds, Joe DiMaggio, Ken Griffey Jr., Willie Mays, Duke Snider, and Hack Wilson.

Beltran, DiMaggio, Griffey, Mays, Dale Murphy, Snider, and Wilson were the only center fielders in major league history to have four consecutive seasons with at least 20 home runs and 100 RBI. Only DiMaggio and Beltran accomplished the feat by their 27th birthdays.

Boras's navy blue Carlos Beltran binder was full of impressive stats and a collection of praise from throughout the baseball industry. The first of eight sections was titled, "Beltran Leads Houston's Playoff Drive."

On the first page of section 1, it read, "He's everything. He can do it all. He's as good as any player I've ever seen. —Houston Astros Manager Phil Garner.

"He is the best player in baseball. I probably should not say that. Man, somebody needs to say it. —Kansas City Royals Manager Tony Peña, 2003 American League Manager of the Year."

The Astros and Mets didn't need Boras's book to understand why they wanted Beltran. Purpura and Smith had crunched their own numbers and came up with essentially the same impressive conclusions. Nonetheless, the baseball industry snickered when it was reported that Boras wanted a 10-year deal for Beltran. Those days in baseball may be over. Nonetheless, Boras had complete control in the process as the Astros gambled their entire winter on chasing Beltran.

Because the Astros had offered Beltran salary arbitration in December 2004, they still had until 11 p.m. on January 8, 2005, to re-sign him or lose any negotiating rights until May 1. After the meeting in Kissimmee, McLane, Beltran, and Boras agreed to take a break from the negotiations until after the Christmas holidays. By December 28, Minaya and the Mets had persuaded Boras to let them meet with Beltran in Puerto Rico. A similar meeting with star free-agent right-hander Pedro Martinez in the Dominican Republic that Thanksgiving had helped Minaya land Martinez for the Mets.

As Minaya set up his meeting in Puerto Rico, McLane wasn't very worried about the Mets. He was more concerned about his own talks with Boras. The free-agent talent pool was already shrinking. Outfielder Moises Alou, who desperately wanted to return to the Astros, had signed with the San Francisco Giants to play for his father, Felipe. Former Astros center fielder Steve Finley, whom the Astros had limited interest in signing as a free agent, had already signed with the Angels.

"We don't want to be left out in the cold if we can't get Beltran," McLane said.

McLane was confident that he'd get an answer from Beltran by the end of the year if not the first weekend of 2005. The Astros told Boras they wanted an answer by end of the last week in 2004, and Smith and Purpura told McLane that Boras assured them the Beltran negotiations wouldn't drag on until the January 8 deadline. The talks definitely dragged on. The Astros spoke with Boras on December 29 and 30, but not much progress was made even though McLane jokingly invited Boras and his family to spend New Year's Eve with him and his wife at their retreat on South Padre Island. Boras passed on the offer, preferring instead to spend his time in Hawaii with family.

The Astros received a tremendous blow when Minaya, Mets owner Fred Wilpon, assistant general manager Jim Duquette, and special assistant Tony Bernazard visited Beltran and Boras in Puerto Rico on January 3. Bernazard, who had been speaking with Boras on a daily basis about Beltran since the last two weeks of December, had known Beltran for a decade. Beltran's parents actually sought Bernazard's guidance before Beltran signed his first professional contract with the Kansas City Royals. Minaya also had ties to Beltran dating back to when Beltran was 18 years old.

The Mets left that meeting without making an offer. A day later, they opened the bidding at around $100 million. The Chicago Cubs reportedly topped out at $80 million. McLane spoke with Boras again on January 5 and then for another 20 minutes Thursday, January 6.

"He kept putting us off and putting us off," McLane said. "Then finally before the Saturday deadline, on Thursday he said I'll call you by 1:30 on Friday. I called him Friday and he said, 'Where are you going to be Saturday at 10:30?' He said, 'I'll call you.'"

McLane started to think he was being put off, and many folks in Houston started wondering if Beltran ever had any legitimate interest in returning to the Astros. Nonetheless, McLane was positive because he assumed Boras was stalling in an attempt to get a better offer than what the Astros had given Beltran. Only later did it leak out of the New York Yankees' camp that Boras was begging the Yankees to give Beltran a six-year, $96 million deal. Boras denies that report, but many people in baseball believe Boras did offer Beltran to the Yankees for $96 million. Whatever the case, the Yankees weren't interested. The Astros entered January 8 competing with the Mets for Beltran's services.

McLane headed to his office in Temple early Saturday, January 8 to prepare for the final stages of the negotiations. He was at his office by 7 a.m. In Houston, Purpura, Smith, and Astros president of business operations Pam Gardner headed to the Astros' Union Station offices at Minute Maid Park. McLane's top officials were optimistic. Other team employees were ready to drive down to Minute Maid Park for a celebratory press conference.

Waiting for Boras, McLane actually fielded more calls from media before 10:30 a.m. passed without starting serious talks that day with Boras. By 10:30 a.m., the negotiations with the Mets and Boras were intensifying. McLane started to feel as though he was getting the brush off, and he didn't appreciate it.

"He didn't call me," McLane said. "I finally really didn't talk to him until, I think, 6 p.m. or 6:30 p.m. was the first real negotiating. How disappointing that was. This was everything to the Houston Astros, and we got put on the back shelf."

At one point that evening, the Mets and the Astros both thought Boras was still trying to get the Yankees involved. As the 11 p.m. deadline neared, Boras informed McLane that Beltran and Jessica would not accept any deal without a no-trade provision. Tired of Boras adding requests as the deadline neared, McLane asked if the no-trade clause would close the deal. Boras said it wouldn't. So although Boras and Beltran said the lack of a no-trade provision was a deal-breaker, they never said a no-trade clause would be a deal-maker once the Astros already had offered a $108 million, seven-year deal that is essentially worth the same as the Mets' deal when New York's taxes are taken into account.

The 11 p.m. deadline hit without a deal, and McLane was stunned.

"It slipped through our fingers in the last, last few minutes," he said. "It was just some sticking points. It should never, never have gotten to this."

At Minute Maid Park, Purpura walked into a briefing room with the other top Astros officials for a quick mock interview session as Lucas prepared him for potential questions. When Purpura took the podium, he could hardly hide his disappointment. It was as though the entire process had sucked the posture out of his body. Sitting in the audience, Smith slumped at his chair. Purpura, Smith, and McLane had spared no expense or avenue in hopes of landing Beltran. Yet, they had still finished second or, possibly even third, in the race. Boras had told McLane that Beltran had chosen the Mets.

Hardly anyone blamed McLane or the Astros. Fans rallied behind McLane and praised him for making such an offer. Although appreciative of the fans' support, McLane was stunned for a few days. He honestly believed that he could sell Beltran on the Astros and the city of Houston. Unable to sleep, he called a reporter at 2 a.m.

"I really thought we had him," he said, a sad trace in his voice. "I really thought we'd get him. You know, I think I'm as good a salesman as anybody, but we never had a chance."

In time, most of Houston began to believe the Astros never had a chance to re-sign Beltran. Some folks blamed Beltran. Most blamed Boras. Even after Beltran said he would have signed with the Astros if they had given him a no-trade clause, only a small pocket of Astros fans sided against McLane.

"I love chocolate cake, and Elizabeth made me a cake," McLane said. "When the deadline came and we found out he was not coming to the Houston Astros, it was just sheer disappointment. I was devastated. The cake didn't have the appeal then. It was several days before I even took a bite out of it, because I was so disappointed. I thought we were going to win it. I really did."

15

Burying the Messenger and the Tombstone

From: Ross Wardlaw
Sent: Wednesday, October 05, 2005 6:59 PM
To: Ortiz, Jesus
Subject: YOU'RE AN IDIOT!!

You ought to be fired for your bashing of OUR home team like you did on June 1st. I hope this email finds you plugged into an EKG machine. Like my good buddy Mike Jones once brilliantly said, "Back then you didn't want them, now they're hot and you're all on them."

Maybe you'll think twice before publicly making a fool of yourself again. GO STROS!

For generations of Western-loving Americans, Tombstone has been associated with the shootout at the OK Corral, the epic gunfight in which Wyatt, Morgan, and Virgil Earp, and Doc Holliday shot and killed three men in Tombstone, Arizona. For Houston Astros fans keeping score at home, the shootout at the OK Corral occurred on October 26, 1881, exactly 124 years before the Chicago White Sox delivered the final blow to the Astros in the 2005 World Series on October 26, 2005, at Minute Maid Park.

That epic gunfight has been celebrated in movies, books, and plays, immortalizing the Earp brothers and Holliday and keeping Tombstone, Arizona, among the most renowned cities of the Old West. Back in Houston, a more infamous tombstone came out in the June 1, 2005, editions of the *Houston Chronicle*. Much to the chagrin of many loyal Astros fans—not to mention Astros owner Drayton McLane and general manager Tim Purpura—the *Chronicle*'s tombstone declared the end of the Astros' season on June 1.

GRAVE CIRCUMSTANCES
The Cold Hard Truth:

Yes, there are 111 games left on the schedule, but the Astros might as well start thinking about next year. It's off

Under those headlines and subheadlines, talented *Houston Chronicle* graphic artist Robert Wuensche illustrated a tombstone with a baseball on top and flowers at the base. Inside the tombstone graphic, it read:

RIP
Astros' season
April 5, 2005–June 1, 2005
Grounds for Burial

Five reasons the Astros won't resurrect their playoff hopes in 2005:

They're last in the majors with 182 runs (3.6 per game).
They don't have a regular hitting above Craig Biggio's .284.
Their bullpen is 2-10 with a 5.34 ERA.
They're on pace to win 15 road games—and lose 66.
That 36-10 finish of last season? Happens once every 43 years.

GOAL TO GO
One goal remaining for the 2005 Astros is to improve their winning percentage enough to avoid the first 100-loss season in franchise history. The Astros teams with the worst starts and how they finished.

Season	51 Games	Final	
1991	18-33	65-97	
2000	19-32	72-90	
2005	19-32	60-102*	(projected record at current pace)
1975	20-31	64-97	
1967	20-31	69-93	
1990	20-31	75-87	

Needless to say, the graphic was off after nearly five months. If we had done it in 1991, we would have nailed it. If the illustration had been done in 1975, not a person would have argued, because that Astros club finished 64–97.

Debates raged on Astros fan forums. On local sports radio, some callers praised the *Chronicle* folks for having the guts to call it like they saw it. Others called to say just how stupid they thought the story was. In the Astros clubhouse, however, not one player complained. Even manager Phil Garner found only one problem with the article, the insinuation that Chris Burke did not have an opportunity to win the starting job at second base in spring training. To this day, not one Astros player has seriously ripped the *Chronicle* for the graphic. Lance Berkman jokingly ripped the tombstone during a rally before the 2005 division series, but he was actually playing up to the crowd. In the story that accompanied the tombstone, Berkman was the most outspoken Astro imploring the team to make changes.

By the time the 2005 season was over, I had received at least 400 emails in response to the tombstone. Here is just a sample of those responses:

From: Jim
Sent: Wednesday, June 01, 2005 4:46 PM
To: Ortiz, Jesus
Subject: Outrageous

Today's column is outrageous. I find it a bit insulting. Did you notice they won last night? *The Chronicle* should be ashamed of your statements. For what it is worth, I have enjoyed most of what you have written in the past because you offer a knowledgeable and intelligent analysis of our Astros. But you have crossed the line a bit today.

I am a lifelong Astros/Colt 45 fan and have been here long before you were and will be here long after you have moved along. I know the Astros are struggling, and are just about the worst team in baseball, but don't rub my nose in it!! The fans (and your customers) don't need a sportswriter, especially one of your caliber, badmouthing our team. Find something a little more positive to write about, don't waste your time and talent insulting your customers.

—Jim

From: ROBERT
Sent: Wednesday, June 01, 2005 1:20 PM
To: Ortiz, Jesus
Subject: June 1 article RIP

Dear Mr. Ortiz,

I, too, am a frustrated ASTROS fan and though I don't truly believe they will make the playoffs this year, stranger things have happened. In 1964 the St. Louis Cardinals were only 2.5 games back on June 2, but by August 23 they were 11 games out. Yet with only 6 weeks left in the season they turned it around and not only won the NL pennant but went on to beat the New York Yankees in the World Series. They had a great young pitcher named Bob Gibson and acquired a speedy young outfielder named Lou Brock that year. They had some good hitters— Ken Boyer, Curt Flood, Bill White, but not nearly the pitching that the ASTROS have. I believe we need to give our young players some playing time. Let's see what they can do. Early in the year the young batters have the advantage over the pitchers as the pitchers don't know the batters' weaknesses and so they hit better (see Willy Taveras and Jason Lane). As the season goes on the pitchers have a record of the weaknesses of these hitters and exploit them—that's the stage we are in now. The hitters then work with their batting coach to learn to improve on those areas and they start to hit again and settle in. I don't want to see the ASTROS trade away their strength—pitching for some temporary fix. Build this club to be strong for the years to come. Build it around Oswalt, Backe, Lane, Everitt [sic], Lidge, Berkman, Taveras, and Burke. In a few years they will be in their prime and ready to dominate the league while the other teams are growing old. I venture to say that June will be a good month for the ASTROS as they get their swings back. They might not make the playoffs, but they will show what they are made of and ready to jump into 2006 knowing where they need to shore up the team in the offseason and where they are set. Let's give them a chance. This team will be over .500 by year's end and nowhere near that 100-loss record you referred to in your column.

From: Richard
Sent: Wednesday, June 01, 2005 11:38 AM
To: Ortiz, Jesus
Subject: ASTROS SEASON
Mr. Ortiz:

I cannot agree that the season is over for the Astros. This team reminds me of the 80-81 team, which had a "Punch & Judy" type offense, good pitching, and an anemic offense. I certainly am disappointed that the team hasn't done better, but let's try to support them and not keep griping about what was not done in the offseason. I do feel that the Astros will give all the teams in the Central Division, except the Cardinals, a run for their money. The new players can only get better. Taveras is having a fair season, but he's only one year away from AA ball. He has to get better. Berkman, Ensberg, Biggio, Everett, and Lamb are due to get it together soon, and if pitching continues, they will start winning.

I know I could talk all day long about the Astros, good and bad, and I will always support the Astros while reading and enjoying the articles you and your fellow coworkers at the *Chronicle* write although I may not always agree with your topic. Keep up the good work and try to be optimistic about our Astros.

An Astro fan at Louisiana Tech University, Ruston, La.,
Richard

Astros fans rallied around the tombstone. Purpura opened his morning's *Chronicle* and was dumbfounded and a bit angered.

"I thought that it was extremely premature," Purpura said. "And in some ways I kind of thought it was a joke that somebody would think that after 60 days of a 180-day season that you could be dead in the water... Berkman wasn't at full force, and we had a bunch of young guys. I thought it was extremely premature. And I guess I was right."

More than a few players believed that the Astros should break up the team. Some of the young guys, after hearing two months of rumors that Roger Clemens would be traded, wondered privately if the team could re-stock the lineup with top young talent if Clemens were indeed traded to the New York Yankees. Berkman was part of the faction on the club that wondered if it wouldn't be a bad idea to sacrifice the 2005 season to see what young guys such as Lane and Burke could do if the team committed to a youth movement. McLane was adamant that his Astros were committed to winning now. He wanted no talk of tearing up the 2005 team.

Purpura also was in no mood to succumb to the chorus of local and national media urging him to break up the 2005 team after only two months. Purpura used the tombstone as a rallying cry, carrying the *Chronicle*'s June 1 sports section with him as he gave his "No retreat, no surrender" speech before that night's game against the Reds.

"The genesis of having that meeting was because there was a lot of talk around town that we need to make trades, we need to break up this team, and we need to start all over," Purpura said. "My message was simple. I believed in our team, and I had full faith that we could get better. I told them I wasn't looking to totally remake the team. I told them I believed in them. The young guys, I had known since they came to the organization, and the older guys like Jeff Bagwell and Craig Biggio I had known for 10 years. I said, 'The organization hasn't lost hope in this team. We haven't lost faith. We're not going to do anything rash.'"

With that said, Purpura ordered some changes. He called Chris Burke back up from Class AAA Round Rock and optioned right-handed starter Ezequiel Astacio to Round Rock. After the game on June 1, Roy Oswalt's personal catcher Raul Chavez was taken into Garner's office and designated for assignment. Chavez had served as Oswalt's personal catcher since 2004, guiding the Astros' young ace to his first 20-win season. Oswalt was definitely upset with the move. He bit his tongue and sulked privately. Catcher Humberto Quintero was promoted from Class AAA Round Rock a day later to take Chavez's place.

Oswalt's lone request after Chavez was taken away from him was that he wanted to throw to Brad Ausmus, the catcher who had ushered him to prominence as a rookie in 2001. Oswalt preferred to throw to Ausmus and settled into a nice groove to become the only pitcher in the majors to collect back-to-back 20-win seasons in 2004 and 2005.

The original plan was to give Quintero a good opportunity to earn a chunk of the starts behind the plate, but he landed on the disabled list on June 18 after suffering appendicitis. Chavez's contract was purchased from the Express on June 18. By then Oswalt had already clicked for good with Ausmus. Dumping Oswalt's personal catcher was the closest Purpura and Garner came to a making a shocking move. That's not to say Purpura wasn't tempted to shake things up more.

"It was very difficult," Purpura said. "You want to do something dramatic because sometimes in this game dramatic things have good results. The example I use was the change in coaches and manager [on July 14, 2004, when Garner, hitting coach Gary Gaetti, and pitching coach Jim Hickey replaced manager Jimy Williams, hitting coach Harry

Spilman, and popular and successful pitching coach Burt Hooton]. You think, 'Is there something you can do to change the mix, change the focus?' And there really wasn't. We brought up Burke, but that's about it."

Staying the course and declaring his belief in the team were perhaps the best things Purpura did for the 2005 Astros. With Oswalt on the mound, the Astros responded to Purpura's speech with a 4-1 victory over the Cincinnati Reds at Minute Maid Park. Oswalt went seven innings, holding the Reds to four hits and one run with four strikeouts while improving his perfect record to 14-0 in his career against Cincinnati. On that day, the Astros started an all-rookie outfield with Burke in left field, Willy Taveras in center, and Todd Self in right. With that victory, the Astros won the three-game series 2-1 against the Reds to win consecutive series for the first time in 2005. They had just taken two of three against the Milwaukee Brewers at Miller Park before playing the series against the Reds.

Oswalt improved to 15-0 in his career against the Reds after the 2005 season, the most victories without a loss for any pitcher against one club in the majors. So if ever the odds were in favor of the Astros, it was on June 1 with the team's ace against a team that has never handed him a loss.

Fans who thought the tombstone was brought out too early would be interested to know that it almost appeared a week earlier. As the Astros appeared in danger of falling to 15-30, *Houston Chronicle* sports editor Fred Faour called to ask if it was time to bury the Astros. It had been 91 years since a team had fallen 15 games under .500 and reached the postseason in the same season. The 1914 Boston Braves were the last team to accomplish the feat, winning the World Series over the Philadelphia Athletics. Since then, the Braves have moved from Boston to Milwaukee after the 1952 season and from Milwaukee to Atlanta after the 1966 season. The Athletics have gone from Philadelphia to Kansas City after the 1954 season and from Kansas City to Oakland after the 1967 season.

In 1914, the Boston Braves were one of eight teams in the National League, joining the New York Giants, St. Louis Cardinals, Chicago Cubs, Brooklyn Dodgers, Philadelphia Phillies, Pittsburgh Pirates, and Cincinnati Reds. They went from 15 games under .500 to winning the NL pennant, $10\frac{1}{2}$ games ahead of the Giants. In the American League, the Philadelphia Athletics won their eight-team league by $8\frac{1}{2}$ games over the Boston Red Sox, 19 games over the Washington Senators, $19\frac{1}{2}$ games over the Detroit Tigers, $28\frac{1}{2}$ games over the St. Louis Browns, 30 games over the New York Yankees and Chicago White Sox, and $48\frac{1}{2}$ games over the Cleveland Naps. The baseball landscape, not to mention America in general, had changed drastically since the Boston Braves rallied from 15 games under .500 to sweep the Athletics 4-0 in the 1914 World Series.

Heck, it would be three more years before Shoeless Joe Jackson and the 1917 Chicago White Sox would win the 1917 World Series over the New York Giants.

Considering the historic burden the Astros needed to overcome, it would have made perfect sense to roll out the tombstone when Faour first suggested it after the Astros lost May 24. Faour, who would likely be practicing law if he had not followed his parents' successful path toward sports journalism, articulated a thoughtful and powerful case for us to roll out the tombstone on May 25. The decision was not made on a whim. The numbers were crunched. History was explored.

Not long after the first tombstone conversation with Faour, the Astros took the field for an afternoon game against the Chicago Cubs at Wrigley Field. The matchup seemingly favored the Astros with Clemens taking the mound against Sergio Mitre, a right-hander fresh from the Class AAA Iowa Cubs, for his debut in the majors that season. Although he had made brief appearances with the Cubs the previous two seasons, Mitre had been stuck in Des Moines. Clemens threw five scoreless innings to extend his road scoreless-inning streak to 26 innings. It wasn't enough. He suffered a strained right groin and did not return to the mound for the sixth inning.

Clemens appeared to have been cruising. He had retired 10 batters in a row since giving up a one-out single in the second inning to Cubs catcher Michael Barrett. That string of retired batters ended when Enrique Wilson drew a two-out walk in the fifth, prompting a visit to the mound from Ausmus, Garner, and athletic trainer Dave Labossiere.

Clemens had managed to hide the injury from the Cubs with the help of Labossiere, who taped the big right-hander's groin between innings in the tunnel leading up to the visitors' clubhouse. There was no disguising the Astros' concern in the fifth inning, especially considering Mitre was the next batter. Something was obviously wrong if the manager and athletic trainer needed to visit the mound with an opposing pitcher at the plate and two outs with a pitcher who had just retired 10 in a row before issuing a walk to the No. 8 hitter. If Garner and Labossiere had not visited Clemens, most of the crowd of 38,805 at Wrigley Field would have assumed Clemens was merely pitching around Wilson to face Mitre.

"I had a little problem in the third [inning]," Clemens said after the game. "We just didn't have time to wrap it in the fourth. I continued to push it. In the fifth inning, again location became the most important thing. Pitch selection and my location became very important. That's what Brad [Ausmus] and I did."

Clemens escaped the fifth inning unscathed by inducing a fielder's-choice grounder to third base from Mitre. Even if he had not been pitching with tightness in his right groin, his line would be impressive because he held the Cubs to a pair of hits and one walk while striking out six. Clemens exited with a 2-0 lead, which had been taken in the fourth inning on Mike Lamb's fielder's-choice RBI chopper to first base and Morgan Ensberg's fielder's-choice grounder to Mitre. Dan Wheeler maintained the 2-0 lead with a perfect sixth inning, and Chad Qualls retired the Cubs in order in the seventh.

Qualls got in trouble in the eighth, an inning that proved fruitless on offense and defense for the Astros. Taveras led off the top of the eighth inning for the Astros with a double down the left field line off of left-handed reliever Will Ohman, who had been brought in to start the inning. Taveras reached third on Self's sacrifice bunt in front of the plate, prompting Cubs manager Dusty Baker to call on right-handed reliever Michael Wuertz. Baker's call paid off. Wuertz struck out Biggio and Berkman to strand Taveras at third base.

"We can't figure it out. We're having one devil of a time getting a run across the board," Garner said then. "We didn't get a ball out of the infield, and we scored two runs. We stressed it. We talked about it. It's in our heads now, and we have to find some way to get it out of our heads. You just don't go through this much and not hit the ball in the outfield or something unless it's in our heads. We have to figure out a way to get it out of our heads."

The bottom of the eighth was even worse for the Astros. Jason Dubois got the Cubs started with a leadoff double to right off Qualls. After Wilson flied out to Berkman in left field, Baker sent Todd Hollandsworth to hit for Wuertz. Hollandsworth cut the Astros' lead to 2-1 with an RBI single up the middle. Garner responded by calling closer Brad Lidge out of the bullpen to face Jerry Hairston Jr. Lidge's first pitch to Hairston was a slider in the dirt, letting Hollandsworth reach second on the wild pitch. Lidge appeared out of sorts. He bounced his second pitch in the dirt. The next one was high and out of the strike zone. Hairston took Lidge's 3-0 offering for a strike and walked on the next pitch.

Then, shortstop Adam Everett made a sensational play in the hole on Neifi Perez's fielder's-choice grounder and threw on the run to third base for the force out. Lidge pitched around Cubs slugger Derrek Lee and walked him, loading the bases for Jeromy Burnitz, the Conroe High graduate who had unsuccessfully lobbied the Astros to sign him in the offseason so he could play for the hometown team he cheered as a child. Burnitz gave the Cubs a 3-2 lead with a two-run single through the right side. With Aramis Ramirez at the plate, Lee added the Cubs' fourth run after Lidge ripped another wild pitch past Ausmus. Cubs closer Ryan Dempster retired the Astros in order in the ninth for the save, officially putting the Astros at 15-30.

As Cubs fans taunted the Astros behind the visitors' dugout at Wrigley Field, Lidge and Qualls sat together in the corner of the dugout. Neither man bothered to look up as their teammates headed down the tunnel that led to the clubhouse. Lidge stared down at the hundreds of empty cups, bubble gum wrappers, and towels at his feet. Qualls stared straight into the Astros cap that he held with his left hand to cover his face. With his right hand, he rubbed his head in complete disbelief. The Astros appeared void of answers, and at that moment Lidge and Qualls embodied the team's agonizing search. Not only had they fallen to 15-30, but they had also lost their seventh consecutive game. That 4-2 loss to the Cubs also dropped the Astros to 2-21 on the road, the third-worst road start in the majors since 1900.

"It does seem like whatever bad can happen, will happen," Lidge said. "So, the biggest thing for us is to just stop it. Get angry. Get something and just stop it."

Hours before that loss, Purpura, Garner, assistant general manager Ricky Bennett, and consultant Matt Galante had closed the doors to the visiting manager's office for over an hour to discuss the team's woes.

"We're just trying to look at every aspect of what we're doing," Purpura said. "We're searching for answers to correct the problems that we have to get us back to where we want to be. There's no answer. There's no easy answers, obviously. I guess the thing I feel good about is that the players and the staff still have the drive and commitment to play good baseball. That's not waned through all of this."

Garner had his theory, and he didn't mind saying he thought his team's lack of hitting was in their heads. Whatever the reason, the numbers told an ugly story.

But the next day Brandon Backe beat Greg Maddux and the Cubs 5-1, beginning the best finish in baseball in 2005.

At that point, though, nobody could predict the future. The Astros won three of five after they fell to 15-30 on May 24.

On May 31 Faour went ahead with the most famous story assignments involving the Astros' franchise. Usually, graphics are built to suit the story. In this case, the story was assigned to fit the tombstone. Understanding the repercussions that his beat writers could face, Faour was very understanding when I said I couldn't bury the team because there was so much of the season left. I promised to ask all of the questions and deliver him a story that asked, "Is it time to pull the plug on the Astros?"

It's June 1; Astros season pretty much over
Copyright 2005 Houston Chronicle
If history is any indication—and history usually shows the way in baseball—the Astros are plugged to an EKG machine this morning. The pulse is weak, and some in the family are preparing the obituary.

The calendar has hit June 1. Is it time to pull the plug on the Astros?

"Absolutely not," said Astros owner Drayton McLane. "Remember last year everybody wanted to bury us at the All-Star break? We made one change. We changed our manager and brought in Phil Garner. That gave a lift to the team."

No, McLane is not thinking of changing managers. The 2004 Astros gave pessimists reason for caution, finishing the season with a 36-10 run to win the National League wild card in one of the most surprising comebacks in major league history.

But as badly as the Astros played last year, they never fell more than four games under .500 with All-Star sluggers Jeff Kent and Carlos Beltran to go along with potential Hall of Famer Jeff Bagwell and All-Star Lance Berkman.

Kent is with the Dodgers, and Beltran is with the Mets. Bagwell is on the disabled list and headed for what likely will be season-ending right shoulder surgery June 7.

Berkman tore the ACL in his right knee playing flag football last October, had surgery November 15 and didn't come off the DL until May 6. Berkman, the only current Astros position player who has been an All-Star this millennium, admittedly is still looking to recapture his swing. But his opinions are in midseason form.

"There's two ways to fix this team," Berkman said. "You have to go in one of two directions, and I'm not smart enough or qualified enough to say when you pull the trigger on either one of these two plans. The first plan is that you have to go to a straight youth movement. You have to make trades and get as young as you possibly can and put together a nucleus of young guys that you think are going to be here for the next four or five or six years and let them play.

"Or you have to say, 'All right, we have enough here with some of the veterans that we have.' You're going to have to go out and add one impact bat and another good professional hitter. Obviously a dream scenario would be like if you traded for a guy like [Kansas City Royals first baseman] Mike Sweeney or a guy like [the Rockies'] Todd Helton if Baggy didn't come back and then signed Brian Giles [away from the Padres] in the offseason. Then you'd have either Sweeney or Helton and me and Giles in the middle of the order with Morgan [Ensberg]. That would be a very good offense.

"You either have to do something like that, or you have to say we're going to go with our young guys and give them a chance to grow into it and be the type of hitters they can be. I think you need to make a determination pretty quickly."

As if missing the team's 2004 RBI leader (Kent), the postseason star (Beltran) and the franchise leader in home runs and RBI (Bagwell) weren't enough, the numbers conspire to throw dirt on the Astros.

Despite Tuesday's 4-3 win against the Reds, the Astros (19-32) are in last place in the NL Central, 14 games behind the division-leading Cardinals.

A's, Marlins beat odds

Only one team trailed by more games on June 1 and reached the playoffs. The 2001 Athletics were 15 games back in the AL West on June 1 and reached the playoffs that year. The 2003 World Series champion Marlins were fifth in the five-team NL East on June 1, 12 games back.

Both those teams earned wild card berths. The A's were 25-26 and the Marlins 22-29 after 51 games.

No other team has reached the postseason after trailing by more than double digits in their divisions June 1, according to the Elias Sports Bureau.

Only six teams that were last in their divisions June 1 made the playoffs: 1974 Pirates (sixth place), 1974 Orioles (sixth), 1989 Blue Jays (seventh), 1995 Dodgers (fourth), 2000 A's (fourth), and 2003 Marlins (fifth).

All those teams were dispatched in the first round except for the Marlins.

"I'm not saying it has to happen immediately, but if we're not in it by the All-Star break and we're not showing significant improvement, I think at that point you've got to give guys looks," Berkman said. "You have to put a Jason Lane in the lineup every day, and you have to figure out a way to get Chris Burke in the lineup, whether in the outfield or somewhere.

"You have to get him some at-bats in the major leagues just to see where you're at."

Not throwing in towel

At least publicly, the Astros aren't ready to concede the season.

McLane refuses to say his team is rebuilding just one season after the Astros got within a win of the first World Series berth in franchise history.

Some young players worry the Astros will try to salvage an unsalvageable season with an ill-advised trade that gets rid of young talent.

McLane and general manager Tim Purpura are adamant that they won't make trades this year unless those players also provide help for the future.

If a poll were conducted in the clubhouse, McLane and Purpura would have realized that several players were clamoring to have top second baseman prospect Burke back up from Class AAA Round Rock.

Burke, who was called up after Tuesday night's game, wasn't given a chance to unseat Craig Biggio at second base in spring training even though the Astros said goodbye to Kent under the premise they wanted to see Burke play daily.

"It's tough to bury us now," said Purpura, in his first season as a general manager. "I know people want to, [but] people in the organization when times are tough, they rally. Whether it's scouts or even people like Nolan [Ryan], we're trying to find answers.

"Chris Burke's name has been talked about a lot lately and trying to find a way to get him in our lineup in a significant way."

Garner focused on present

Astros manager Phil Garner is adamant that he is under a mandate to try to win now. He is more concerned about winning on a daily basis instead of trying to prepare younger players for the future.

"That's not my task," Garner said about managing to rebuild. "My job right now is to try to win the pennant. So until things change, that's what we have to do. What we have to do is keep our pitching pretty much the way it's been. We have one-third of the season gone.

"We can be equally as devastating for another third of the season and then play decent ball another third and be where we need to be.

When you have good pitching, you can get hot. But all the talk in the world won't get it done. We have to get it done. Truly, we have to start getting our offense clicking."

As the Astros' season progressed, many readers forgot that the story accompanying the tombstone graphic didn't say the Astros were dead. Almost in each broadcast of an Astros playoff game, the *Houston Chronicle*'s front page of the sports section was shown with the tombstone.

Carl Dukes, a popular sports radio personality in Houston, went on the air in June and also essentially declared the Astros done. He vowed to sit atop a billboard in Houston with his clothes off if the Astros reached the postseason. Fortunately for the great people of Houston, Dukes decided to keep his clothes on.

Each time the national media would try to get the Astros to rip on the *Houston Chronicle* during the playoffs, the Astros admitted that it didn't take a tremendous leap to consider them dead on May 24 or June 1.

"As you know, I feel a little bit more comfortable in the underdog world," Garner said. "I don't know how I feel in the dead role too much, but there is a certain amount of satisfaction in having proven people wrong. I don't mean that in a malicious way by any sense of the imagination, but the truth of the matter is we did look dead. We didn't look like we were going to go anywhere. And you can't fault anybody for writing what looks like to be the truth. But to your credit, to our team's credit we didn't let that bother us. We stepped up and answered the challenge."

16

Garner's Shriveled Prunes

Astros manager Phil Garner had seen enough. In all his days in baseball, he doesn't recall many times when he was more furious with his team than he was on May 27, 2005, at Milwaukee's Miller Park. For the second time in a span of five games and the eighth time over the first 47 games of the season, his Astros had been shut out. Seven of those shutouts had been suffered on the road.

At five feet, 10 inches and 180 pounds and with a thick mustache stuck in 1970, the Astros manager doesn't mince words. Hypocrisy isn't in his nature. If he's pissed, he'll tell you about it. If he's really pissed, he'll tell you about it—*loudly*. On May 27, he was growing angrier by the inning as the Astros mounted a season's worth of weak appearances at the plate against the lowly Milwaukee Brewers.

Despite a stiff back that forced him out of the game after only six innings, Astros ace right-hander Roy Oswalt had limited the Brewers to only one run. That run was enough to hang the 3-0 loss on Oswalt, the eventual 20-game winner who fell to 5-6 that evening. Milwaukee left-hander Doug Davis, who hasn't exactly earned any comparisons to Randy Johnson, Andy Pettitte, or any other top left-hander in the majors, escaped with the victory on a day he walked five Astros and struck out only two.

Davis literally walked away with seven scoreless innings, and his teammates pulled away with their final two runs off right-handed reliever Chad Qualls, who lasted only a third of an inning while giving up two hits and a walk. Soon after Milwaukee right-hander Derrick Turnbow secured the save with two strikeouts and a ground out while giving up a hit in the ninth, Garner unleashed his rage on his players.

"Inexcusable," Garner's players remembered him saying.

Ever the poet, Garner left a lasting impression on his players with one of his best putdowns. Berkman still laughs when he remembers Garner telling the Astros that when they were at the plate with runners on base, they "shrivel up like a bunch of damn prunes and act like 'I'm scared to death.'"

There was little doubt which direction Garner pointed his criticism. The pitching staff—as was the case for all but a few rare instances in 2005—had done its job. In 2005, the offense was the Astros' definite weak link on a team with star pitchers like Oswalt, Roger Clemens, Pettitte, and Brad Lidge.

Only a few minutes after his outburst, Garner returned to the manager's office and came to the conclusion that he had probably been a tad too harsh in his assessment. Just as quickly, though, Garner rationalized that his players needed to hear that appraisal. Nobody argued. The Astros had just dropped to a major league-worst 3-22 on the road and 16-31 overall for the worst record in the National League Central, the second worst in the league and the slowest start in franchise history.

"It's absolutely frustrating to no end, I'll tell you," Garner told the Chronicle's Brian McTaggart after the loss. "They're frustrated; we're all frustrated. We've got to figure out a way to stop it."

Berkman, who actually raised his average six points to .206 by going one for three on May 27, broke the ice with Garner a day later.

"Man, that was pretty harsh," Berkman told Garner. "I've never been compared to a prune before."

Berkman is one of the Astros' wittiest players. He keeps teammates laughing with his jokes, voice imitations, and even blunders on the bases. But he realized rather quickly that day wasn't a time for jokes.

"I tell you what, Phil wasn't in a laughing mood," Berkman said.

Garner isn't sure just how much of an impact his fit after the 3-0 loss on May 27 had on the Astros. There's no denying, though, that his players responded. They returned to Miller Park on May 28 and beat Brewers ace right-hander Ben Sheets 9-6 as rookie left-hander Wandy Rodriguez allowed four runs over six innings for his first major league victory.

On May 29, Pettitte threw six scoreless innings with a then-season-high eight strikeouts to beat the Brewers 2-1 as the Astros finished 6-3 on the trip through Arlington, Chicago, and Milwaukee. By winning the final two games in Milwaukee, the Astros improved to 5-22 on the road and won consecutive road games for the first time since 2004. Until then, the Astros had not won a road series in 2005.

After Garner's speech, the Astros went on their first five-game winning streak of the season and posted the best record in the majors after that loss. After falling 16-31, the Astros were 73-42 to finish 89-73 and one game ahead of the Philadelphia Phillies for the National League wild card berth.

"Maybe," Garner says of May 27, "we were just hitting rock bottom. It was almost like we hit rock bottom, and the next day we started building."

Garner had jokingly vowed not to have anymore team meetings a few weeks earlier when his players responded to one of his closed-door lectures with one of their worst performances of the year two days later. The Astros were reeling when they started a four-game series against the Atlanta Braves at Turner Field on May 5. Franchise icon Jeff Bagwell was out of the lineup and essentially on his way to the disabled list with right shoulder problems after being unable to play on May 4 against the Pittsburgh Pirates because of severe shoulder pain. A day after going zero for five with one strikeout in a 7-4 loss to the Pirates at Minute Maid Park, Bagwell had to cut his batting practice short because of pain.

Bagwell had played through right shoulder problems since the 2001 season, needing surgery that November to insert pins to attach his labrum to his right shoulder capsule. Although at times he needed teammates to help him lift his right arm to put his uniform on, Bagwell had endured the pain until May 4, 2005. With Bagwell out of the lineup on May 5, right-hander Brandon Backe took the mound against the Braves only two days after he had been in a Houston-area hospital with pneumonia.

In between coughs, the weakened Backe gave up nine hits and seven runs over 5⅓ innings to suffer the 9-3 loss against Atlanta left-hander John Thomson. The Astros mustered only three hits—only one after the first inning—as Thomson threw a complete game. The next day, Berkman came off the disabled list. If the Astros had been playing really well, Berkman might have remained on the disabled list a little longer to recover more from the right knee surgery he underwent in November to repair a torn right anterior cruciate ligament. But the Astros were struggling, and Berkman was needed.

Berkman, who had led the Astros with a .316 average and 30 home runs while earning his third All-Star nod in 2004, offered little help in his first game back on May 6, 2005. He was hitless in four at-bats and contributed to the team's poor defense with an error that led to two unearned runs in the fifth inning. With Berkman at first base, Mike Lamb played left field with all of the grace of a man out of position and misplayed what was ruled an RBI triple by Rafael Furcal in the Braves' three-run rally in the second inning. Rookie center fielder Willy Taveras also struggled, misreading Marcus Giles's line drive that fell in for an RBI double as Oswalt looked on in disbelief while the Braves took a 5-0 lead, which increased to 6-0 on Chipper Jones's RBI double.

"We had a couple of balls that should have been caught tonight," Garner said afterward. "We have to do better at that. Lamb's learning on the job. He's going to have a couple of balls that are going to be tough for him. I believe that he can do it."

Radio reporter Joe Walker, who has covered baseball in Atlanta for decades even though he is legally blind, was so dismayed by the Astros' poor defense that he said they looked like minor leaguers. That minors-like defensive performance was a major reason Oswalt gave up a career-high seven earned runs and nine runs overall on 10 hits over five innings. Perhaps because he didn't want to point fingers at the poor defense that failed him, Oswalt admitted the Astros were rebuilding.

Garner offered a harsher assessment after that 9–4 loss, telling his players they looked as though they were playing scared. Garner's meeting didn't exactly inspire his players to play better. Despite seven strong innings from Pettitte, the Braves beat the Astros 4–1 on May 7.

It got much worse the next day when former Astros left-hander Mike Hampton threw a two-hitter while the Braves completed the four-game sweep with a 16–0 rout, dropping the Astros to 1–14 on the road with the most embarrassing of the Astros' major league-worst 17 shutouts.

"The low point, to be honest with you, to me was when we got beat 16–0 by the Braves," Berkman said seven months later. "I had never been beat like that on a baseball field. I don't know where that put us as far as record goes, but as far as how we played after that, to me that game was the low point of our season."

A few days after the 16–0 rout, Garner laughed and promised not to call anymore team meetings because he'd hate to see his team respond to his lectures with another 16–0 loss.

"Then we have about eight more meetings," Berkman joked. "After he vowed he'd never have another meeting, he had at least eight more."

The Astros left Atlanta and snapped their six-game losing streak the next day when Clemens threw seven scoreless innings to beat A.J. Burnett and the Florida Marlins at Dolphins Stadium. The victory was the 330th of Clemens's career, passing Hall of Famer Steve Carlton for ninth on the all-time victories list while becoming the winningest pitcher alive.

"He's one of the best left-handers ever," Clemens said of Carlton after appearing at Dolphins Stadium for the first time since his supposed retirement. "To have my name alongside of him, that's where I consider him. Even though I'm in front of him, I still feel I'm right there with those guys."

Clemens's victory snapped the Astros' six-game losing streak and an 11-game road losing streak, but the problems continued as the team lost the next two against the Marlins and the first two of a four-game series at Minute Maid Park against the Barry Bonds-less San Francisco Giants. Clemens served as the stopper once again on May 14, throwing a season-high eight innings while holding the Giants to one run on five hits as the Astros snapped a four-game losing streak with a 4-1 victory.

With bench coach Cecil Cooper in charge the next day while Garner was at home with the flu, Morgan Ensberg tied the Astros' single-game record with three home runs, and Backe threw a four-hitter to beat the Giants 9-0 with his first career shutout. Looking back at the 2005 season, Garner rates May 15 as one of those key dates in the Astros' return to respectability.

"Morgan hit those three home runs against San Francisco, and that was big," Garner said. "Morgan got hot, and we won a lot of ballgames, and then Lance got hot, too."

After splitting the series with the Giants at two apiece, the Astros dropped two of three against the Arizona Diamondbacks before heading to Arlington from May 20 to 22 and suffering a three-game sweep against the Rangers. The second game at Ameriquest Field was a complete disaster for the Astros, who watched helplessly as the Rangers hit a franchise-record eight home runs, the most ever allowed in an inter-league game. The Astros left Arlington and lost two of three against the Cubs before that fateful 3-0 loss to start the three-game series against the Brewers on May 27.

Ensberg had hit only four home runs in 2005 before he went four for four with three home runs on May 15, raising his batting average to .325. He hit eight home runs in May, putting his season's total at 10 homers over the first two months of the season. He added 10 more homers and 28 RBI in June, making a tremendous case to earn a place at Detroit's Comerica Park for the 2005 All-Star Game on July 12.

With Ensberg leading the offense, the Astros capitalized with a 16-9 record in June after going 9-13 in April and 10-9 in May. On June 29, Craig Biggio made history when he was hit by a pitch from Colorado Rockies right-hander Byung-Hyun Kim, setting the modern record for most hit by pitches in a career with his 268th plunking. Kim became the 203rd pitcher to hit Biggio with a pitch and the second Kim (Sunny Kim was the other). Interestingly enough, the modern-day record that was held by former Rockies manager Don Baylor fell in Colorado against the team that has drilled Biggio more than any other.

Biggio was free to celebrate the record without any remorse, because Oswalt had thrown seven scoreless innings with six strikeouts to win 7-1 at Coors Field. With that victory, Oswalt solidified his case for his first All-Star nod by improving his personal record to 10-7. In that game, Ensberg hit a two-run home run to put his RBI total for the month at

28 in June, only one RBI shy from the franchise record that was set in 1984 when Jose Cruz drove in 29 runs that June. Since 1986, Atlanta's Chipper Jones (1997), Kansas City's Jeff King (1997), San Francisco's Matt Williams (1990), and Seattle's Jim Presley (1986) are the only third basemen in the majors to have driven in 29 runs in the month of June.

Ensberg and Oswalt headed into July with impressive statistics. By going 5-1 with a 1.40 ERA in June, Oswalt improved his record to 10-7. Ensberg entered July with 20 home runs, 54 RBI, and a .280 batting average. Nonetheless, Oswalt and Ensberg were not on the initial list of National League All-Stars. Clemens and Lidge were the only two Astros to make the NL All-Star squad in voting by their peers.

Ensberg finished sixth in fan balloting even though he was leading National League third basemen with 22 home runs and 59 RBI when the teams were announced. Perennial Gold Glove winner Scott Rolen of the St. Louis Cardinals was voted as the starter by the fans, who ignored the fact that he had been injured most of the year. Chicago Cubs third baseman Aramis Ramirez was put on the All-Star team from the players-coaches ballot.

Ensberg accepted the news with grace as his teammates expressed their dismay by saying he had been robbed.

At 10-7 and a 2.54 ERA that stood as the third best in the NL at that point, Oswalt had a glimmer of hope because he at least was named as a finalist for the last opening on the team. Oswalt, former Astros closer Billy Wagner of the Phillies, San Diego closer Trevor Hoffman, Phillies starter Brett Myers, and Arizona's Brandon Webb were the five competitors for the fifth spot in online balloting.

With home-field advantage in the World Series on the line, Clemens implored Houston fans to get on their computers and vote for Oswalt.

"The fans need to get behind him," Clemens told the *Chronicle*'s Brian McTaggart. "This kid needs to go. He's never been, and he needs to be a part of the All-Star Game. Now you're playing for keeps, playing to win the game."

Oswalt did his part on July 4, the first full day of online balloting for the final spot, with a complete game while allowing only one run and five hits in a 4-1 victory over Hoffman's Padres at Minute Maid Park. With that victory, Oswalt improved to 11-7 and dropped his ERA to 2.44 with his fifth consecutive victory. Led by Brad Ausmus, Oswalt's teammates also rallied behind him, spending countless hours voting for Oswalt on their laptops, home computers, or the two computers in the trainer's room at Minute Maid Park.

"Ausmus would be in there and really everybody on our team contributed," Lidge said. "When a guy is as deserving as Roy and you don't make a good effort to try to get him in, you're not a good team-mate."

Equally important for Oswalt's candidacy, Astros fans logged on and put him on top of the other four candidates. A year after drawing three million fans, the Astros benefited once again from having made Houston a baseball town.

"We have tremendous team camaraderie," Berkman said. "Of all the teams I've played on in the big leagues, the 2005 Astros are easily the closest team as far as guys liking each other and pulling for each other. I think that's a big part of our success. When you have that much respect for your teammates and care that much about them, you pull for them. At least with the way the Astros do things or how our clubhouse is, we would have supported anybody like we did Roy. That's just the way we operated. I was very impressed [that] the city of Houston got behind Roy. Houston is not known as a baseball town like New York, Chicago, or St. Louis. But with the support Roy got to get in the All-Star Game, I think it shows we're trying to take some steps in that direction."

Even with Oswalt, Lidge, and Clemens on the NL All-Star team, there was a sense in the Astros clubhouse that the NL All-Star team wouldn't be complete without Ensberg. Lidge readily admits that he kept telling Ensberg that he had been robbed by the snub. That problem was rectified soon after the Astros beat the Dodgers 6-5 on July 10. As Ensberg and his wife, Christi, headed to Bush Intercontinental Airport for a flight to Lake Tahoe to start their All-Star break, Ensberg received a call from Astros general manager Tim Purpura. St. Louis Cardinals manager Tony La Russa, the NL manager in 2005, had called Purpura to inform him that Rolen had opted to skip the event because of injury.

The Ensbergs were only a mile away from the airport when they turned back home to repack for the All-Star festivities in Detroit. On their way home, they hurriedly called their loved ones to inform them of the good news and ask some of them to join them in Detroit. They also had to call Padres reliever Scott Linebrink and his wife, informing their good friends that they wouldn't be joining them in Tahoe after all.

"I can't really wipe the grin off my face," said Ensberg, who had been humbled earlier that morning by all the fans in the stands with signs telling him he deserved to be an All-Star. "It's hard to explain. You're kind of shocked. I don't know what to make of it."

The All-Star Game also served as an opportunity to finally put to rest the trade rumors involving Clemens. Not long after Clemens re-signed with the Astros on January 21, Long Island's *Newsday* reported in February that Clemens had a secret deal with the Astros to be traded if the team fell out of contention. *Newsday* also reported that Pettitte likely wouldn't be ready for the start of the season. Both parts of the story turned out to be tremendously false.

Nonetheless, each month seemingly brought along more Clemens trade rumors. One day he was supposedly headed to the Yankees, the next to the Red Sox or Rangers, and on and on and on. As off base as those rumors were, irresponsible reporters might as well have had Clemens going to the Dallas Cowboys, Houston Texans, or Los Angeles Lakers.

The Astros entered the All-Star break with a 44-43 record and second in the NL Central, 11½ games behind the Cardinals. Oswalt had won six in a row to improve to 12-7. Clemens had the best ERA in the majors at 1.48, and Pettitte was just starting to heat up. Just as important was the fact that no one was running away with the NL wild card race.

Of the four Astros at the All-Star Game, Lidge stood out by striking out the side. Oswalt gave up two runs over one inning. Clemens pitched a scoreless inning. Ensberg was zero for two with a strikeout as the American League extended its undefeated streak to nine games against the NL with a 7-5 victory. Oswalt was the third NL pitcher and the first Astro to appear in the 76th All-Star Game when he took over in the third inning with a 1-0 deficit. Boston Red Sox slugger David Ortiz's RBI single and All-Star Game MVP Miguel Tejada's RBI ground out brought in both runs Oswalt gave up as the AL took a 3-0 lead.

The AL made it 5-0 in the fourth inning with two more runs off Livan Hernandez, but Clemens finally set down the AL in order for the first time that evening. Clemens had volunteered to sit the game out so other pitchers could participate, but La Russa asked him to pitch the fifth inning.

"He's experienced this many times, and there are guys in here that need to experience it," La Russa said. "But this is a fans' game, and a big part of their enjoyment and entertainment was to watch Roger Clemens pitch. As long as he was healthy and rested, which he was, we wanted him. And as it turns out, we got the young guys in the game. So Roger pitched, and so did the young guys, so it worked out all right, except that we lost."

Marlins ace left-hander Dontrelle Willis gave up two more runs to the AL in the sixth. Lidge didn't have any problem in the seventh as he struck out Melvin Mora, Mike Sweeney, and Garret Anderson, joining Clemens as the only two NL pitchers to throw perfect innings that night.

"At that point in my career, it was the most unbelievable thing that ever happened to me," Lidge said of striking out the side at the All-Star Game. "That's something that nobody can ever take from me. I'm an All-Star. I was a major league All-Star. That reality for me was overwhelming."

The night was made even more memorable for Lidge when he returned to the NL clubhouse and saw Clemens waiting for him. Clemens's smile and congratulatory nod gave Lidge a sense of warmth and pride.

"After I came in from the game after I pitched that inning, I was so pumped up," Lidge said. "It was just nice to see Roger's face in the clubhouse. He was smiling at me and he just said, 'Yeah.' It meant so much to me to see Roger Clemens."

Clemens stuck around at Comerica Park just long enough to visit with Lidge after the seventh inning. As he tried to exit with his wife, Debbie, and two oldest sons, Koby and Kory, he was surrounded by nearly 50 reporters, who came at him in waves with essentially the same question at least a dozen times.

"Roger, will you accept a trade to the …?"

Because Clemens had missed the All-Star workout the previous day because of a charity golf outing, the media at the All-Star Game didn't get him until hours before the first inning. The Astros hardly resembled the team that had appeared done in May. Since almost suffering a no-hitter against Pedro Martinez in a 3-1 loss to the Mets at Shea Stadium on June 7, the Astros had gone 23-8 to enter the All-Star break a game over .500.

"It's the furthest thing from my mind right now," Clemens said of accepting a trade away from the Astros. "We've put ourselves back in contention for this wild card. And that's a good thing."

Clemens insisted the trade questions should be posed to Astros owner Drayton McLane. He said he'd rather have McLane asked if there was a chance that the Astros could acquire another offensive player at the July 31 trading deadline.

In case there was any misinterpretation, Clemens hinted at the June 2004 trade in which the Astros acquired Carlos Beltran to make it clear what kind of deal he hoped for. Clemens's mind was on adding to the Astros, not on bailing out.

The July 31 trading deadline went by without a major bat landing in Houston, but the Astros hardly missed a step. The Astros went 22-7 in July for a .759 winning percentage and their best July in franchise history. The Astros limped out of the All-Star break by suffering a three-game sweep against the Cardinals at Busch Stadium from July 15 to 17. They rebounded and pushed toward the wild card lead with a four-game sweep over the Pirates at PNC Park. They followed that sweep by taking three of four against the Washington Nationals in the franchise's first visit to Washington D.C., July 21 to 24. The series finale went 14 innings before the Astros won 4-1. Rodriguez held Washington to one run over seven innings and Backe was used as a pinch hitter. Eric Bruntlett hit the game-winning three-run home run over the left-field wall at JFK Stadium in the 14th inning.

The Astros returned to Minute Maid Park and swept a three-game series over the Phillies. In winning the first game of the series 7-1, Biggio and Berkman became the first Astros teammates to hit a pair of back-to-back homers in the same game. The next two games were decided by one run. Oswalt won that game 2-1 with a complete-game eight-hitter, but he was in line for a no-decision until Mike Lamb hit a walkoff home run in the ninth. Clemens won the next night 3-2, pushing the Astros within one game of the wild card lead.

With the Phillies out of the way, Beltran and the Mets were finally in town for the series many Astros fans had awaited. As proof that hate sells, Astros fans packed Minute Maid Park for the right to jeer Beltran for spurning the Astros. Beltran was booed at every turn. Even the New York media, who have seen fans at Shea Stadium throw batteries and obscenities at opponents and even their own players over the years, made note of the harsh treatment Beltran received. The Astros won three of the first four games in the series against the Mets.

In the first game of the season, rookie Ezequiel Astacio matched Pedro Martinez just long enough so that the Astros could eventually win 3-2 before the second-largest crowd of the season at Minute Maid Park. Rodriguez took the 5-2 victory the next night, and Pettitte threw eight scoreless innings to win the third game of the series 2-0 before a season-best crowd of 43,596 at Minute Maid Park, where the fans were still riding Beltran. The Mets avoided the four-game sweep by winning the finale 9-4, but the Astros had already started to take the shape of a playoff contender.

They had started to pull for each other even though they had doubts about their abilities to contend at times. In a sense, the anemic offense jelled in their quest to reward their vaunted pitching staff.

"We want Roy to do well or we want Andy to win or we want to get Roger a win," Berkman said. "We would say, 'We may have an early offseason, but we're going to give our best effort for whoever is on the mound.' In our little small groups, it was definitely the topic. I guarantee you there were several nights I spent in a hotel room talking to Andy Pettitte, Chris Burke, and Jason Lane, and saying, 'We really stink. This is looking really bad. How are we going to get better?'"

17

Tests Away
From the Field

Responding to the Indian Ocean tsunami that killed approximately 275,000 and left over a million homeless throughout Sri Lanka, Indonesia, Thailand, and South India in late December 2004, the Astros put together a Leadoff Luncheon to support the Bush–Clinton Fund for Tsunami Relief on April 8. In a matter of weeks, the Astros in Action Foundation organized the lunch and raised $75,000. With Hall of Fame broadcaster Milo Hamilton as emcee, the Astros' entire 25-man roster and coaching staff turned out along with many of the city's top business leaders. Some businesses donated as much as $10,000 a table to attend the event. Astros owner Drayton McLane, manager Phil Garner, Roger Clemens, Morgan Ensberg, and Lance Berkman addressed the crowd, speaking on the importance of helping others less fortunate.

Ensberg talked about being a citizen of the world and understanding that he was put on this Earth to do more than play baseball. Everybody talked about giving back to their communities and helping their fellow man. As the season progressed, the city of Houston and the Astros lived those words as they rallied behind the New Orleans evacuees who landed in Houston after Hurricane Katrina.

At times, it's easy for some major leaguers to lose perspective. With all that fame and money, some stars forget they'll face some of the same obstacles their less famous neighbors confront. In 2005, Mother Nature tested the city of Houston and the Astros often, pushing the team closer through the struggles away from the field.

The Astros were concluding a six-game, seven-day trip through Southern California when they learned a hurricane of potentially biblical proportions was headed toward New Orleans. Most of the Astros' young stars had played with the Class AAA New Orleans Zephyrs. Berkman, Roy Oswalt, Ensberg, Jason Lane, Adam Everett, Brad Lidge, Chad Qualls, Chris Burke, and several others had spent at least half a season in

New Orleans before reaching the Astros. Hitting coach Gary Gaetti and his family live in Covington, which is in St. Tammany Parish, just north of New Orleans. Astros pitching coach Jim Hickey spent seven seasons as the Zephyrs' pitching coach before he was promoted to his major league job on July 14, 2004.

Hickey and Gaetti have family or close friends in the New Orleans area, and several of the players still had friends there. Although the Astros had ended their agreement with the New Orleans Zephyrs after the 2004 season to move their Class AAA affiliate to Nolan Ryan and Don Sanders's Round Rock's Express, New Orleans holds a special place in the hearts of many of the current Astros. The Astros also held a special place in the hearts of New Orleans residents who kept track of the former Zephyrs players in Houston.

By the time the Astros lost the final two games in a three-game series against the San Diego Padres at Petco Park on August 23 and 24, Tropical Storm Katrina had already formed in the Bahamas and started toward Florida.

Some Astros such as Jeff Bagwell, Brad Ausmus, and Jose Vizcaino remained in the San Diego area. Most of them headed north to Los Angeles to enjoy their day off on August 25. Christi Ensberg held a surprise cruise birthday party for Morgan, who assumed he and Christi were going to have an intimate dinner with Adam and Jennifer Everett. By that night, Tropical Storm Katrina had become a Category 1 hurricane and hit Southern Florida.

By Ensberg's birthday on August 26, Hurricane Katrina had claimed nine lives in Florida and moved into the Gulf of Mexico as it pushed toward New Orleans while Andy Pettitte beat the Dodgers at Dodger Stadium 2-1. As the Astros filtered into Dodger Stadium the next afternoon, many of them intently monitored Katrina's path. By then waves of residents from the New Orleans area were booking hotel rooms in Houston after the hotel rooms in Baton Rouge filled up.

Oswalt, whose parents and wife, Nicole, braced for the aftermath of Katrina in Weir, Mississippi, was hammered 8-3 in one of his worst performances of the year on August 27. The 20-game winner gave up five runs in the first inning while tying his career high with seven runs allowed. He lasted a season-low four innings. The next day, Gaetti checked in with his wife, Donna, who had decided to wait the hurricane out with friends and their three-year-old daughter, Gigi.

On August 28, Jeff Weaver dominated the Astros with eight scoreless innings of seven-hit ball with 10 strikeouts to beat Clemens 1-0. Clemens's teammates had been shut out for the 16th time and the eighth on a day he started in 2005. As the Astros went home after that loss, many

New Orleans residents were already headed up Interstate 10 to Houston to escape their fish bowl. By then, the first batch of New Orleans residents had already settled throughout Houston-area hotels and with relatives spread around the city and its suburbs. Ultimately, at least 150,000 of the 1.4 million who lived in the New Orleans area sought refuge in Houston. The National Weather Service predicted on August 28 that Hurricane Katrina would become the fourth Category 5 hurricane to hit land in the United States. Thousands of New Orleans residents responded by filtering into the Superdome.

On that day, New Orleans mayor C. Ray Nagin warned his community and the rest of the world that the storm surge would likely crush the city's poorly maintained levee system. Later that afternoon, the torrential showers ahead of the hurricane began to pound New Orleans.

"We are facing a storm that most of us have long feared," Nagin told the *Houston Chronicle*. "The storm surge will most likely topple our levee system."

Katrina arrived in New Orleans with all its rage on Monday, August 30, stunning the nation with the cruel destruction it left behind. New Orleans's Superdome's roof was ravaged, stranding over 10,000 in an unlivable mess. For days and weeks, the images out of New Orleans seemed as though they were filtering through from some Third World city.

Making humanitarian efforts the top priority, Houston mayor Bill White and his staff rallied. The city opened the Astrodome for evacuees from the Superdome. The George R. Brown Convention Center, which only a year earlier had served as the FanFest site for the 2004 Major League Baseball All-Star Game and for the 2004 Super Bowl, was also turned into a shelter. The entire September slate of conventions scheduled for the George R. Brown were postponed, moved, or canceled. According to the *Chronicle,* the conventions that were affected were: "La Cumbre, a travel industry show; the Texas Association of School Boards/Texas Association of School Administrators Convention; the Houston Minority Business Council's Expo 2005; the Houston Antique Dealer's Association show; and the Turbomachinery Symposium."

Houston's two million residents rallied, providing more than 100,000 volunteers at many of the shelters around town. The lines of refugees at the Astrodome and the George R. Brown Convention Center were matched with long lines of volunteers hoping to help. There were so many volunteers that many of them were turned away until the local relief effort could find ways for them to help. On September 2, Astros fans raised $18,000 for the Red Cross's Katrina Relief Fund during

Hurricane Katrina Relief Night against the St. Louis Cardinals at Minute Maid Park.

During that three-game series against the Cardinals, the Astros' wives also helped collect canned goods, books, clothing, and toys to help the Houston Food Bank and the Salvation Army's Katrina relief efforts. Nicole Oswalt, Jennifer Everett, Stephanie Wheeler, Kasey Lamb, Jennifer Taveras, Kristin Gallo, and Mary Pat Bailey participated in the event.

Houston's entire sports community helped Katrina relief efforts in some way. Bob McNair, the owner of the National Football League's Houston Texans, donated $1 million to Katrina relief efforts and held a telethon during one of the team's preseason games to raise another $1.5 million. Coach Van Chancellor of the WNBA's Houston Comets took his team on a visit to the evacuees at the Astrodome. Les Alexander, the owner of the NBA's Rockets and the WNBA's Comets, opened up Toyota Center and provided his staff's services on multiple occasions to support the relief efforts. The Rockets held a three-day HopeFest from September 6 to 8 to collect and distribute necessary goods and services to evacuees from Louisiana, Mississippi, and Alabama.

On September 6, Van Gundy and several Rockets were on hand from 7 a.m. until 9 p.m. at Toyota Center accepting donations, asking their fans to contribute baby formula, diapers, sanitary wipes, peanut butter, bread, canned vegetables, soups, Raman noodles, can openers, hot plates, bottled water, pillows, bedding, stuffed animals, toys, school supplies, clothes, and footwear. All-Star forward Tracy McGrady, David Wesley, Mike James, Bob Sura, Jon Barry, Luther Head, and Derek Anderson attended the event.

"This unprecedented natural disaster has affected our entire country," Alexander said. "This is a time for our community to rise to this challenge and help our neighbors move forward with their lives. We're trying to coordinate this event so we can really make a meaningful impact on the lives of others. We are focusing our efforts not only on providing immediate assistance, but also on long-term solutions to help with job training, employment opportunities, and housing assistance."

On September 7 and 8, evacuees were invited to Toyota Center to receive the donated items. The Rockets also set up Toyota Center with experts to provide the Katrina victims with job skills training, job placement, housing assistance, medical services, counseling, and school registration.

Alexander also made the Toyota Center and his staff available on September 11 for former Rockets star guard Kenny Smith's celebrity basketball game to benefit Katrina relief. All but a few of the biggest stars in the NBA donated at least $10,000 for the opportunity to play in the event.

Stephon Marbury, Kobe Bryant, Kevin Garnett, Carmelo Anthony, LeBron James, Allen Iverson, Dwyane Wade, Steve Francis, and the Rockets' McGrady, James, and Anderson were only a few of the stars who participated in the NBA Players Hurricane Relief Game. Hundreds of evacuees were let in for free to join the boisterous crowd of 11,416.

Marbury, who vowed to give $1 million to the relief effort, spent several hours with evacuees at the Astrodome. Countless stars visited the evacuees in Houston, including Oprah Winfrey and rap star Kanye West, who attended the game and gave an impromptu concert. Smith, who starred on the Rockets' teams that won two championships in the 1990s and serves as a popular studio host with TNT, set up four tours for players to visit evacuees at Houston shelters.

"It was inspirational," Bryant told Michael Murphy of the *Houston Chronicle*. "I mean, when I say it was inspirational, when we walked into the shelter, we thought it was going to be a really bad sight, and you are going to feel really bad for the people there. But when you walk in, it was really spirited. There was a lot of energy in there and a lot of resolve to bounce back."

The Astros passed the hat around the clubhouse and came up with $50,000. Clemens matched that $50,000 donation through the Roger Clemens Foundation, and McLane matched his players' $100,000 combined contribution to donate a total of $200,000 to Katrina victims. Clemens has donated millions through his foundation and helped raise at least $1 million more by attending countless charity events throughout his 22-year career.

He was raised by his mother, Bess, in a modest home in Houston, and he has kept the less fortunate on his mind throughout his career.

With a mean grin and an imposing commitment to own the plate with his fastball, Clemens has been the picture of strength on the mound since he was helping the University of Texas win the College World Series in the early 1980s. He has a record seven Cy Young Awards and 341 career victories to show why many consider him the greatest pitcher of his time if not ever. He got his fighting spirit from his mother, Bess, who fought through emphysema for a decade.

Clemens decided to play his 22nd season overall and second with the Astros only after his ailing mother signed off. When he announced that the 2003 season with the New York Yankees would be his last, he made that announcement in part because he wanted his mother to be around for his induction ceremony at the Hall of Fame in Cooperstown. With 310 victories through the 2003 season, Clemens had already earned his

Roger Clemens attributes his will to watching his mother, Bess, while he was growing up. Clemens shared the honor of his seventh (2004) Cy Young Award with her in 2005.

place among the greats of the game. All he needed was the five-year wait after retirement for the Baseball Writers' Association of America to vote him in on the first ballot.

Clemens didn't want to play too long and risk denying his mother the opportunity to watch him accept his plaque at Cooperstown.

"I wanted her to hang on so I could thank her properly at the Hall of Fame," Clemens said. "I said that so many times. I keep playing this silly game, and I love it. I just hope and I know she enjoyed some of the games. I don't know what to say. Like I said, she played both parts for me."

Bess Clemens gave Roger her blessings for him to put off retirement and sign with the Astros on January 12, 2004. Telling him she wanted him to finish on top, she gave her blessings again in January 2005.

It was clear that something was on Clemens's mind as he had one of his worst performances of the season on September 9 against the Milwaukee Brewers. He gave up five runs over three innings and lost 7-4 at Miller Park. A day later, he left the team and rushed to be at his mother's side in Georgetown, Texas. Andy Pettitte, Clemens's best friend on the team, remained optimistic that all would be fine. Bess had fought through critical conditions a few times over the last few years, and Pettitte thought she'd pull through again in September.

Clemens's teammates all grew more optimistic on September 13 when they were assured that Clemens said he would not miss his start the next evening against the Florida Marlins.

Bess Clemens–Booher loved and lived baseball. She understood her son and the Astros were in the middle of the pennant stretch and frantically climbing up the National League wild card standings. As Clemens sat with her on the night of September 13 and early into the wee hours of the morning, she made him promise before she died at 4:30 a.m. that he'd be on the mound for his start that night.

Bess remained lucid throughout her final moments, and she peppered her son with questions about Pettitte's surgically repaired left elbow. She mentioned Shoeless Joe Jackson, the slugger from the infamous Chicago White Sox who was accused of fixing the 1919 World Series in the Black Sox scandal.

"I told her last night I needed to go to work, and she told me to go to work," Clemens said. "When I left the room, she told my sisters again to go to work. It was nice. I don't know what to say. I'm just very thankful. I thought it was the neatest thing."

Clemens arrived at Minute Maid Park on September 14 about two hours before the first pitch and was on the mound less than 15 hours after his mother died at the age of 75.

"I feel very blessed she's at peace now," he said. "The last 10 years were hard on her. The last two or three days were grueling. She was very tough to the end. She didn't want to give up."

Walking in from the bullpen along with catcher Brad Ausmus, Clemens slumped his shoulders and kept his head down on his way to the dugout. After the national anthem and the ceremonial first pitch, Clemens lumbered out of the dugout and jogged half-heartedly to the mound. He appeared void of his normal swagger, which was to be expected from a man who had just lost the person who raised him.

"She was my strength," Clemens said. "She's always my will. She gave me so much. It was very painful. She was really my mother and my father. She played both roles."

His first pitch to Marlins leadoff hitter Luis Castillo at 7:05 p.m. was clearly out of the strike zone. The next three also were out of the strike zone, and Castillo walked on four consecutive 91-mph fastballs.

"I was lost as soon as I climbed on the mound," he said. "I was lost a little bit. I knew I had to gather up really quick so I could get through that."

The Marlins' next hitter, Jeff Conine, singled to center. Clemens caught a bit of a breather to compose himself because Burke, who was starting in center field for the first time, suffered a dislocated left shoulder trying to make the diving catch on Conine's sinking line drive. Miguel Cabrera followed with an RBI ground out to third, giving the Marlins a 1-0 lead. Clemens induced a grounder to first from Carlos Delgado for the second out. After he walked Juan Encarnacion, Damian Easley popped out to third base to end the inning.

Clemens settled in after that rough first inning and didn't give the Marlins another run before a crowd of 30,911. Even though he had hardly slept in the previous three nights, Clemens held the Marlins to one run and five hits over 6⅓ innings to win 10-2. With the victory, Clemens put the Astros within a half-game of the wild card lead by dropping the Marlins into a tie with the Philadelphia Phillies atop that race.

Clemens gave himself his first lead during the three-run second inning. With the bases loaded and one out in the second, Ausmus drew a walk from Burnett to tie the score 1-1. Clemens, who had gone six starts without a victory, broke the tie with an RBI walk. Biggio followed with an RBI single to left. Those three runs were more than enough on this night from an Astros squad that scored 10 runs despite playing without the injured Ensberg and Willy Taveras, as well as Burke, who had to be replaced after the first inning.

The crowd gave Clemens a respectful and somewhat subdued standing ovation after Phil Garner called on Qualls with two on and one out in the seventh inning. Qualls induced a double-play grounder from Paul Lo Duca to end the inning.

"He's obviously committed to this job and to this team," Berkman said. "I can tell you this, I probably wouldn't be here. In fact, I know I wouldn't be here. Part of the reason is that it's a pretty major deal."

Clemens had no choice. His mother had ordered him there. From her deathbed, she asked him to return to work.

"That woman had baseball in her heart," Roger's wife, Debbie, said. "She was very much in a good mood and very loving and sweet throughout the whole time. She would have been proud of Roger tonight."

The Astros couldn't afford to be without Clemens. Ensberg had not played since two innings after he suffered tissue damage on his right hand when Philadelphia's Brett Myers hit him with a pitch on September 5. Taveras sat out September 14, a day after suffering a laceration on his right hand's middle finger when Josh Beckett hit him with a pitch. Taveras needed five stitches to seal the laceration, and he didn't return to the starting lineup until September 21.

After dislocating his shoulder, Burke, Taveras's replacement, didn't start again until September 22. Starting shortstop Adam Everett left the team after the Astros' 4-1 victory over the Marlins on September 15 to be with his wife and daughter in Atlanta the next day for the eight-month-old's surgery to remove a benign tumor from her spinal cord.

Everett missed four games while his daughter, Peyton Rebecca, recovered. There was a risk of paralysis if the surgery had not been a success. Everett rejoined the Astros at Pittsburgh's PNC Park on September 20. Everett, Ensberg, and Taveras were all back in the starting lineup on September 21 for the first time since September 5.

By then, the Astros and the city of Houston had much greater concerns. Hurricane Rita was ripping through the Gulf of Mexico and on a path toward Galveston. The images of all of the destruction and loss of life from Hurricane Katrina were fresh in everybody's mind throughout the Houston–Galveston area. Having learned a lesson from the folks who didn't evacuate in time from New Orleans, Houstonians packed the airports and highways out of town as soon as they received warnings about Hurricane Rita.

Throughout the entire four-game series at PNC Park from September 19 to 22, the Astros players and coaches were glued to the Weather Channel. Many of the players hurriedly made plane reservations for their families to join them in Chicago from September 23 to 25, the weekend that Rita was expected to hit the Galveston–Houston area. Because the Astros don't let families on the team flights once rosters expand on September 1, many of the players' wives had remained in Houston when the team headed to Pittsburgh for the start of a three-city, nine-game, 10-day trip through Pittsburgh, Chicago, and St. Louis.

With the looming threat of Hurricane Rita, general manager Tim Purpura relaxed the policy and told the players their families could travel with them. Placing a call into Houston those days was practically impossible on the first try, and frustration grew as the Astros struggled to reach their worried families. Right-hander Brandon Backe's father, Harold, had evacuated the night of September 21, but it was impossible to know if he got very far because it was not unusual for trips that normally lasted only 15 minutes to last hours on the crammed highways as residents fled Rita's predicted path.

Backe is the only Astro from Galveston, and he spent hours on September 21 trying to reach his father and several good friends in Galveston. He woke up early the next morning and tried to reach his father again with no luck. Frustrated, Backe put the phone down and began preparing for his noon start against the Pirates on September 22.

While trying to put the situation at home out of his mind, Backe pitched seven strong innings to beat the Pittsburgh Pirates 2-1.

"I'm sure he's fine," Backe said of his father after the game. "He's that type of guy. But it's irritating when you can't get in touch with somebody [when] you have to."

Backe held the Pirates to one run on two hits with six strikeouts and a hit batsman to win the series 3-1 and maintain the Astros' two-game lead in the wild card standings.

"Once we start the game, my focus is on baseball," said Ausmus, who was in charge of guiding Backe through the outing. "But the moment before I left the clubhouse and the moment I came back to the clubhouse, my focus is on the Weather Channel to see what's going on with the hurricane. Brandon Backe has family in Galveston. It's a great deal of concern for us, a very powerful storm."

At the airport that day, Purpura's wife and mother were stuck along with thousands of others in a mad dash. Lane's wife and mother-in-law also were stuck at the airport for hours. The scene at the airport was a miserable one in many cases. At Bush Intercontinental, lines to check in snaked through and outside packed terminals. If a traveler arrived a few hours early for a flight on September 22, he or she likely missed it because of long security lines. In Pittsburgh, the Astros frantically tried to reach their loved ones after dispensing of the Pirates. More often than not, their phone calls were greeted by, "All circuits are busy."

After they finally got through, the frustration built because many of their loved ones weren't making much progress on the road. Like the rest of their neighbors, they were stuck in the mother of all traffic jams.

"The traffic jams are so bad," Brad Lidge said after collecting the four-out save on September 22. "This hurricane is on the forefront of our minds, for sure."

Lidge's wife, Lindsay, packed their 10-month-old daughter, Avery, and their black lab, Nutmeg, into a car and set out toward former Astros left-hander Jeriome Robertson's home in Round Rock at 4 a.m. on September 22. Eight hours later, she was still stranded in the Houston suburbs.

Ensberg's wife, Christi, eventually reached Round Rock and received refuge at the home of former Astros reliever Scott Linebrink of the Padres.

As her car overheated with the baby and the dog, Lindsay Lidge began to worry. She caught a break when speaking to the wife of Class AAA Round Rock utility player Royce Huffman. Huffman's wife called her father-in-law, Royce Huffman Sr., who secured a small plane from a family friend. Lindsay abandoned her car in Brenham and caught a flight on that small plane.

Some of the Astros' family members braved it out, catching a break along with the rest of the city when Hurricane Rita missed Houston. Others were already at their other year-round homes, but all of them felt the stress of loved ones and neighbors awaiting the unknown on the packed highways and airports of the city they called home.

"We're lucky," Oswalt said. "We were lucky."

18

Oswalt on the Line for the Wild Card

As the anti-war movement grew stronger throughout the United States, Billy Joe Oswalt knew there was only one thing for him to do when his number was called in 1968 for the Vietnam War. He wasn't exactly celebrating, but in Weir, Mississippi, the boys are raised to respect and defend their country. He was only one of two men from the Jackson area whose numbers had been called in their draft classification. Allowed to make his own choice, he likely would have picked the Army. He didn't have a choice. He was drafted into the Marines, and it didn't take him long to buy into the Semper Fi mantra.

"We don't leave our dead behind," he still says 37 years later. "We're just a little tighter group."

Billy's tour of duty in Vietnam was originally scheduled to last 13 months. After serving 10 months in Vietnam, he had completed his tour. Although Billy strongly believes that it would be beneficial for every able man in America to serve some time in the armed forces, he hasn't spoken much to his children about his time in Vietnam. Sure, Roy Oswalt realizes his father believes the Marines and the other branches of the armed forces are good places for boys to mature, become men, and appreciate the freedoms often taken for granted in parts of this country. Oswalt doesn't need to ask his father what he thinks of those folks who disgrace the flag in the name of freedom of speech.

All Oswalt needs to know about his father's tour of duty is the emotion Billy shows during church services each Veterans' Day. The tears rolling down Billy's cheek during Veterans' Day services are essentially the most he'll say of his buddies who didn't return from Vietnam.

"You see people disgracing the flag, they've never been there and seen their fellow man killed in war," Billy Oswalt says. "A person that's seen many men killed, that's just something not to really talk about. You want to remember your buddies, but I don't know."

Billy Oswalt, who will celebrate his 60th birthday in 2007, was one of the lucky ones who came back in one piece from Vietnam. He hadn't been in the Marines more than a month when his wife, Jean, found out she was pregnant with their first child. He was already fighting in Vietnam when Jean gave birth to Patricia Lynn in 1969. His daughter was nine months old when he held her for the first time, and he vowed to appreciate every moment the Good Lord gave him with his children.

He was determined to follow the example his father, Houston, and mother, Delcy Mae, had set. Billy's parents were born in Ackerman, Mississippi, a few miles away from Weir. Houston Oswalt was born in 1910, and he moved with his wife to Weir in the 1930s. After starting off in farming, Houston began making his living in what they call cutting the short wood before dedicating himself full-time to logging. A few years later, the Oswalts began cutting large timber.

If his children were participating in an athletic event, Houston made sure his work was done early enough for him to attend his children's activities.

After retiring from logging at age 72, Houston dedicated his time to growing watermelons to keep his grandchildren busy. He'd wake them up at 6 a.m. to plant or water the watermelons, depending on the time of year. Although he didn't miss many of the athletic events that his children or grandchildren participated in, Houston considered sports diversions. He didn't view baseball as a realistic career opportunity for Roy or any of his grandchildren. As far as he was concerned, Roy was merely trying to figure out what to do with his life when he signed with the Astros.

"He was the type that believed hard work was a way of life," Oswalt said of his paternal grandfather. "You can ask anybody who lived around here in Weir that. He'd work six days a week and take Sundays off. He was never a real outspoken person. He always believed in work. He didn't know that you could actually play a sport and make money. He thought I was still wondering what I was going to do. He was thinking I would play one or two years until I got going, and my dad started showing him different news clippings about me.

"I think the biggest thing you learned from being around my grandfather was the respect he got from people in the community. I think he got so much respect because anytime he said he was going to do something, he always did it. If he gave his word, he was going to do it. It never crossed his mind that he wouldn't do it. It never crossed his mind to expect anything in return."

Billy Oswalt and his wife were the same way with their three children, Patricia Lynn, Brian, and Roy. As long as it didn't rain, Billy would work every day of the week. By daylight he'd already be hard at work so that his evenings would be free for him to devote his time to his children's sporting events. Around Weir, folks would warn Billy against spreading himself too thin.

"A lot of people kept telling me I'd never make it if I kept trying to make all those events," Billy recalls.

Billy ignored the critics. Only a lack of athletic facilities could stand in his way, but even that wasn't enough to deter him and his children. Patricia Lynn became a good softball player, joining her mother on an adult-league team on the weekends in nearby Ackerman. Weir, with a population of about 550, didn't get a baseball field until Brian's senior year at Weir High in 1993. By then, Patricia Lynn had already graduated. There was no softball team for Patricia Lynn to join in high school, but she got plenty of practice pitching to her younger brothers at home. Brian is two years older than Roy, the youngest of the family.

Jean bought her boys a small pitching machine when they were young. Jean, Billy, or Patricia Lynn would go out into the yard and pitch to Roy and Brian, or play ball with them. Jean's organized sports experience was limited to her outfielder's spot at the local women's softball league. As a child, she'd play baseball with other children out on the pastures in Weir. But her parents, Edward and Nina Threet, had essentially no interest in sports. Jean can trace her family's roots 100 years in Weir, and her children's generation was the first from her side of the family to participate much in organized sports. Edward and Nina Threet had six children, four boys and two girls. Edward Threet worked as a truck driver, traveling the country for weeks at a time on his runs. Nina stayed at home and raised the children.

"My folks never cared anything about baseball or football or anything like that," said Jean, who goes by her middle name because she doesn't much care for her first name of Martha. "Daddy worked all the time. He was gone a good bit, cross-country. We'd go down to the pasture and play softball, but that was the only ball we ever knew."

Jean made up for her lack of sports activities as a youth with her children, doubling as somewhat of a sports psychologist. She was constantly working on her children's confidence, telling them there was little they couldn't accomplish with solid work ethic and dedication.

Now, she blushes with pride each time she sees Oswalt standing tall on the mound with no trace of fear.

"When he steps on the mound and I can tell he's just built with so much confidence, it just causes my pride," she said. "I sometimes tear up because he's so secure in himself. I really don't know where he got that from. When they were coming up, I'd always try to build their confidence. I've always tried to build my kids up."

The Astros needed a confident Roy Oswalt on the mound on the final game of the season on October 2, 2005. Heading into the season-ending four-game series against the Chicago Cubs at Minute Maid Park, the Astros led the Philadelphia Phillies by 2½ games in the wild card standings. The Astros' magic number stood at two, meaning any combination of losses by Philadelphia and victories by Houston totaling two would clinch the wild card for the Astros. The Cubs beat the Astros 3-2 in the opener of the series on September 29. After Lance Berkman's two-run home run in the eighth inning the next day, the Astros were primed to cut their magic number to one as closer Brad Lidge took the mound in the ninth inning with a 3-2 lead.

Entering that night, Lidge had recorded 40 saves in 2005 and converted his previous 24 save opportunities in a row to set a new franchise record for consecutive save opportunities converted. He'd have to wait one more day for his 41st save of the season. Struggling to find the strike zone with his usually trusty slider, Lidge struggled mightily. Matt Murton greeted him with a leadoff single through the left side. Slugger Jeromy Burnitz, the Conroe High graduate who had tormented the Astros all season after they refused to sign him over the winter, followed Murton with a single through the right side. With runners at the corners, Michael Barrett doubled off the left field wall to tie the score 3-3.

Lidge caught a break for the first out when first baseman Berkman fielded Corey Patterson fielder's-choice grounder and threw home to force Burnitz out at home. Lidge's control problems continued as he fell behind in the count 3-0 against pinch hitter Todd Walker. Walker broke the tie by sending Lidge's 3-0 fastball through the right side for an RBI single. Ryan Dempster took care of the Astros in the bottom of the ninth, and the Astros' magic number remained at two.

"They were hitting some sliders that were staying in the zone," Lidge said afterward. "It's definitely frustrating. Good news is we have two more games, and I hope I throw both of them."

Until then, it seemed as though manager Phil Garner would have the privilege of skipping Oswalt in the final game of the season to set him up for the first game of the division series against the National League East champion Atlanta Braves. Oswalt needed one victory to collect the second 20-win season of his career and become the first pitcher to have back-to-back 20-win seasons in the majors since Randy Johnson and Curt Schilling accomplished that feat in 2001 and 2002 for the Arizona Diamondbacks. Oswalt made no secret of his desire to go after his second consecutive 20-win season, but he agreed with Garner that it would be best for the Astros if he rested and waited for Game 1 of the division series if they clinched before the final game of the season.

With Lidge's blown save and the Phillies' 4-3 victory over the Washington Nationals, skipping Oswalt on the final game of the season no longer seemed like an option for Garner heading into the penultimate game of the season.

Craig Biggio put the Astros ahead right away on October 1 by depositing Jerome Williams's first pitch into the Crawford Boxes for a leadoff home run, raising his National League record for leadoff home runs with the 44th of his career, tying Brady Anderson for second on the all-time leadoff home run list behind Rickey Henderson. The home run also was Biggio's 26th of the season, extending his career high for home runs in a season. Roger Clemens collected the 4,500th strikeout of his career when he struck out Jose Macias in the third inning. Clemens retired the first batter in the fourth, but Nomar Garciaparra, Burnitz, and Barrett hit consecutive one-out singles to the outfield to load the bases. Garciaparra tied the score 1-1 on Matt Murton's deep sacrifice fly to the warning track in right field. With Williams on deck, Clemens reloaded the bases by intentionally walking Patterson. Williams stranded the bases loaded when he struck out looking at Clemens's 94-mph fastball.

The Astros regained the lead in the sixth, which Willy Taveras led off with a rare double off of the left-center field wall. One out later, Berkman reached base when Williams hit him with a pitch. Williams collected the second out on Mike Lamb's fielder's-choice grounder to first. Jason Lane came through with a two-out RBI single through the left side to give Clemens a 2-1 lead. Adam Everett opened the seventh inning with an infield single to short, and Chris Burke followed with a bunt single toward first. One out later, Everett scored on Jeff Bagwell's pinch RBI ground out to third base, making the score 3-1.

Clemens, who had not started since September 19 because of back and hamstring problems, held the Cubs to six hits and one run over seven strong innings. Dan Wheeler handled the eighth, and Lidge took care of the ninth before an appreciative sellout crowd of 42,021. The Phillies kept their wild card hopes alive with an 8-4 victory over the Nationals later that Saturday evening, so Garner sent Oswalt to the mound Sunday.

"I don't think that guys need to even be concerned with if Washington's going to help us out or not," Clemens said. "Just go out and do it."

Garner had lined up his starters since late August just so he'd have his top three starters ready for the final weekend of the season. Cubs manager Dusty Baker altered his starting rotation so that 318-game winner Greg Maddux would have a chance to claim another 15-win season. By the final game of the season, Maddux no longer had a shot at 15 victories. He merely wanted to avoid his first losing season since he was a rookie. Oswalt's incentives were obviously much greater.

As if clinching the National League wild card weren't incentive enough, Oswalt also had a chance to join Joe Niekro as the only Astros to ever collect consecutive 20-win seasons. Actually, Niekro had been the only Astro to collect two 20-win seasons for the franchise. Other than Niekro and Oswalt, only six other Astros pitchers have collected 20-win seasons, starting with Larry Dierker's 20-13 campaign in 1969.

"Obviously we all believe in Roy and have a ton of confidence," Lidge said. "It's just nice that if you have one game that you have to win, you get to have Roy Oswalt pitching."

Once again, Biggio got the Astros going with a leadoff double down the left field line in the first inning. Biggio reached third on Taveras's sacrifice bunt, and Ensberg drove him in with a single to left field. Berkman moved Ensberg over to second with a ground out to first base, and Lamb made it 2-0 with an RBI single to right field. Oswalt pitched in and out of trouble in the third inning after Neifi Perez hit a one-out blooper for a double to left field. Perez reached third on Berkman's error in left field.

Oswalt ruined Baker's call for a suicide squeeze by busting Maddux with a fastball inside on the first pitch. Maddux fouled that pitch back, and the suicide squeeze play was called off. Running on contact, Perez was thrown out at home by Everett, who fielded Maddux's fielder's-choice grounder cleanly. Maddux moved into scoring position when Oswalt uncorked a wild pitch to Patterson, who eventually reached when Oswalt hit him with a fastball that tailed inside. Maddux and Patterson were stranded on Macias's grounder to third. The Astros weren't as forgiving in the fourth inning. Lamb and Lane jumped on Maddux with consecutive singles to center. The threat stalled on Brad Ausmus's double-play grounder to short. With Oswalt at the on-deck circle, Maddux gambled with an intentional walk to Everett. The move backfired. Oswalt singled to the hole in short, taking a 3-0 lead.

Oswalt's nemesis, Michael Barrett, who challenged Oswalt to a fight twice in the 2004 season, cut the Astros' lead to 3-1 in the fifth inning with a leadoff home run to left field. Murton kept the rally going with an infield single to third base. Perez put runners at the corners with a single to right. Maddux hurt his cause with a horrible sacrifice bunt attempt, which he hit too hard toward the mound. Oswalt fielded the ball cleanly and threw to second base, beginning a double play. Patterson cut the Cubs' deficit to 3-2 with an RBI double to left field. Oswalt maintained the lead by inducing Macias's ground out to short.

The Cubs took a 4-3 lead with two more runs in the sixth. Garciaparra began that rally with a one-out single to right field, and Burnitz blooped a single to left field. Barrett's single through the right side of the infield tied the score 3-3. After Murton flied out to center field, the Cubs went ahead 4-3 on Perez's single to right field. Not one of the Cubs' hits that inning was very impressive, but the damage had been done.

Maddux didn't enjoy the lead very long. Lane led off the bottom of the sixth with a home run into the Crawford Boxes behind the left field wall, tying the score 4-4. After Ausmus grounded out to third, Everett hit a single to left field. Garner responded by calling on Bagwell to hit for Oswalt, and the Cubs helped out with terrible defense. Perez fielded Bagwell's fielder's-choice grounder without any problem. As Everett charged toward second, Perez rushed an errant throw past the outstretched Macias at second. Everett capitalized on the error and scored as the ball carried toward the railing along the right field line. Fortunately for the Astros, the fan who tried to retrieve the ball along the railing was not able to touch it. If he had, Everett might have been called back to third base. Instead, Bagwell was standing at third base with a 5-4 lead.

"They weren't going to turn a double play, I felt," Bagwell said. "Probably they might have, but I [knew] it was a tough play. Adam got such a great jump. When you force the issue, get good jumps, and do what Adam did, get a good secondary lead and run hard, things like that can happen."

The Cubs' comedy of blunders continued after Garner sent September call-up Charles Gipson to run for Bagwell. With a 1-1 count, Cubs reliever Michael Wuertz sent a slider in the dirt. Barrett couldn't keep the ball in front of him, and Gipson gave the Astros a 6-4 lead on the wild pitch. Chad Qualls retired the Cubs in order in the seventh, and Wheeler did the same in the eighth.

As had been the case all season, the Astros were tested until the end. Murton led off the ninth against Lidge with a single through the right side. After Ben Grieve struck out, Walker hit a potential double-play grounder to short. Second baseman Eric Bruntlett bobbled Everett's throw and failed to get the force out at second. Patterson's ground out to short put the potential tying run at second base and the go-ahead run at the plate with two outs. Even the final out gave the Astros a scare. Fortunately for the Astros, Bruntlett was in perfect position for Macias's line out to second, starting a celebration on the field as the Astros won the NL wild card for the second consecutive year on the final game of the season.

"I guess you could say it was all a little microcosm," Garner said of the 6-4 victory. "It was pretty much the way things have been."

In that maddening ninth inning and throughout that entire afternoon, the Astros teased their fans with an example of their difficult march from 15-30 on May 24. The Phillies had already won 9-3 against the Nationals, but Oswalt, Lidge, and the Astros made sure there was no need for a one-game playoff at Citizens Bank Park. Back on May 24, a post-season berth or even a one-game playoff for the wild card would have been impossible to imagine. In the National League, the Astros were looking up at every team in the standings except the lowly Colorado Rockies, who were stuck at 13-30 when the Astros were at 15-30 and 11½ games behind in the wild card standings. Back then, the Phillies were five games ahead of the Astros in the wild card race, and the eventual NL Central champion St. Cardinals were already leading Houston by 14.

"It didn't seem so bad once we got it going," Garner said. "It got to be fun when we were playing and scoring a lot of runs. Then we kind of hit a stall a little where we lost a lot of that when we were winning six or seven games in a row and then losing one. Then you didn't know what was happening. We managed to hang on. Down the last couple of weeks, the lead changed hands [in the wild card standings] a couple of times. When I thought we were going to take off, we didn't. When I thought we were going to crater, we didn't. Then it came down to the last day, and we did what we had to do."

19

Division Series, Five Games in Four

They had driven in from Louisville, Kentucky, expecting to watch Chris Burke play for the Astros at Turner Field against the Atlanta Braves during the 2005 regular season. They weren't dreaming about majestic home runs or franchise-defining moments. Chris Burke's parents, wife, siblings, in-laws, nieces, aunt, and uncle just wanted to see the rookie play.

With the Astros scheduled to play a four-game series from May 5 to 8 against the Braves at Turner Field, Burke's relatives assumed he'd at least get in one of the four games. Burke's wife, Sara, took time out from her classes at the University of Louisville Law School to make the seven-hour drive to see her husband. Sara didn't see much of Burke during the school year. Burke's parents, Al and Mary Jo, also made the trip along with Chris's brother, Paul, and Paul's wife, Nicole, and their daughter, Caroline. Chris's sister, Erin, and her daughter, Claire, also were there. Even Aunt Kate and Uncle Phillip Zoercher drove up from Gainesville, Georgia, which is 55 miles south of Atlanta.

Although he couldn't beat out Craig Biggio for the starting job at second base in the spring of 2005, he played well enough in spring training to earn a spot on Phil Garner's opening day, 25-man roster as a backup outfielder–infielder a season after hitting .315 with 16 home runs and 52 runs batted in with Class AAA New Orleans.

Burke didn't get much playing time, though, in the first month of the season. Furthermore, his statistics weren't very impressive in the few games he played. He was hitting .222 over 45 at-bats with three RBI, three walks, and five runs scored for the season heading into that series in Atlanta. He remained on the bench as the Astros were pummeled 9-3 in the first game of the series.

The next morning, more of Burke's supporters were due in town. Joe Bergaminni, Burke's former varsity basketball coach at St. Xavier High in

Kentucky, was headed to Atlanta to celebrate his birthday with three friends by watching Burke play at Turner Field. Bergaminni's wife had set up the weekend as a birthday gift, and Burke promised to give the group tickets.

Burke arrived at Turner Field early that afternoon for extra batting practice. He was brought into the manager's office to speak with Garner and general manager Tim Purpura after early batting practice was over. All of the Astros' young players knew somebody would be sent down to make room for Lance Berkman to come off the disabled list. It was assumed a pitcher, like struggling relievers Brandon Duckworth or Chad Harville, would be optioned to Class AAA Round Rock because the Astros were carrying 12 pitchers already.

Burke understood there was a possibility that he'd be sent down, but he liked his odds. He and his family were shocked when he learned that he was the one chosen to make room for Berkman. Burke called his family from the stadium and rushed to meet them at the team hotel after staying around just long enough to speak with the media requesting comments from him. He handled his demotion with class and vowed to return.

"People keep asking me, 'Would you rather be here and not playing or be at Triple A and playing?'" he said. "The answer has usually been neither. It's a situation that the scenario that I would like is not available. It's just kind of frustrating from that standpoint. You just don't know whether the situation is ever going to pop up or where it's going to pop up."

Most of his teammates empathized with the popular Burke, especially the younger stars, who on countless occasions went public with their belief that the Astros would be foolish to trade Burke.

Dejected, he had his father call his old basketball coach to say there wouldn't be any tickets for him in the Astros' family section at Turner Field that day or any other that weekend. After about an hour, he and his family drove south to Kate and Phillip Zoercher's home.

"I got to hang out with my family," he said. "It was good for everybody to get on the same page. After about two days of licking my wounds I was able to regroup. I was so down. I told my dad to call my coach. They were disappointed. The first day I didn't play, and the second day I got sent down. That was one of the hardest moments in 2005. That was a really, really hard day from the standpoint of not knowing what the future had in store for me. As frustrating as it was for me, it was really hard because we all knew Lance was coming off the disabled list. In the back of my mind I always knew the chance was there. I guess nobody on the team was talking about it or nobody thought it would be me. Even members of the media speculated it might be a pitcher. It wasn't shocking. The timing was as bad as the actual situation."

Burke didn't sulk at Round Rock. He hit .311 (28 for 90) with six doubles, two triples, nine stolen bases, two home runs, and 11 RBI over 22 games. He was back up in the majors on June 1, the day the Astros responded to the *Houston Chronicle*'s infamous tombstone cover by seeing if the team's fortunes could change with more of a commitment to steady playing time for Burke and Jason Lane.

Burke, the Astros' first-round pick out of the University of Tennessee 2001, had convinced Astros officials that he no longer had anything to prove at Class AAA. A former All-America shortstop at Tennessee, he shifted to second base early in his minor league career. At five feet, 11 inches and 180 pounds, he was athletic enough to play all of the outfield positions well in 2004 at New Orleans and during spring training in 2005. Scouts predicted that he'd grow with the league, meaning he'd get better each month until he settled into a productive career.

Burke also has a swagger. He oozes confidence, and he doesn't shy away from the big moments. He's so confident that Purpura actually compared All-Star and two-time 20-game winner Roy Oswalt favorably to Burke, saying Oswalt had that same desire that Burke had to be in the big-game situation. Some famous players shrink when the stakes are highest. Guys like Oswalt and Burke rose with the stakes, and Astros fans everywhere realized that fact in time.

As New York Mets ace right-hander Pedro Martinez toyed with the Astros on a no-hitter into the seventh inning, Burke broke up the no-hitter with a home run over the left field wall at Shea Stadium for his first major league homer on June 7. Burke raised his average to .219 with that hit after seeing it dip to .192 after an zero-for-three performance on June 3 against the St. Louis Cardinals. Burke's average dipped back to .198 after another zero-for-four performance June 12 against the Toronto Blue Jays at Minute Maid Park.

He went zero for five the next day in a loss to the Baltimore Orioles at Camden Yards and zero for four the day after that in another loss. Suddenly, concern set in as Burke wondered when Garner and Purpura would bring him back into the manager's office with another ticket to Round Rock. He was out of the lineup the next day against the Orioles, and the doubts picked up as the Astros were swept.

"I started wondering if was blowing it," he said. "You feel like at any point you could be sent back down. You just don't know if you have any kind of leeway and they're going to give you any grace period."

Garner and Purpura gave Burke the rest of the season and, fortunately for Astros fans, the postseason, too. Burke bought himself some confidence with a career-high 11-game hitting streak from June 27 to July 6, hitting .350 (14 for 40) during that span. Only two other rookies had longer hitting streaks in the majors in 2005. He finished the season with a .248 average, five home runs, 19 doubles, two triples, 26 RBI, and 11 stolen bases. After hitting .229 before the All-Star break, he hit a respectable .270 in the second half of the season.

And when the Astros returned to Turner Field on October 5 for Game 1 of the best-of-five division series against the NL East champion Braves, Al and Mary Jo Burke were guaranteed to see their son play at one point during the series, because he was one of Garner's top players off the bench.

Burke didn't see any action in Game 1 as Morgan Ensberg sparked the Astros to a 10-5 victory before a crowd of 40,590. Andy Pettitte, who had to watch the previous postseason from the dugout while recovering from season-ending left elbow surgery, earned the victory with seven strong innings.

Pettitte held the Braves to four hits and three runs with two walks and six strikeouts. Garner was rewarded for flipping Berkman and Ensberg back to third and fourth in the lineup after having Berkman hit cleanup and Ensberg third in the final 11 games of the year.

Ensberg greeted his return to the cleanup spot with a three-for-four performance while tying Carlos Beltran's franchise single-game post-season record with five RBI. Berkman went zero for two with three walks as Tim Hudson and the rest of the Braves' pitching staff set out to pitch around him. The Astros held a 5-3 lead before pulling away with a five-run rally in the eighth inning. Adam Everett started the five-run rally with a leadoff single to right field off of reliever Chris Reitsma. Brad Ausmus followed with an infield single to second base. After Pettitte sacrificed, Reitsma intentionally walked Craig Biggio, prompting Garner to send Jeff Bagwell to hit for Willy Taveras. Bagwell, who rushed his rehab from right shoulder surgery to be ready for the postseason even though he had not started a game since May 3, came through with an RBI single to left field.

Braves manager Bobby Cox called left-hander John Foster to relieve Reitsma and turn the switch-hitting Berkman to his weaker right side. Foster struck out Berkman, but Ensberg followed with an RBI walk.

Foster let another run score when he threw a wild pitch to Lane. Foster intentionally walked Lane to reload the bases, and Orlando Palmeiro capitalized with a two-run single to left field. Everett kept the inning going with a walk, prompting Cox to call on right-hander Jim Brower, who struck out Ausmus to end the inning.

The Braves countered with a run in the bottom of the eighth off of Dan Wheeler and another run in the ninth off of Russ Springer to make the game seem closer than it was.

"I was surprised that we put the runs on the board," Pettitte said. "I'm not going to lie to you. Credit to our hitters."

Ensberg was the key player that afternoon, punishing the Braves for each walk they issued to Berkman. After Tim Hudson issued a four-pitch walk to Berkman with one on and one out in the first inning, Ensberg gave the Astros a 1-0 lead with a single to center. After Biggio hit a one-out double and Taveras followed with a walk in the third inning, Hudson pitched around Berkman and walked him to load the bases. Ensberg followed with a two-run single through the left side. Pettitte led off the seventh with a rare double to left, lumbering to second. Biggio, who was two for three with one RBI and three runs scored, pushed him to third with a sacrifice bunt. After Taveras grounded out to short for the second out, Hudson intentionally walked Berkman. Ensberg put the Astros ahead 5-1 with an RBI single to left.

"They're not trying to get to me per se," Ensberg said. "I think really what was going on there was they're trying to get a righty-on-righty matchup, and Lance obviously is an outstanding left-handed hitter. He's very dangerous. When you have the option to go after another right-handed batter, I think you just do it. So I think the only difference in those situations, one is that there's virtually no pressure on me, because he's the one that's got to throw the ball over the plate. Two is you want to put a good swing on a good pitch, and I actually got good pitches to hit in those situations."

John Smoltz dominated in Game 2 on October 6, limiting the Astros to seven hits and one run with one walk and five strikeouts over seven innings to beat Roger Clemens 7-1 before a crowd of 46,181. Clemens lasted five innings after giving up five runs on six hits and three walks with two strikeouts.

Already pitching with two small tears in his back and a tender left hamstring, Clemens paid dearly for his decision to pitch to rookie catcher Brian McCann with two men on, two out, and Smoltz on deck in the second inning. Clemens's troubles began when he gave up Andruw Jones's leadoff single to left field. Adam La Roche sacrificed and Jeff Francoeur followed with a walk. Clemens struck out Ryan Langerhans for the second out, but he fell behind in the count 2-0 on McCann.

Clemens challenged with a 2-0 fastball, and McCann turned on it for a three-run home run that carried 409 feet to right field to give the Braves a 3-1 lead. Not bad for McCann's first postseason swing.

"You know, that won't sink in for a while," said McCann, who was born on February 20, 1984, the year Clemens made his debut in the majors. "You know, he's one of the greatest pitchers of all time. Just to get a pitch, up out of the plate, and I connected, it was neat."

Considering Smoltz was on deck, Clemens regretted giving McCann anything to hit in that situation.

"Well, the home run's what killed us," Clemens said. "I mean you can't afford to make that mistake there. It was a fastball [meant to be] down and away, and it cut back over the zone. I mean it's just a very hittable pitch. You know the pitcher's on deck. You don't want to give them that momentum."

Smoltz held the Astros to six singles until Burke made his postseason debut with a pinch two-out double to left field in seventh. Until then, the Astros hadn't put a runner in scoring position since the first inning. Starting for the first time since September 23 because of a tired right shoulder, Smoltz was rusty during his 22-pitch first inning.

The Astros had their only chance to take control during Smoltz's struggles in the first inning. Smoltz got in trouble immediately after striking out Astros leadoff hitter Biggio on three consecutive sliders. Taveras hit a one-out single to right field, and Berkman followed with another single to center. One out later, Lane gave the Astros a 1-0 lead with an RBI single to left field. Smoltz intentionally walked Palmeiro to load the bases and take his chances against shortstop Everett. The move paid off. Everett struck out on three pitches—two fastballs and a slider— and Smoltz never looked back.

"The further along he gets in the game the more dominant he gets," Everett said. "He's got pinpoint control, and you got to take advantage when you get the chance."

Although they couldn't capitalize on an opportunity to take a commanding 2-0 lead in the best-of-five series, the Astros returned to Houston confident with 20-game winner Roy Oswalt on the mound for the first time since he clinched the wild card berth.

Oswalt grew up a Braves fan. He knew as much about the Braves' record 14 consecutive division titles as any Astros player. And at 28, he already had become arguably the most clutch pitcher in franchise history. A year earlier, he earned the victory that pushed Houston past the Braves in Game 5, helping the Astros win a postseason series for the first time in franchise history. He pitched the United States to the gold medal game at the Sydney Olympics, earning a gold medal after Ben Sheets beat the Cubans in the final. And he had just completed his second consecutive 20-win season.

Oswalt had been beating the odds his entire life, refusing to let his small-town roots serve as an excuse for being held back. He may not carry a chip on his shoulder, but he'll also tell you he doesn't take a backseat to anybody in baseball, not Clemens, Randy Johnson, Bagwell, Biggio, or anybody else. He learned early on from his father not to believe all of the folks who told him he couldn't be special because he came from a town of about 550 people or because Weir High School wasn't even big enough to be considered a small school.

"I always heard that I was too small," he said. "I always heard that I wasn't from a big school. But I like challenges. I always have. I've always been the guy who likes big games. All the way from high school or Little League or the minors, I always liked big games."

Oswalt holds a special place in legendary Hall of Famer Nolan Ryan's heart. In Texas, that means something. By now, the story has been retold hundreds of times about the time Ryan first laid eyes on Oswalt at Round Rock's Dell Diamond on May 25, 2000. The Astros had Oswalt make a spot start for an injured pitcher at Round Rock, which was in its inaugural season as the Astros' Class AA affiliate in the Texas League.

Oswalt had a 4-3 record and a 2.98 ERA at Class A Kissimmee at the time. Believing Oswalt needed more seasoning at Kissimmee, then-general manager Gerry Hunsicker had Purpura buy him a roundtrip ticket with the return date of May 26. Oswalt responded with a five-hit shutout and 15 strikeouts against Class AA San Antonio. Ryan, Purpura, and Ryan's son, Reid, were among the sellout crowd at Dell Diamond that day.

Reid Ryan is the president of the Round Rock Express, which became the Astros' Class AAA affiliate in 2005. When informed that Hunsicker wanted to send Oswalt back, Reid Ryan got on a walkie-talkie and called his father.

"Hey, Dad, Tim says that Roy's going back to Kissimmee tomorrow," Reid told his famous father.

After a few seconds of silence, Nolan Ryan's Texas drawl came back with a simple sentence, "Sounds like I need to make a phone call?"

Purpura told Nolan Ryan that his call wouldn't be necessary. Purpura called Hunsicker, and Hunsicker agreed that Oswalt could not be sent down.

For the second time in his life, Oswalt had outrun the law.

As a teenager, Oswalt and his buddies literally outran the law in Mississippi. Oswalt chuckles at the memory and prays that his daughter, Arlee Faith, who was born on September 6, 2004, won't ever be so foolish.

Oswalt was 14, and his good friend Scott Shivers was 15 when they borrowed a 21-year-old friend's brand new 1992 Honda Accord. The young lady who owned the car had purchased it only a week earlier.

Oswalt and Shivers stopped to pick up Nicole Green, Oswalt's future wife. Another friend named Kevin Brown was along for the ride in the backseat. They headed toward the town of Mathinson, 20 miles away from Weir. A new game hall with pool tables and music had just been built there. Oswalt, Shivers, and Green wanted to check it out. Oswalt wondered out loud how fast the Accord could go, and Shivers obliged by stepping on the accelerator. A Mississippi trooper was waiting over the hill, and Oswalt and Shivers knew they were in trouble as soon as they spotted him.

"We were going so fast," Oswalt said. "Scott looked at me and said, 'What should I do?'

"I said, 'Pull over.'

"He said, 'I don't have a license.'

"He floored it."

Going over 90 mph on a gravel road, they lost the trooper by driving back on another road and slipping in between other cars. Straight out of *The Dukes of Hazzard,* the local police set up a roadblock. The trooper who had chased them wasn't at the roadblock, though. Oswalt's group got through by pretending as though they had done nothing wrong.

The trooper's patrol car had a video camera on it, though. The Accord's owner was tracked down rather easily, and the group was caught three days later. Oswalt was grounded, and the driver received about $500 in fines.

"We were probably going 115 mph," Oswalt said. "And we were probably running 95 on the gravel road. It's kind of funny now when you look back at it, but I'd hate for my kid to do it."

For the Astros organization in the playoffs, the Braves had always been the equivalent of the troopers who caught up with Oswalt's group in 1992. No matter how fast they went in the regular season, the Astros were usually caught and punished after a few days in the division series against the Braves. In 1997, 1999, and 2001, the Braves had eliminated the Astros. In 2004 with Oswalt pitching the winner-take-all Game 5, the Astros bounced the Braves.

Oswalt was in the Braves' way again in Game 3 of the 2005 division series. He responded with $7\frac{1}{3}$ strong innings, holding Atlanta to six hits and three runs with two walks and seven strikeouts to win 7-3 and push the Astros within one victory of the National League Championship Series. Biggio contributed three doubles while going three for five with two runs as the Astros set a division series record with seven doubles before a sellout crowd of 43,759 at Minute Maid Park.

Ensberg was two for four with two RBI, and Lane was three for four with two RBI. The Astros took a 2-0 lead with Ensberg's RBI double and Lane's sacrifice fly in the first inning against hard-throwing right-hander Jorge Sosa. The Braves countered with two runs in the second inning as Oswalt struggled with his command.

Andruw Jones led off the second for the Braves with a single to left. La Roche followed with a walk on a 3-1 pitch out of the strike zone after plate umpire Jeff Nelson ruled that Oswalt had balked with a quick pitch. Nelson claimed that Oswalt made the pitch from the set position without coming to a stop. Per Major League Baseball's Rule 8.05, La Roche could have declined the result of the pitch. He took the pitch for a walk, negating the balk call that would have put Jones at second anyway.

After Jeff Francoeur grounded into a double play to third, Oswalt walked Langerhans on four pitches. McCann, the Braves' rookie star in Game 2, cut Oswalt's lead to 2-1 with an RBI bloop single to left. Oswalt's problems continued when he let Sosa hit an RBI single through the left side to tie the score 2-2. Mike Lamb atoned for Oswalt with a home run to right field in the third inning, giving the Astros a 3-2 lead.

"Lamb has been big for us all year, coming off the bench, playing here and there," Oswalt said. "He's been doing a real good job. But to get us a one-run lead gets you right back into the game for us. You don't have to be so fine as to throwing a ball, you know, around the plate. You can still be aggressive and make them hit the ball early."

The Braves kept it close only because the Astros stranded runners in scoring position in each of the first six innings except the third and fourth. The Astros finally pulled away with a four-run rally in the seventh off four Atlanta relievers.

Biggio led off the seventh with a double off of Reitsma. After failing to execute a sacrifice bunt, Taveras hit an infield single over Reitsma's head. The left-handed John Foster relieved Reitsma so the switch-hitting Berkman would hit from his weaker right side. Berkman responded with an RBI single to left. Rookie Joey Devine was brought in to face Ensberg, who responded with an RBI double. Devine intentionally walked Lamb to load the bases for Lane, who drove in another run with a single to left, forcing Cox to dig into his bullpen again with right-hander Jim Brower.

"Well, the flow of the game felt pretty good, but you do begin to wonder how many opportunities you're going to let slide by before you tack a bunch of runs on the board," Phil Garner said. "But we did that in the seventh inning obviously, get a nice inning going and put runs on the board. I wouldn't exactly say ice the game, but we did feel more comfortable at that point. But we did a nice job tonight of continuing to add on, even though we let some opportunities slip away. We're not the type of team that's probably going to score 15 runs, but, you know, in tonight's game, seven was pretty good."

The Astros returned to Minute Maid Park the next morning with an opportunity to clinch the series at home. They never imagined they'd need almost every player on the 25-man division series roster. Pettitte was sent home before the game, because Garner and the training staff didn't want him to spread the stomach virus that had kept Pettitte's family up all night.

Pettitte drove to his home in Deer Park and went right to sleep. When he woke up several hours later, the Astros had already played nine innings and Garner was going through his roster as though he was in the middle of September with a bench full of September call-ups.

A sellout crowd of 43,413 arrived at Minute Maid Park for their early Sunday afternoon game on October 9 ready for a celebration. The Braves sucked the energy out of the stadium in the third inning as Brandon Backe faltered. Backe retired Hudson to start the third, but he walked Rafael Furcal. Backe erased Furcal on Marcus Giles's fielder's-choice grounder to third base. The middle of the order handled the rest with some help from Backe's struggles with the strike zone. Backe walked Chipper Jones and hit Andruw Jones with a pitch to load the bases.

Not wanting to fall behind against La Roche, Backe tried to jam La Roche with a 1-1 fastball up and in. The fastball tailed toward the middle of the plate. La Roche pounced for a grand slam to right field, giving the Braves a 4-0 lead with the first grand slam ever allowed by the Astros in postseason history.

The Braves added another run in the fifth inning on Andruw Jones's sacrifice fly to left field after Giles singled and Chipper Jones hit a double to start the inning. Then, left-hander Mike Gallo relieved Backe. Gallo induced a ground out to first from La Roche and intentionally walked Francoeur. He hit Langerhans with his first pitch, loading the bases. Gallo got out of the inning when McCann grounded out to second base. The Astros got a run back in the bottom of the fifth on Palmeiro's bases-loaded sacrifice fly to center. Springer kept the deficit at 5-1 with two scoreless innings of relief, but the Braves made it 6-1 in the top of the eighth with McCann's leadoff home run to right field off of rookie left-hander Wandy Rodriguez.

Ahead 6-1, Cox decided to stay with Hudson to start the eighth inning instead of calling on his porous bullpen. The move backfired. Pitching on three days' rest instead of the usual four, Hudson had already tired. He issued Ausmus a leadoff walk. Eric Bruntlett followed with an infield single to shortstop, prompting Cox to call on his bullpen. Hard-throwing right-handed closer Kyle Farnsworth induced Biggio's fielder's-choice grounder to third for the first out. Pinch hitter Luke Scott followed with a walk, loading the bases. Farnsworth fell behind in the count 2-1 against Berkman and challenged him with a 97-mph fastball. Berkman turned on the fastball and sent it the other way to cut the Braves' lead to 6-5 with a grand slam into the Crawford Boxes behind left field, marking the only playoff game in history to have a grand slam by each side.

Farnsworth struck out Ensberg and induced Lamb's fly out to end the inning. Chad Qualls retired the Braves in the top of the ninth. Farnsworth kept the Braves ahead 6-5 after Lane grounded out to third and Jose Vizcaino struck out in the bottom of the inning. Ausmus followed to the plate as the Astros' last hope. A home run didn't seem very likely from a man with only three home runs in the entire regular season. Since reaching the majors in 1993 with the San Diego Padres, Ausmus has hit 71 home runs. He has never hit more than nine home runs in a season, which he accomplished in 1999 with the Detroit Tigers. As an Astro, he has never hit more than six home runs in a season.

In 2005, Ausmus hit his first home run in May and didn't hit another until he hit two in September. He entered the postseason swinging the bat well. His 66 hits after the All-Star break were the most by any catcher in the National League. The Dartmouth graduate hit .286 with the two home runs and 11 RBI in the crucial month of September. Nonetheless, few among the sellout crowd could have expected him to save the Astros in Game 4 of the division series with a home run. Needing only one out to send the series back to Atlanta for a winner-take-all Game 5, Farnsworth nibbled and fell behind in the count 2-0. His next pitch was a fastball, and Ausmus lined it over the yellow stripe along the left-center field wall for a game-tying home run.

"The last half of this season, he's gone somewhat unnoticed in his contribution to the club," Garner said of Ausmus. "You know other guys. Lamb has gotten hot, you know, Lance was swinging the bat pretty good. Brad just kind of slid under the radar. But he's been really swinging the bat well and come up with major hits for us. He's hitting down in the lineup, where it's not easy to hit. When you're in the eighth spot, people will pitch around you. But he absolutely tattooed it."

The Braves threatened in the 10th against Qualls when Langerhans hit a one-out double to right, but Qualls struck out McCann and induced a ground out to first from Kelly Johnson. The Astros put their own man in scoring position in the bottom of the 10th when Berkman hit a two-out double to left-center field. After Garner sent Burke to run for Berkman, Braves reliever Reitsma intentionally walked Ensberg. Garner countered with pinch hitter Jeff Bagwell, who flied out to left. The Astros didn't get another hit until the 18th.

The Braves threatened in the 11th against Brad Lidge, who issued a leadoff walk to Furcal and a one-out walk to Chipper Jones. Lidge struck out Andruw Jones and induced a ground out to second from Julio Franco. Atlanta left another man in scoring position in the 12th.

By then, Garner had already turned to Clemens and asked how the 43-year-old legend's right arm felt. Clemens pitched the final month of the season with two small tears in his back, a tender left hamstring, a sore groin, and more determination than anybody who has ever worn a Houston Astros uniform.

He went down the tunnel that leads to the clubhouse and walked to the indoor batting cages. He called his oldest son, Koby, out of the Clemens family suite at Minute Maid Park and asked him to come down to help him loosen up. He returned briefly to the dugout with the answer Garner had hoped for.

Nobody would have blamed Clemens if he could not have pitched. He had labored through 92 pitches over five innings three days earlier while giving up five runs in the 7-1 loss in Game 2 at Turner Field. In that outing, he threw only 39 of his pitches for strikes. And on only two days' rest, he carried his battered body to join the dwindling relief corps. He sat in the lonely left corner of the bullpen behind right field by himself, quietly posing a gigantic shadow over each passing inning.

Wheeler took over in the 13th for the Astros and retired the Braves in order before loading the bases in the 14th. Andruw Jones led off the 14th with a walk, and Franco followed with a bunt single toward the mound. After Francoeur sacrificed, Wheeler intentionally walked Langerhans in hopes of setting up the double play. Wheeler struck out McCann and induced a fielder's-choice grounder from pinch hitter Pete Orr.

By then, Garner had already run out of position players. Berkman had been pulled in the 10th inning. Center fielder Taveras was pulled for a pinch hitter in the eighth. Starting first baseman Lamb and shortstop Everett also were already done for the afternoon. Backup catcher Raul Chavez had replaced Ausmus behind the plate, moving Ausmus to first base as Wheeler pitched. Vizcaino, who took over for Everett at short in the eighth, had moved from short to first base back to short. Bruntlett, who entered as a pinch hitter in the bottom of the eighth, had moved from center fielder to short to center field. And Berkman, the Astros' top hitter in the postseason, was in the dugout after starting the game in left field and moving to first base.

"Yeah," Burke said, "the game turned into a little bit of a three-ring circus."

Garner still had the main attraction waiting in the bullpen.

"To be honest with you, I think they were just down to the last straw," Hudson said. "They really didn't have anybody else to get it to. I don't think they really wanted him to come back on two days' rest. Regardless who you are, I don't care what kind of warrior you are, what kind of Hall of Famer you are, you're not going to pitch on two days' rest unless they desperately need you to. But he was able to come in, step up, get the job done, and make some good pitches. He just kept us at bay until they were able to score."

The Astros were definitely in a desperate situation, so Pettitte frantically called team officials to let them know he was headed back to Minute Maid Park. Pettitte was too sick to pitch, though. Garner had settled on outfielder Lane if he needed a pitcher after Clemens. Lane had pitched in college and actually earned the victory on the mound when the University of Southern California won the 1998 College World Series.

Clemens, who had not pitched in relief since he was a rookie with the Boston Red Sox in 1984, warmed up in the top of the 15th and strolled to the dugout in the bottom of the 15th inning. After Biggio drew a leadoff walk from right-hander Jim Brower, the sellout crowd went wild as Clemens strolled to the plate as a pinch hitter. The legendary pitcher who spent the first 20 seasons of his career with the designated hitter rule in the American League was now being called upon to bat. Clemens dropped a sacrifice bunt to the right side.

"If Roger had [homered], they'd have just shut the game of baseball down. We wouldn't even have bothered to play the World Series, because you couldn't have topped it," Berkman said.

Brower walked Burke, but that threat ended when Ensberg grounded into a double play. Ausmus returned behind the plate to catch Clemens. Chavez, who had entered in the double switch with Wheeler in the 13th, moved to first base. With a consistent 94-mph fastball that was missing from his arsenal in Game 2, Clemens took the mound for the first postseason relief outing of his career and struck out the first two batters and retired the side in order in the 16th. Brower retired the Astros in order in the bottom of the inning and gave way to pinch hitter Brian Jordan, who hit a one-out double to center in the 17th. Clemens stranded Jordan in scoring position by inducing a ground out to second from Furcal before striking out Giles.

Devine, who was born the year before Clemens made his major league debut, took over in the bottom of the 17th and retired the Astros in order. After Chipper Jones led off the 18th with a ground out to second, Andruw Jones reached on Vizcaino's error at short. Franco popped up to short for the second out. Francoeur struck out on a 94-mph fastball to end the inning.

Clemens led off the bottom of the inning and struck out while swinging from his heels, nearly falling at one point after one of his powerful, yet ineffective swings.

Burke, the man who earlier in the year wondered if he would get a chance to contribute in the majors, followed to the plate. He sent everybody home when he ripped Devine's 2-0 fastball over the left field wall, pulling his teammates in a rush toward the plate as he rounded the bases. Five hours and 50 minutes after the longest game in playoff history started, the kid who wasn't even allowed to play in the Astros' four-game series at Atlanta in May had finally pushed the Astros to the National League Championship Series with a line drive into the Crawford Boxes.

"I don't know how to explain it," Garner said. "It's been the darnedest thing I've ever seen. It looked like it was over. It looked like we were down and out. We came back. How do you explain that game? It's like the Sunday afternoon softball game where everybody on your block gets to play."

As the crowd danced in the stands, Burke gave first base coach Jose Cruz a high-five and sprinted toward second base without realizing the moment's impact. He knew he had just won the game 7-6. He just didn't realize he also had eliminated the Braves until he saw third base coach Doug Mansolino's eyes.

"I was a little bit lost in the moment until I saw Doug's face," Burke said. "All of his emotions shot into me. From that moment on it was a tidal wave of emotions that didn't settle down until a few days afterward. I almost failed to realize that series was over. The emotion was so much. Until they were jumping on me and I had a minute and a half to think, I realized the series is over. Then you realize we're going to the NLCS."

When it was all over, the Astros had set a division series record by using 23 players. The Braves used 19 players, joining the Astros to combine for the most players ever used in a division series game. Garner used eight pitchers, and Cox called on six as the combined 14 pitchers used tied the record for most in a division series game. Only Oswalt, who started and won the day before, and Pettitte, who was sick and in line for the potential Game 5, did not participate for the Astros. The game was the longest in postseason history in terms of innings and time. It was a

Chris Burke celebrates the game-winning series-clinching home run in the 18th inning against the Braves.

minute longer than the New York Yankees and Boston Red Sox played in 2004 during Game 5 of the American League Championship Series.

"Maybe this game was the perfect example of our entire season, that battle, that grind," Ensberg said. "Then all of a sudden you got Rocket going into the bullpen, getting ready, coming back out to sacrifice bunt before going out on the mound. Those are situations that he's not in. The guy's a flat-out gamer."

20

Houston Oswalt, a National League Champion

"And now it's my time (now it's my time)
It's my time to dream (my time to dream)
Dream of the sky (dream of the sky)
Make me believe that this place isn't plagued by the poison in me
Help me decide if my fire will burn out before you can breathe
Breathe into me
I stand alone
Inside
I stand alone"

—Third verse of Godsmack's "I Stand Alone"

A s they walked into the T.G.I. Friday's restaurant in downtown St. Louis, Nicole and Roy Oswalt could hardly believe what they were hearing a few hours before he started Game 6 of the National League Championship Series against the St. Louis Cardinals. Godsmack was playing over the restaurant's sound system. Nicole, who had a dream that her husband would beat the Cardinals 1-0 in Game 6, nudged Roy and asked him if he realized what song was on. Oswalt couldn't quite remember the name of the song, but the lyrics were as familiar to him as his 95-mph fastball, his biting curveball, and Nicole's soothing voice. Ever since Godsmack wrote and performed "I Stand Alone" for the sound-track to the movie *Scorpion King* in 2002, the hit had been played for

Oswalt at Minute Maid Park each time he took the mound or went to
the plate.

> Now I've told you this once before
> You can't control me
> If you try to take me down you're gonna pay
> Now I feel your every nothing that you're doing for me
> I'm picking you outta me
> you run away
> I stand alone
> Inside
> I stand alone

Throughout St. Louis, there was much talk about momentum.
Oswalt and his Astros teammates, it seemed, could not turn on their tele-
vision sets without some local newscaster showing a replay of St. Louis
Cardinals All-Star Albert Pujols's game-winning, three-run home run in
Game 5 of the NLCS.

As closer Brad Lidge moved the Astros within one out of clinching
the National League pennant on the 45th anniversary of the day Major
League Baseball awarded Houston the first major league franchise in
Texas history, Minute Maid Park rocked in anticipation on October 17.
Backup infielder Jose Vizcaino and backup catcher Raul Chavez were
actually dancing in the Astros' dugout, celebrating about 48 hours too
soon. Most of the sellout crowd of 43,470 stood on its feet while former
Astros Nolan Ryan and Enos Cabell watched in the general manager's
suite with general manager Tim Purpura, Astros president of baseball
operations Tal Smith, and front-office executives Dave Gottfried and
Ricky Bennett. Ryan, Cabell, and Smith knew better than to celebrate
prematurely. They were there in 1980 when the Astros lost a gut-
wrenching five-game NLCS against the Philadelphia Phillies after taking
a 2-1 lead in the series. Needing only one victory to reach the 1980
World Series, the Astros lost Game 4 5-3 in 10 innings before a stunned
crowd of 44,952 at the Astrodome on October 11, 1980.

A day later, the Phillies scored five runs in the eighth inning to erase
a three-run deficit and take a 7-5 lead. The Astros countered with two
runs in the bottom of the eighth, tying the score 7-7 and leading to the
fourth consecutive extra-inning game in that NLCS. Ryan gave up six
runs over seven innings, but he was taken out of the decision when his
teammates scored twice in the bottom of the eighth. Garry Maddox
ruined the Astros' hopes in the 10th with the game-winning RBI double

off Frank LaCorte. Ryan, still considered by many the greatest pitcher from Texas, understands just how easily an inning and a lead can disappear in the postseason. He appeared in firm control on October 12, 1980, when he went out for the eighth inning with a 5-2 lead.

He faced four batters without recording an out in the eighth, prompting a call to the bullpen. Joe Sambito pitched a scoreless third of an inning before he was relieved by Ken Forsch, who had not pitched since Game 1. Forsch had delivered a gutsy performance in Game 1 while holding the Phillies to three runs over eight strong innings while keeping the Astros close against Steve Carlton, who lasted seven innings and won 3-1. Five days later, Forsch relieved Sambito and gave up two hits and one run over two-thirds of an inning to lose the lead.

Twenty-five years and five days later, Lidge was on the mound in Game 5 of the 2005 NLCS hoping to complete the job. Andy Pettitte had held the Cardinals to two runs over $6\frac{1}{3}$ innings, giving way to reliever Chad Qualls with a 2-1 deficit, one out in the top of the seventh and one man on. Pettitte received no favors in the seventh inning from his defense. Leadoff hitter David Eckstein had reached on an error by shortstop Adam Everett. After Pettitte picked off Eckstein, Jim Edmonds reached safely when first baseman Mike Lamb dropped a pop up for the Astros' second error of the inning. It was as though the ghosts of Game 5 of the 1980 NLCS were haunting the Astros all over.

What if Nolan Ryan had not deflected that potential double-play grounder up the middle in the eighth inning in 1980? Would he have escaped that inning with the lead and provided the needed push toward the World Series 25 years earlier? Nobody will ever know.

In 2005, Qualls atoned for his teammates and kept the Astros within one run by inducing consecutive ground outs to third base from Pujols and Reggie Sanders.

The Astros responded with three runs in the bottom of the seventh against 2005 Cy Young Award winner Chris Carpenter. After Orlando Palmeiro led off with a ground out to short, Craig Biggio reached on an error by third baseman Hector Luna. Chris Burke, the hero of Game 4 of the division series against the Atlanta Braves, followed Biggio with a single to right field. With tension building at Minute Maid Park, Lance Berkman strolled to the plate. Carpenter challenged Berkman with a 93-mph fastball.

Berkman put all of Texas on that ball, ripping it the other way for a home run into the Crawford Boxes behind the short porch in left field. Just like that, the Astros led 4-2, and Berkman's home run seemed destined to go down as one of the most magical moments in the city of Houston's sports history.

"My thought was getting a ground ball, and I had not thrown him a pitch down and away all night," Carpenter said. "I was throwing him in all night and the ball kept coming back a couple of times on the balls he got hits on. First and third there, I'm thinking, you know, make a good quality pitch down and away and get a ground ball. I made a good, quality pitch down and away, and he hit it into the seats. So obviously it wasn't the result I was looking for. I was confident in the pitch, I was confident in the location, and the result wasn't what I wanted. Fortunately, the big man [Pujols] came back to hit a homer and win the game."

Left-hander Mike Gallo took over in the eighth and retired Larry Walker on a weak grounder back to the mound. With the lefty-lefty matchup out of the way, Phil Garner called right-hander Dan Wheeler out of the bullpen to finish the inning. Wheeler retired Mark Grudzielanek on a fly out to center and catcher Yadier Molina on a grounder to short. Folks who had been at the raucous Astrodome for Game 5 of the NLCS could not ignore the similarities with the thunderous roars that built at Minute Maid Park after Berkman's home run.

"The noise in the Astrodome was very much like it was this year at Minute Maid Park," said Smith, the general manager of the 1980 Astros.

Lidge had no trouble with John Rodriguez, who struck out swinging. John Mabry also struck out swinging, and it seemed as though Houston's long wait for the World Series was essentially over. Only the five-foot-seven, 165-pound Eckstein stood in Lidge's way. Eckstein, who struck out only 44 times in 2005, is one of the best players in baseball in terms of putting the ball in play. Back in the press box, Major League Baseball had already collected the ballots for the NLCS Most Valuable Player trophy. Richard Justice, the *Houston Chronicle*'s lead sports columnist, and I were asked to vote on the award. There was no debate. Lidge got our vote, and everybody else's for that matter. Astros media relations intern Charlie Hepp was assigned the duty of securing Lidge for the MVP presentation. Hepp was in the tunnel leading up to the home dugout, and he was ready to sprint after Lidge as soon as the final out was recorded. Inside the clubhouse, the champagne was ready, the television sets and locker stalls had already been covered in plastic. Only one out— actually one more strike—was needed for the celebration to begin.

Eckstein flicked Lidge's 1-2 slider for a single through the left side of the infield. Edmonds followed with a walk on five pitches.

"The mistake is walking Edmonds," Garner said after the game. "You have to let Edmonds hit the ball. You can't walk him, and Brad knows that."

With Pujols lumbering to the plate, Garner visited with Lidge and Ausmus on the mound after Edmonds's walk.

Garner's message was simple, "It doesn't matter if we walk him."

Garner made it clear that Lidge didn't have to give in to Pujols. Although the tying run would be at second base if Pujols received a walk, Garner was willing to take his chances. All season, Garner had told his pitching staff that he wanted somebody other than Pujols to beat them when they played the St. Louis Cardinals. Pujols had offered a little prayer in hopes that he would at least have a chance to make the final out. If he had been walked, somebody else would have had that chance.

"I know I was the fifth guy coming up in that inning, but I put my batting gloves on knowing that if I have the opportunity, I just did a little prayer that hopefully I might be the last guy to make the out," Pujols said. "That's the attitude that I had out there. I was praying, 'Just give me the strength, Lord, to get one at-bat and hopefully I can come through for my teammates.' Earlier in the game I had some chances to drive some runs in and I didn't come through it. Couldn't be better than this. Eckstein had a great at-bat plus Jimmy, taking that pitch. They were pretty close, and he just drew that walk."

Garner didn't have much time to settle into the home dugout. Lidge threw a first-pitch slider for a strike. He went with his slider on the next offering, too. That slider hung, and Pujols showed the Houston fans why he was the National League's Most Valuable Player in 2005. Only the closed roof at Minute Maid Park kept Pujols' three-run home run from clearing the stadium.

"He hit it a mile," Lidge said, only slightly exaggerating.

With one powerful swing, Pujols accomplished what seemed impossible only seconds earlier: silence. The sellout crowd stood in stunned disbelief. Up in the general manager's suite, nobody said anything. Cabell, Ryan, and Smith had visions of 1980 all over again.

"Even when Pujols came up, we all just stood," Purpura said. "I don't remember a word being said. It came out of the park, and I can't remember a word being spoken. We all just sat down again. The air let out of a tire. It was a like a punch to the gut."

By the time they started speaking again after Jason Isringhausen had retired the Astros in the bottom of the ninth to send the NLCS back to St. Louis for Game 6, Cabell turned to Ryan and told him he was tired of winning the "Almost there" trophy. The "Almost there" trophy is the one the Astros had to settle for in 1980 and 2004, seasons in which the franchise got within one victory of the World Series.

"One minute you're on the verge of clinching and going to the World Series," Tal Smith said. "A couple of minutes later, the wind is knocked out of you. Just complete silence. Everybody was just stunned and obviously very disappointed."

Godsmack's "I Stand Alone" might as well have been playing in the Astros clubhouse that disappointing night.

> You're always hiding behind your so-called goddess
> So what you don't think that we can see your face
> Resurrected back before the final fallen
> I'll never rest until I can make my own way
> I'm not afraid of fading
> I stand alone
> Feeling your sting down inside of me
> I'm not dying for it
> I stand alone
> Everything that I believe is fading
> I stand alone
> Inside
> I stand alone

Lidge had collected saves in all three of the Astros' victories in the 2005 NLCS. He collected a two-inning save in Game 2 for Oswalt to tie the best–of–seven series at one apiece. He gave up a run in Game 3, but he held on for the save in that 4–3 victory. Until that point, Lidge had gone 31 consecutive innings without giving up a run to the Cardinals, a streak that extended to September 14, 2003. Lidge also had thrown $16\frac{2}{3}$ scoreless postseason innings, dating back to the 2004 postseason, until he gave up the run on Mabry's RBI double to left field in the ninth inning of Game 3. With the help of superb glove work from Everett and backup second baseman Eric Bruntlett, Lidge escaped with the save in Game 4 as the Astros held on for a 2–1 victory to move within one victory of the World Series.

Suddenly, the Astros' All-Star closer appeared vulnerable even though he said all of the right things afterward.

"It's tough, but I told everybody in this clubhouse, I'm looking forward to going to St. Louis and winning it there," Lidge said. "This is a bump in the road, but no way is this going to get anybody down."

Actually, quite a few Astros and thousands of their fans were feeling down after losing Game 5. Berkman walked over to Lidge, hugged him, and told him he loved him. Lidge's teammates rallied around him, especially his bullpen-mates. There was no denying the crushing blow, however.

"This is devastating," Berkman said. "We were going to the World Series."

Instead, they were heading back to Busch Stadium in the same position they had been in the previous year. There was one major difference, however. Instead of starting journeyman Pete Munro in Game 6, as they did in 2004, the Astros had their 20-game winner, Oswalt, on the mound for that outing in 2005. Momentum in baseball is only as good as that day's starting pitcher, and Oswalt didn't seem very concerned.

Even Oswalt's mother was confident. Jean Oswalt didn't bother joining her husband, Billy Joe, on the drive to St. Louis from Weir, Mississippi, for Game 6. Bothered by flu-like symptoms, Jean told Billy and Roy that she'd wait to see her son in Game 3 of the World Series at Minute Maid Park.

The Astros didn't mope around after the deflating loss in Game 5. Brad Ausmus and Jeff Bagwell, the Astros' two leaders, wasted little time lightening the mood for their teammates. Once the players settled into their seats for the charter flight to Houston, Astros traveling secretary Barry Waters approached Purpura with a request. Bagwell and Ausmus wondered if Purpura would mind if they had the pilot pull a prank on Lidge. Purpura approved the gesture.

Once the plane reached cruising altitude, the pilot informed the Astros that if they looked out the left side of the plane they'd see the ball Albert Pujols hit flying past them. For a brief second, some of Lidge's closest teammates were upset at the pilots' comments. Pitching coach Jim Hickey was furious. With so much at stake, Hickey couldn't believe a pilot would take a shot at Lidge after such a disappointing loss. But everybody laughed heartily, once they realized Ausmus and Bagwell were behind the joke.

"Well, since I didn't get in the game, it's hard for me to contribute [that] night," Oswalt said in his pregame press conference a day before Game 6 and a day after Game 5. "But as far as [Game 6], I'm going to pitch the same way I pitch. I never go out there with the mindset I'm going to lose. I always go out there to win. Doesn't matter what happened yesterday. A lot of guys get caught up in what happened yesterday. You have to go do your job that day you're out there. Can't worry about yesterday."

If ever a man was destined to put the Astros in the World Series, it was Houston Oswalt's grandkid. Each time Oswalt takes the mound on the road, he is reminded of the man who taught him about work ethic. Houston died in 1999, when his now-famous grandson Roy was a little-known top prospect in the Midwest League. As a rookie with the Astros two years later, Oswalt smiled when he put on the Astros' road uniforms.

Across the front of his No. 44 jersey, it said Houston. On the back, it read Oswalt. Houston Oswalt, welcome to the major leagues.

At Busch Stadium on October 19, 2005, the Astros wore their solid grey road uniforms against the Cardinals. Among the crowd of 52,438 for what would be the last game played at Busch Stadium, Billy Joe Oswalt sat with his oldest daughter, Patricia Lynn; his daughter-in-law, Nicole; and Oswalt's longtime agent, Bob Garber.

Left-hander Mark Mulder, who lost to Oswalt in Game 2, retired the Astros in order in the top of the first inning in Game 6. Oswalt countered by retiring leadoff hitter David Eckstein before issuing a walk to Edmonds in the bottom of the first. Oswalt struck out Pujols and induced a grounder to third base from Larry Walker to end the first. Oswalt got all of the runs he needed in the Astros' two-run third inning. Ausmus led off the third with a single through the left side. Everett followed with an infield single to short. Oswalt followed with a sacrifice bunt toward the mound, chopping the bunt a bit too hard. Mulder fielded the ball cleanly and spun toward third and then second to see if he could get a force out. Mulder might have gambled correctly if he had thrown to third base without hesitation. He went for the sure out at first instead.

Mulder unraveled soon thereafter. His first pitch to Craig Biggio almost hit Biggio. Since 1900, no man has taken more plunkings for the team than Biggio, who has been hit 273 times in his career. Biggio didn't take one for the team this time, however. He got out of the way for the team, letting Mulder's pitch go in the dirt and behind him for a wild pitch. Molina had no chance of saving Mulder, and Ausmus sprinted home to give the Astros a 1-0 lead. Everett also advanced on the wild pitch, and Biggio drove him in with a single to left. Mulder escaped further damage by inducing a line out to right from Willy Taveras and a fielder's-choice grounder to short from Berkman.

"That's big getting the early runs," Oswalt said. "Once you get the early runs, you put pressure back on them to do something. And the more guys you can keep off base, the less the crowd is going to get into it."

The Cardinals mounted their own threat in the bottom of the third. After retiring the first two batters in the inning, Oswalt hit Eckstein with a pitch. Edmonds worked the count to 3-2, and the sellout crowd of Busch Stadium began to rock with anticipation because Game 5 hero Pujols and his powerful bat were waiting on deck.

Oswalt had escaped a similar situation six days earlier in Game 2. With two men on and Pujols on deck in the fifth inning of Game 2, Oswalt flicked a slider in against Edmonds for a called third strike to end a threat. Ausmus and Oswalt deemed that slider and called third strike the biggest pitch Oswalt made in Game 2. Six days later, Edmonds, who had become quite successful at sitting on Oswalt's superb curveball, surely had to think that Oswalt would be confident enough to throw him a slider with the count full in the third inning of Game 6.

This time, Oswalt challenged Edmonds with a 96-mph fastball. Edmonds couldn't turn on the fastball. He merely popped it up to Berkman at first base to end the inning. Jason Lane made it 3-0 with a home run to left field in the fourth inning. Oswalt carried a no-hitter into the fifth, but Oswalt hit Mark Grudzielanek with a pitch. Molina followed with a single to right field, giving St. Louis its first hit. Oswalt and his teammates received a boost from the umpires after Abraham Nunez followed Molina with a fielder's-choice grounder to the mound.

Rushing to field Nunez's grounder, Oswalt slipped on the mound. He recovered in time, but he rushed his throw in hopes of the force out at second. Shortstop Everett had to abandon second base to keep Oswalt's throw from sailing into the outfield. Noticing Everett's predicament, Molina tried to run around Everett's tag. Everett countered with an acrobatic, circus lunge at the burly Molina. To the dismay of the Cardinals and their fans, second base umpire Greg Gibson thought he saw Everett tag Molina. Gibson called Molina out, drawing Molina's wrath. Cardinals manager Tony La Russa sprinted out of the dugout to argue the call. Replays indicated that Everett never applied a tag, but Gibson stuck to his call.

Instead of having the bases loaded and nobody out, St. Louis had runners at the corners with one out. John Rodriguez's pinch sacrifice fly to center got the Cardinals within 3-1. Oswalt kept the lead at 3-1 by getting Eckstein on a 94-mph fastball for a called third strike. The Astros countered in the top of the sixth against reliever Jason Marquis, the third pitcher of the night for the Cardinals.

Chris Burke and Ausmus jumped on Marquis to put runners on first and third with consecutive one-out singles. Burke sent his single through the left side of the infield, and Ausmus sent his to right field to put runners at the corners. One inning after his phantom tag, Everett came through at the plate and gave the Astros a 4-1 lead. Marquis got Oswalt on a called third strike to end the sixth, but the Astros jumped on him again in the seventh. Biggio led off the seventh with a single to left, and Taveras sacrificed him over to second. La Russa called left-hander Randy Flores to face Berkman.

After Flores induced the second out on Berkman's fly out to right, La Russa went to his bullpen again. Right-hander Julian Tavarez was brought in to face Morgan Ensberg, who greeted him with an RBI single to left field. An inning after Oswalt got Reggie Sanders on a called third strike to strand Walker at second base, Oswalt retired the first two batters in the bottom of the seventh. Nunez hit a two-out single up the middle, but Oswalt induced a grounder to first from So Taguchi. Oswalt raced to first base, received the toss from Berkman, and beat Taguchi by a foot for the final out of the seventh.

Oswalt responded to that out by pumping his right fist violently at his side in one of his rare shows of emotion. Chad Qualls handled the Cardinals in the eighth, and Dan Wheeler took over in the ninth. As Lidge watched from the bullpen, Wheeler retired Walker on a called third strike for the first out. Mabry struck out swinging for the second out, and for the second game in a row the Astros were within one out of the World Series. Grudzielanek kept the Cardinals' slim hopes alive with a two-out single to left field. That's as close as St. Louis got to another upset. Time had indeed run out on the Cardinals and Busch Stadium. Wheeler induced a fly ball to right field from Molina, and Jason Lane settled in under it at 10:22 p.m. on October 19, 2005, for the moment Houston baseball fans had awaited since the franchise had been awarded 45 years earlier.

"I wasn't quite sure what was actually happening," Wheeler said. "I saw Jason make the catch and I was like, 'Is that the third out? Is this game over and are we going to the World Series?' It's tough to comprehend."

Finally, the Astros were left to comprehend a trip to the World Series instead of another crushing loss. Houston Oswalt's kid kept the Cardinals silent and pushed the Astros franchise to the biggest stage.

"They had a lot of things as a team that they did well to win four games," La Russa said of the Astros. "But I thought the first and maybe the most important key they had was the fella that pitched today, pitched Game 2, and just worked us over, got them even. And today when we were trying to get to Game 7, he just worked us over again. He pitched outstanding, and as long as this game is played, when a pitcher out there is pitching that way, you're not going to do much. It makes your team look like, 'What's going on?' You can't get on base. You can't string any hits together. Just outstanding pitching. I think Oswalt was one of the differences."

By holding the Cardinals to three hits, one walk, and one run with six strikeouts over seven innings in Game 6 after holding them to five hits and one run over seven innings in Game 2, Oswalt earned the NLCS Most Valuable Player Award. When the award was handed to the Astros' No. 44, the jersey said Houston on the front, and Oswalt on the back.

"Well, there's a reason the clubhouse was loose today," Garner said. "When you're running Roy out there, you've got to feel pretty good

Roy Oswalt receives the NLCS MVP trophy, which he gave to his father, Billy.

about your chances. I also think that we see a true competitor here with Roy, and the way he went about his business tonight gave us great confidence. He went after them, he challenged them. This is a powerful ball club. They are powerful from top to bottom, and Roy didn't back down. He struggled—not really struggled but labored a little bit—in the middle part of the game, not because he was weak or pitching around anybody. They are just a good-hitting team. They foul off a lot of pitches, they get you deep into the count and they are tough. But he never gave in, and I think that set the tone for the whole ballgame. We just kept picking away a bunch of singles and came up with some big hits when we needed them. I think maybe a big point in the game is when they scored the one run, was it the third inning? They scored a run in the bottom of the third, we came right back out and put a run right back on the board. To me that stopped any sort of potential momentum on their side of the game. I thought Roy did what he does so well, shuts the offense down on their side, and we did a nice job on our side offensively."

Oswalt celebrated with his teammates in the visitors' clubhouse for a few minutes after the victory, but he ducked out while the champagne baths were in full swing. With a firm grip on the MVP trophy, he snuck out of the clubhouse and headed to the visitors' family room a few feet away. As his teammates' family members patted him on the back, he hugged his wife, Nicole, who couldn't say a word through her joyful tears. Roy hugged his sister and three good friends who had made the six-hour drive from Mississippi with Billy.

Jeff Bagwell celebrates with his teammates the franchise's first World Series berth.

Houston Oswalt never was much into sports, but he always found time to get away from work to watch his son, Billy, play football. Billy carried that trait into adulthood, always getting to work at dawn so he could finish in time to watch his children play their sports. Whether it was Patricia in softball or Brian and Roy in baseball and football, Billy and Jean always found time to attend their sporting events.

When others shared their rude doubts, Billy and Jean worked on building their children's confidence. Roy has never forgotten the sacrifices his father made to shuttle him to baseball practices. Those sacrifices were fresh on Oswalt's mind as he made eye contact with his father after Game 6.

With Nicole still hanging on tightly around his waist, Oswalt lifted the NLCS MVP trophy with his right hand, hugged his father with his left, and handed the trophy over to his father.

"I've won this for you," Roy said.

Through tears of joy, Billy thanked his son with a tight embrace but few words.

"He got up at 5:30 a.m., got back home at 5:00 p.m. to get me to the game by 7:00," Oswalt said of his father. "To give it to him that meant more to me than winning it. He didn't want to take it, but that's the way he is. It was more special, though, for me to see his face once I gave it to him, and just the way he believed in me. Growing up, people used to come by and ask why he spent so much time with me out in the yard throwing the ball. Hopefully those guys see that on TV today."

Oswalt and the rest of the Astros boarded a plane back to Houston after winning the National League pennant. Billy, Nicole, and Patricia Lynn returned to Mississippi. Thinking nothing of it, Billy Oswalt walked out of Busch Stadium holding the NLCS MVP trophy in plain sight. Thousands of fans lingered outside Busch Stadium for a few hours after the game, providing a sea of red welcoming Billy as he walked out. After a few steps, Garber suggested that Billy cover the trophy. Billy took off his jacket, put it over the trophy, and walked toward his car. Local police who were nearby gave them an escort. Once again, an Oswalt was working his way easily through the Cardinals with the major prize.

The Astros were finally headed to the World Series, and Houston Oswalt's grandkid pushed them there.

21
The World Series

United States attorney general Alberto B. Gonzales grew up in a home of modest means in Houston. His family couldn't afford to attend any games when Major League Baseball hit town in 1962. He attentively followed the new Colt .45s from afar through their inaugural 1962 season. He marveled in 1965 when the franchise opened the Astrodome and changed the team's name to the Astros. He appreciated the spectacle as the Astros played the first game in Major League Baseball history indoors on April 9 in an exhibition against Mickey Mantle's New York Yankees.

Gonzales watched on television and dreamed of one day having enough money to attend a game at the building referred to as the Eighth Wonder of the World. He realized his father Pablo's budget didn't provide enough discretionary income for taking the family to watch the Astros in the 1960s.

Texas was welcomed into the majors when MLB announced on October 17, 1960, that Houston and New York would receive two expansion National League franchises. On that day, Houstonians started dreaming about landing in the World Series. Since then, several generations of Texas boys and girls turned grey waiting for the World Series to land in the Lone Star State. Most fans remain young in spirit as they recall their first trips to Colt Stadium, the Astrodome, or Enron Field–Minute Maid Park.

They cherished the memories left behind by Nolan Ryan and Mike Scott, Larry Dierker and Jose Cruz, Don Wilson and J.R. Richard, Roy Oswalt and Roger Clemens, Andy Pettitte and Lance Berkman, Carlos Beltran and Jeff Kent, and Jeff Bagwell and Craig Biggio.

Some of the legendary names in baseball history passed through the Astros clubhouse—Ryan, Clemens, Joe Morgan, Leo Durocher, Yogi Berra and Milo Hamilton—either as players, coaches, managers, or broadcasters. Almost everybody in Houston has a favorite player or memory.

For Gonzales, that first kiss, so to speak, happened in 1967 or 1968. He cannot remember the exact date, game, or opponent. He remembers the family ties, and isn't that what baseball is all about anyway? At the time, the Astros had a program that gave free tickets for youths who received straight As in school. Gonzales won his family's first tickets that way. He picked up the tickets at his elementary school and rushed home to wait for his father.

"I remember waiting in the road, and my dad finally came," Gonzales said. "We finally came, and I still remember the image of seeing the field for the first time."

Gonzales has watched countless Astros games live since then. Like every other loyal Astros fans, he had been waiting by the side of the road as other teams reached the World Series since 1962. Astros fans watched with dismay as their expansion twins, the New York Mets, won the 1969 World Series with a Houston kid named Nolan Ryan. They watched the Mets reach the World Series again in 1973 and again in 1986, pushing past the Astros in the 1986 National League Championship Series to meet Clemens's Boston Red Sox. They watched the Mets get there again in 2000. And after getting within one victory of the World Series in 2004 with Beltran leading the way, Astros fans entered 2005 disappointed after the Mets courted Beltran and landed him in Queens.

To be an Astros fan is to understand coping with heartbreak. For that is what the 1980 NLCS brought when the Astros got within one victory of the World Series before losing two straight against the Philadelphia Phillies. Disappointing is the only way to explain 1998, the year the Astros were loaded on offense and on the mound. That team won a franchise-record 102 games, picked up ace Randy Johnson at the trading deadline, and had Biggio, Bagwell, and Moises Alou in their primes. Seemingly destined to reach the World Series a year after losing in the division series, Johnson's Astros were done after four games in the 1998 division series against the San Diego Padres.

If the Astros ever reached the World Series, Gonzales and many of their most loyal fans vowed to be there watching somehow. They had been waiting for the World Series so long there was a sense of disbelief after Oswalt dominated the St. Louis Cardinals at Busch Stadium in Game 6 of the NLCS to win the Astros' first National League pennant.

"Even after they won Game 6 in St. Louis, it was almost as if it wasn't real," Gonzales said. "I just felt so proud and so happy. It was just unbelievable."

The Astros line up for the pregame festivities at the first World Series game played in the state of Texas.

The attorney general made plans to leave Washington D.C. and attend the Astros' first World Series games at home. Before those games at Minute Maid Park, however, the Astros had to start the World Series on the road with two games against the American League champion Chicago White Sox at U.S. Cellular Field.

After winning the American League Central with an AL-best 99–63 record, the White Sox cruised through the postseason with their outspoken and somewhat whacky manager Ozzie Guillen leading the way. They eliminated the 2004 World Series champion Boston Red Sox from the division series in a three-game sweep. They beat the Los Angeles Angels in five games in the American League Championship Series.

As the Astros prepared to play the St. Louis Cardinals in Game 6 on October 19, the White Sox had already clinched their place in the World Series three days earlier. The White Sox were merely working out in the mornings waiting to see whom they'd face. Some White Sox fans wanted to face the Cardinals, the only team rival Chicago Cubs fans hated as much as they hated the South Siders at U.S. Cellular Field. Others wanted to face the Cardinals because they wanted to see St. Louis manager Tony La Russa, a former White Sox manager.

After finally beating La Russa's Cardinals on October 19, the Astros were so high it wouldn't have taken much to lift them up for the 50-minute flight to Chicago. They wanted to share the moment with their fans in Houston, though. The Astros left Busch Stadium after Game 6 and headed home to regroup and sneak in a night at home before heading to the Windy City. When they landed in Houston at 4 a.m., hundreds of fans awaited them at the airport with signs thanking them for reaching the World Series.

Thousands more arrived at Minute Maid Park the morning of October 21 to send the team off to Chicago for that afternoon's workout.

"Well, I wanted to go home," Houston manager Phil Garner said. "I wanted to see what was going on in Houston. Our players generally are homebound guys. We had a big pep rally when we left Houston. And that's exciting."

The White Sox and their fans had five days to lather up for the Fall Classic. Some Sox officials were pulling for St. Louis because it would set up a lovefest between La Russa and White Sox chairman Jerry Reinsdorf, who still adored La Russa despite firing him in 1986. Such a matchup also would rub salt in the collective wounds of Cubs fans, who would have had to watch and read about their two biggest rivals playing on baseball's largest stage.

The Astros brought enough intrigue. Chicago media and Sox fans didn't need much prodding to remember Garner's teams in Milwaukee and Detroit were in bitter feuds with the Sox in the 1990s that featured former Sox manager Terry Bevington getting Garner in a headlock under a pile, and Garner challenging Sox announcers Ken Harrelson and Tom Paciorek to a fight for accusing Garner of ordering his pitchers to throw at the White Sox's batters.

Not all of the memories going into the World Series were bitter. There were just as many relationships renewed. Houston general manager Tim Purpura grew up in Oak Lawn, a South Chicago suburb, cheering for the White Sox. Purpura's father, Jim, raised him as a devout White Sox fan, and the pair attended hundreds of White Sox games together over the years. Purpura still displays the wedding picture he and his wife, Shari, took with White Sox hats on, following a tradition established by his parents. Purpura secured 30 tickets to Games 1 and 2 of the World Series for friends and relatives, passing them out only after his family members disowned the White Sox.

Jim Purpura taught Tim about baseball, usually by using the White Sox as examples. He'd point out the scouts and the general manager in the stands. Jim Purpura set his son on the course to become a general manager one day, and he would have been proud on November 1, 2004, when his son was promoted from assistant general manager to the general manager of the Astros. Jim Purpura died on August 1, 1991, when his son was still in law school after enrolling on the advice of former White Sox general manager Roland Hemond.

Purpura visits his father's grave annually. In 2005, he visited his father's grave on May 24 before the Astros hit their famous 15-30 mark later that evening in a loss to the Chicago Cubs at Wrigley Field.

"Basically I just went there and said a prayer and thought about him," Purpura said of his May 24 visit to his father's grave. "It was the first time I had visited him since I became general manager. You think, 'Boy I wish you could be here and experiencing this.' I guess I didn't think about the fact that we were 15-30. He would have been extremely proud. He's the one that first made me aware of people like scouting directors and farm directors and general managers. We'd go to games and he'd teach me about the players, but also about the general managers."

The World Series also was a reunion of former Yankees pitchers Clemens and Pettitte and the White Sox's Jose Contrera and Orlando "El Duque" Hernandez. Clemens and his Game 1 opponent Contreras were teammates with the New York Yankees in 2003. Contreras, a Cuban defector, never forgot how Clemens treated him, Japanese native Hideki Matsui, and rookie Nick Johnson to dinner during the 2003 spring training.

"I wish I had him on my team, but too bad we have to face him," Contreras said before Game 1.

The White Sox had been interested in signing Clemens as a free agent when he left the Boston Red Sox after the 1996 season. White Sox executives had backed off because they thought Clemens was a medical risk.

That was after the 1996 season and before Clemens won the last four of his seven Cy Young Awards, starting with the 1997-1998 seasons with Toronto. The White Sox skipped on Clemens and signed Jaime Navarro, who had three losing seasons and was out of baseball after the 2000 season, the year Clemens collected his second consecutive World Series ring with the Yankees.

The White Sox were finally right about Clemens's health concerns nine years later entering Game 1. Chicago scouts had been tracking the Astros since late September. They noticed he was hardly agile in the NLCS and wondered how his legs would fare in the 50-degree temperatures.

Their suspicions were confirmed when Clemens had to leave Game 1 of the World Series at U.S. Cellular Field after two innings because of a left hamstring strain that had bothered him for six weeks. Clemens was taxed by a 24-pitch first inning in which he allowed an opposite-field home run to Jermaine Dye that gave the White Sox a 1-0 lead. Clemens's problems were more apparent when he gave up two runs on three hits during a 30-pitch second inning. Scott Podsednik worked Clemens over on a 12-pitch at-bat before striking out on a 92-mph fastball.

"I had the problem in the second inning, and fought my way through that inning, got through that inning," Clemens said then. "I came up here [to the clubhouse] as quick as I could to take my [hamstring] sleeve off and [to] have them check it and see if there was anything I could do so I could continue. And the fluid already started to build up in my leg. So they gave me some medication, and I'm going to treat it and that's all I can tell you from there."

As far as the White Sox were concerned, getting to Houston's bullpen early was a big break because the Astros lined up their rotation with Pettitte starting Game 2 in Chicago and the formidable Oswalt at Minute Maid Park in Game 3. The Astros were hardly fazed by losing Clemens early. They battled back on a solo home run to center by Mike Lamb, who ripped the pitch over the head of his former Cal State Fullerton teammate Aaron Rowand to cut Chicago's lead to 3-1. Berkman pulled an off-speed pitch down the right field line for a two-out, two-run game-tying double in the third inning.

Rookie left-hander Wandy Rodriguez, who had thrown only 16 pitches in October and did not appear in the NLCS, relieved Clemens to start the third. He made only one mistake in his 3⅓ innings of relief, giving up a home run to Joe Crede in the fourth inning as the White Sox took a 4-3 lead. The Astros missed golden opportunities to at least tie the score in the sixth, seventh, and eighth. Willy Taveras led off the sixth with a double. He was stranded after Berkman grounded to first, Morgan Ensberg grounded to third, and Lamb grounded to second.

Contreras, who already had thrown 25 postseason innings, started to fatigue in the seventh. He hit Bagwell to lead off and Brad Ausmus one out later. Bagwell moved into scoring position on Adam Everett's fielder's-choice grounder to short, but Crede haunted the Astros again with his glove. Crede made a quick stop of Biggio's grounder to end the rally one inning after he stopped a potential game-tying hit by Ensberg.

"We play pretty good defense almost every day," Guillen said. "And Joe is a Gold Glover. One thing about it is that's why I told my pitchers, 'Make sure we keep it in the ballpark and we have a chance to catch it.'"

The Astros' frustrations grew in the eighth. Taveras led off with his second double, prompting Guillen to call on left-handed reliever Neal Cotts to flip the switch-hitting Berkman to his right side. Berkman pulled a single to left field. Taveras had to stop at third. Cotts, a former middle reliever who emerged as the White Sox's primary left-handed specialist, recovered to strike out Ensberg and Lamb in succession.

That set up a classic showdown between Bagwell, the greatest hitter in Astros history, and rookie Bobby Jenks, the White Sox closer. Jenks's 100-mph fastball had overshadowed his poor behavior in the past, on and off the field, which had led the Los Angeles Angels of Anaheim to waive him in December 2004. White Sox general manager Kenny Williams picked him up, and Jenks found a home with the White Sox.

The 24-year-old Jenks showed no fear in going right after Bagwell, whose ailing right shoulder deprived him of the quickness and power that had made him one of baseball's most feared sluggers. Bagwell had not started since May 3 because of his right shoulder problems. He had had career-saving right shoulder surgery in June, and many assumed he'd likely never play again. By September, he was off the disabled list.

Bagwell accepted the starts as the Astros' designated hitter for Games 1 and 2 of the World Series only after Garner assured him the move was not made for sentimental reasons.

"Phil's been nothing but great with me," Bagwell said. "He's really been straight up with me. He's helped me along at times here, and I appreciate the confidence. That's why I'm in there. I told Phil this cannot be a charity case or a sentimental pick, which I know Phil's not about. This is what he wanted. He wanted me to be here and get the opportunity to play. He thinks I can do something, and I hope I reward him for it. I was excited. This is what I tried to come back for. The thing in the back of my mind was if I [could] get to the World Series, I could DH, and I [was] going to get the opportunity."

A month earlier, Bagwell had shown the Astros he could still hit. In what was one of the most exciting moments of the Astros' season, Bagwell came off the bench in the bottom of the ninth inning on September 16 against the Milwaukee Brewers. He had only made one pinch-hit appearance since coming off the disabled list September 9. With the score tied 1-1, a man on third, and two outs, Bagwell hit a walk-off single to right field as his teammates rushed out to celebrate.

A little more than a month later, there was no celebration for Bagwell or the Astros against Jenks.

Bagwell couldn't catch up to a 100-mph fastball that sent a sold-out crowd of 41,206 into delirium. The White Sox added an insurance run off Russ Springer in the bottom of the eighth to beat the Astros 5-3.

"If I see that pitch 250 times," Bagwell said, "I'm still not going to hit it."

Bagwell's at-bat was not the reason the Astros lost Game 1. The Astros went two for 11 with runners in scoring position, a trait that would haunt them throughout the World Series.

"I thought we did a pretty good job of hitting the ball well against Contreras," Garner said. "We hit some balls a foot one way or the other it might be a different ballgame. But it wasn't. They made the plays. Part of this game is throwing the ball over the plate and making your opposition put the ball in play. And they did that better than we did."

Wet weather raised the possibility of a postponement in Game 2, but the rains let up long enough to start that game after only a seven-minute delay. With Pettitte carrying a 14-9 lifetime postseason record, the Astros stood a decent chance of coming home with the Series tied 1-1. Ensberg gave Pettitte a 1-0 lead in the second inning with a home run off left-hander Mark Buehrle. The bottom of the White Sox's batting order countered with two runs in the bottom of the inning on an RBI single by Crede and an RBI ground out by Rowand.

Berkman continued his production with a game-tying sacrifice fly in the third inning and a two-run double in the fifth to give the Astros a 4-2 lead. The Astros carried a 4-2 lead into the bottom of the seventh. Although Pettitte had been finished after six, the team was in a good position, needing only nine more outs.

The Astros couldn't hold the lead in one of the zaniest finishes in World Series history. The White Sox loaded the bases in the seventh. Juan Uribe doubled; Tadahito Iguchi walked. Astros reliever Dan Wheeler hit Dye with a pitch with two outs. Or so home plate umpire Jeff Nelson thought. Television replays revealed that Wheeler's pitch hit Dye's bat. Dye admitted as much later.

"It didn't hit me," Dye said. "It hit my bat. I turned around, and the umpire told me to go to first. I wasn't going to argue with him."

Although Garner was surprised that Nelson didn't ask for help on the call, he didn't lose sight of the situation as he summoned Chad Qualls from the bullpen to face cleanup hitter Paul Konerko, who batted only .176 in situations in which he had two outs and the bases loaded during the regular season. Konerko ripped Qualls's first pitch over the left field fence for a grand slam, giving the White Sox a 6-4 lead that seemed secure with Jenks ready.

"I came in and threw one pitch, and all of a sudden the game's in their favor," Qualls said. "It's just the situation I've been put in. I've done it over the whole season, and I've succeeded, but tonight it just didn't work out. I don't know. For whatever reason, it just happens that way sometimes. As soon as he hit it, I said, 'Uh-oh.' Other than that, I was just trying to make my pitch, and I didn't make my pitch."

Jenks started the ninth inning for the White Sox, and Bagwell gained some revenge from the previous night with a compact swing for a leadoff single to center. After Lane struck out, Chris Burke walked. The runners moved up on Ausmus's ground out to first. Jose Vizcaino, a valuable member of the New York Yankees' last world championship team in 2000, came up to pinch-hit for Adam Everett.

The switch-hitting Vizcaino poked an opposite-field single to left. Burke sprinted in and barely beat catcher A.J. Pierzynski's tag for the tying run. With the temperature dropping to around 40 degrees, the game had the makings of an extra-inning affair. Garner summoned closer Brad Lidge to pitch the ninth.

Lidge was on the mound for the first time since he gave up St. Louis Cardinals slugger Albert Pujols's game-winning three-run home run in Game 5 of the NLCS at Minute Maid Park. He had gone six days between appearances, and his rust was evident. Uribe, who hit two doubles in the game, flied out to center. Podsednik, who didn't hit a home run in 514 regular-season at-bats, followed Uribe.

Lidge fell behind early, and Podsednik assumed he had nothing to lose if Lidge came in with a 2-1 fastball instead of his suddenly shaky slider. Podsednik correctly guessed he'd see a 2-1 fastball. He jumped on the offering and hit a drive to center. Taveras and right fielder Lane broke immediately to the fence. Not even the steady rain could knock down the ball and avoid one of the most unbelievable endings in World Series history—a game-winning home run by Podsednik.

"I was really surprised it was Podsednik," Lidge said. "You don't expect him to do that. He's not a home run guy during the regular season, but I guess in that situation he was going for a home run, so I'll learn from that and make a different pitch next time."

Podsednik, a West Texas native who spent the previous two seasons with the Milwaukee Brewers, has hit seven of his 22 career home runs against the Astros. None was greater than the one he deposited over U.S. Cellular Field's center field wall to give the White Sox a 7-6 victory in Game 2, giving Chicago a 2-0 lead in the best-of-seven World Series heading to Houston.

"Well, we're certainly not in a good spot," Garner said. "We had a chance to win this ballgame tonight. As badly as we played, we had a chance to win this ballgame. And that would have been a feel-good experience. We have to go home and regroup and see what we can do now. This is not the best situation, but it's the one we're in… We'll bounce back. We'll make a Series out of this."

The Astros came home to play their first home World Series game with anger and disappointment. They were disappointed after losing two games they could have won. Several players also were mad that a fan pulled the hair of Biggio's wife, Patty, during Game 2 at Chicago. The

Biggios elected not to press charges, but Guillen offered an apology to Biggio the next day.

"My brother-in-law ended up putting him against the wall," Craig Biggio said. "That's pretty sorry. You don't slap a New Jersey girl and get away with it."

When the World Series shifted to Houston for Game 3, Astros officials put all of the White Sox's immediate family in adjoining sections, 113-114, at Minute Maid Park. The Astros make it a policy not to separate the seats of their opponents' immediate family members. The White Sox didn't offer the Astros the same courtesy.

White Sox officials spread the Astros' immediate family members throughout U.S. Cellular Field for Games 1 and 2. Patty Biggio and her family were sitting next to Jennifer Everett in seats sprinkled with White Sox fans. Other Astros players had their family members all over the stadium, and there were multiple horror stories about vulgar treatment from White Sox fans. If you were wearing any Astros gear at U.S. Cellular Field during the World Series, you were probably harassed or taunted in some way.

One White Sox follower referred to White Sox fans as 10th-rate soccer hooligans, and some White Sox followers lived down to that reputation. Whatever the case, the White Sox fans didn't behave with the same cuddly, classy demeanor the Astros had grown accustomed to seeing when visiting the North Side's Wrigley Field to play the Cubs.

"Some of the treatment that the Astros' families received at U.S. Cellular Field was a huge black eye for the city of Chicago," Ausmus said. "Now, I understand that's not indicative of all the people in the Chicago area, because I have friends and relatives there. I know people of Chicago are overwhelmingly good people. But if I was from Chicago, I'd be embarrassed by the way the Astros' families were treated by White Sox fans."

The Astros' discontent was further fueled by Major League Baseball's decision to order the opening of the retractable roof at Minute Maid Park for Game 3 under cool, but clear skies.

"We operate the postseason," said Jimmie Lee Solomon, Major League Baseball's executive vice president of baseball operations. "The clubs operate the regular season."

The Astros were 40-18 when the roof was closed, compared to 15-11 with the roof open and 2-0 when the roof was opened during the middle of the game. For two years, Major League Baseball let the Astros use their own discretion as to when they'd close the retractable roof at Minute Maid Park. The pitching staff preferred the roof closed, believing the ball didn't carry as much with the roof open. The Astros hitters liked it closed too because they would benefit from playing in a controlled environment.

Asked during the 2004 division series if he thought the Astros should open the roof, Atlanta's John Smoltz sided with the Astros after he and the Braves snapped the Astros' 19-game home winning streak in Game 4 of that division series.

"No, that's their call," he said. "That's why it's home-field advantage. That's why they play here. It's whatever they [want], you know. This is a place where, obviously, 18 in a row or 19 in a row until today, they can do whatever they want here. They feel they're unbeatable, and they pretty much are so far."

The Astros had won four of five postseason games at home with the roof closed in 2005 and eight of 10 dating to the 2004 postseason, and the Astros didn't hide their disappointment with commissioner Bud Selig's office. For years, people in baseball had said Selig was Reinsdorf's puppet. Many people had said Reinsdorf put Selig in power, and the Astros' cries about the roof fell on deaf ears. Astros owner Drayton McLane pleaded with Selig to let him keep the roof closed. McLane, Purpura, and Astros president of business operations Pam Gardner lobbied Solomon to no avail.

"I think it's a joke," Ausmus said. "Nobody tells teams how long they need to grow their grass. They don't mandate what uniform a team has to wear during the course of a game. They way overstepped their bounds."

Ausmus's teammates joined him in those sentiments. Nonetheless, there was enough reason for the Astros to feel confident about possibly getting back in the World Series with Oswalt staked to a 4-0 lead after four innings in Game 3. Moreover, there was much to be proud of as Houston held the first World Series game in the state of Texas.

Former president and first lady George and Barbara Bush, attorney general Gonzales, and Nolan Ryan were in attendance among the sellout crowd of 42,848. Drayton and Elizabeth McLane's two sons and daughters-in-law were also in from Dallas and Birmingham, Alabama.

"The fact that we're in Houston and that it's the first time in Texas, it's exciting to see the fans so enthusiastic and excited about it," Ryan told the *Houston Chronicle*. "For me, another perspective is [that] so many of the players who are on the Astros team have come through Round Rock, and I've watched them develop and play in a World Series."

The roof was a mere afterthought once Oswalt threw the first World Series pitch in the state of Texas at 7:39 p.m. to Podsednik. Oswalt caught Podsednik looking at a called third strike. Iguchi followed with a single through the right side. Oswalt escaped the inning when he induced Dye's double-play grounder to short.

Perhaps fittingly, Biggio led off the first inning with a double to left, collecting the first World Series hit in the state of Texas at 7:47 p.m. The man who has played the most games for a Texas franchise collected the first hit for a Texas team in the Series. After Taveras popped his bunt attempt to the third baseman, Berkman gave the Astros a 1-0 lead at 7:51 p.m. with a single to left. The Astros jumped on White Sox right-hander Jon Garland again in the third. Everett led off the third with an infield single to short. He was almost caught stealing, but Uribe hit him with his throw to first as he ran back to the bag. Oswalt sacrificed Everett over to second, and Biggio drove him in with a single through the right side at 8:25 p.m. Garland struck out Taveras for the second out. Berkman followed with a single to right, and Ensberg made it 3-0 with a single through the left side. The Astros went ahead 4-0 when Jason Lane led off with a shot to left-center field in the fourth for the first World Series home run in Texas at 8:47 p.m.

Oswalt had allowed five runs in his previous 25⅓ innings and entered the fifth inning with a 4-0 lead. He gave up only two runs through 14 innings against the Cardinals to win the NLCS MVP trophy, so there was reason for the Astros to assume they'd get their first World Series victory on this night.

Forty-six pitches later in the fifth, the White Sox led 5-4. Crede continued to haunt the Astros with a leadoff homer in the fifth. Oswalt threw one pitch that inning for each year that had passed since the White Sox were last in the World Series. Oswalt needed only 54 pitches through four innings, so he'd never imagined he'd need a career-high 46 throws to get out of the fifth. After Crede's homer to right field, Uribe singled to center. Oswalt struck out Garland for the first out. Podsednik followed with a single through the right side, and Iguchi made it 4-2 with an RBI single up the middle. Dye's blooper to center cut the Astros' lead to 4-3. After Konerko flied out to center field for the second out, Pierzynski gave the White Sox a 5-4 lead with a two-run double to right-center field. Oswalt walked Rowand, the ninth batter of the inning. His control problems continued when he hit Crede with a pitch, loading the bases and prompting a nasty stare from Crede.

Crede's reaction sparked some screams from the Astros dugout before Uribe flied out to right field for the final out of the inning. Garner yelled at Crede as he walked toward first after Oswalt had hit him. Volatile White Sox designated hitter Carl Everett, who was relegated to the bench because of National League rules that don't employ a designated hitter,

Brad Ausmus's body language says it all after the Astros lost Game 3.

leapt to the dugout rail to shout at Garner. White Sox general manager Ken Williams fired the sharpest words at Garner.

"It's best that I don't talk about Phil Garner," Williams told Chicago reporters. "I had problems with him even before he said those things about my players, and it's just best kept between the two of us. I have no reason or desire to speak to him about anything."

The next day, Garner apologized to the fans who may have read his lips when he and Everett were caught screaming obscenities at each other during the Fox telecast.

"Well, Crede was hit with a pitch and popped off to Oswalt," Garner said. "I took exception to that. We made a whole bunch of pitches in the middle of the plate, and they've been hitting pretty good. And you haven't seen any of our guys yelling. When you miss a pitch inside a few inches, take it and go [to first], plain and simple.... I do need to apologize. I don't apologize for my passion, but I do apologize."

The Astros eventually tied Game 3 in the eighth inning on Lane's RBI double, but they were in one of their worst slumps. They stranded the tying or go-ahead run in five consecutive innings while using seven relievers. The Astros had a chance to win it in the ninth when Burke drew a one-out walk off of Hernandez. Burke reached second on Hernandez's errant pickoff throw to first base and stole third base on a 1-0 pitch to Biggio. Hernandez walked Biggio, but he struck out Taveras. Guillen visited Hernandez and ordered him to pitch around Berkman. Hernandez fell behind in the count 2-0 and then intentionally walked

Berkman to load the bases. Ensberg stranded the bases loaded when he struck out. The Astros stranded two more runners in the 10th and two more again in the 11th.

The Astros' lack of offense finally caught up to them in the top of the 14th inning. Geoff Blum, who shared the third base job with Ensberg in Houston in 2002 and praised former Houston manager Jimy Williams for giving him his first opening-day start, haunted his former team. Blum, acquired from San Diego in a July deadline deal merely as insurance for Crede's aching back, hit a two-out, pinch-hit homer off of rookie Ezequiel Astacio. Garner responded to Blum's home run by tossing a chair down the dugout's tunnel.

The Sox added another run en route to a 7-5 win that took five hours, 41 minutes to complete. As fate would have it, the first World Series game played in Texas, where everything is said to be bigger, officially tied for the longest game in terms of innings in World Series history. A World Series game had not gone as many innings since the Boston Red Sox beat the Brooklyn Dodgers in Game 2 of the 1916 World Series. In terms of time, the five hours and 41 minutes easily outdistanced every game in Series history.

"It's the stuff dreams are made of," Blum said. "I've had about a hundred of these at-bats in my backyard with my younger brother. But to do it on this stage and in this situation makes this year incredibly worthwhile."

The Astros, obviously, weren't very thrilled on a night they wasted many opportunities.

"That's some pretty poor hitting, absolute rotten hitting," Garner said. "We had our chances. It's amazing. I don't know how you win a ball-game when you can't hit the ball. We didn't even hit the ball [well] except for Jason. We managed to stay in the ballgame, but we might have played 40 innings, and it didn't look we were going to get a runner across the bag. Very frustrating."

National media that had not followed Garner all year assumed he was throwing his players under the proverbial bus. The fact of the matter, however, was that Garner had acted the same way all year. He wasn't ripping his players as much as he was giving his genuine feelings. All of the focus, though, turned on his raw emotion.

"I'd like to put on a better show," Garner said. "It's embarrassing to play like this in front of our hometown. It was just not a good game for us tonight."

It was as though the national media wanted Garner to act as though all was fine after such a disappointing loss.

Brandon Backe was the least heralded of the Astros' starting pitchers, but he made one of the best performances of the postseason in Game 4. A year after his masterful eight scoreless innings in Game 5 of the National League Championship Series against the Cardinals, Backe stepped up with the Astros' best pitching performance of the World Series.

Backe limited the White Sox to five hits through seven innings and seemed to get stronger with each inning. After allowing Dye's leadoff hit in the fourth, Backe struck out the next five batters and retired 11 consecutive batters. Garner stuck with him after Rowand singled and Crede doubled with two out in the seventh. Garner was rewarded when Backe struck out Uribe on a slider to end the threat. The Astros' offensive woes carried over from Game 3, though.

Garner played for one run early against former Astros prospect Freddy Garcia. His players couldn't push a measly run across the plate despite putting a runner in scoring position in three of the first six innings against one of the three players the Astros had given to the Seattle Mariners in 1998 in the Randy Johnson trade.

Garcia, a right-hander from the Astros' Venezuelan Academy, escaped a bases-loaded jam in the sixth by striking out Lane. Garcia was pulled after retiring the side in order in the seventh, leaving after seven scoreless innings of four-hit ball with seven strikeouts. Garner took no chances after Backe exited. He called on Lidge, his closer, to start the eighth. Garner was banking that Lidge could go two innings, and the offense could forge one run to win.

The Astros came up short again. Willie Harris, making his first plate appearance of the World Series, led off with a single and moved to second on Podsednik's sacrifice bunt. Harris reached third on pinch hitter Carl Everett's ground out to second. On a 1-1 count, Dye hit a clean single up the middle to give the White Sox a 1-0 lead with what proved to be the only run of the night.

The White Sox thought so much of Berkman that they intentionally walked him with one out and Taveras at second in the bottom of the eighth. The move paid off when Ensberg flied out to center, and left-hander Neal Cotts retired Jose Vizcaino on a grounder to short. The Astros, who scored their last run of the World Series in the eighth inning of Game 3, took their last shot in the ninth off Jenks.

Lane led off the ninth with a single and moved to second on Ausmus's sacrifice bunt. Burke hit for Adam Everett and sent a foul pop toward the left field line. Uribe, known more for his arm than his range, sprinted from short toward the railing along the left field line and leaned into the stands to catch the foul pop among a throng of fans wearing

Astros gear. Down to their final out, pinch hitter Orlando Palmeiro went up to the plate to face Jenks.

Palmeiro hit a grounder that barely got by the robust Jenks. Uribe, playing with a definite sense of urgency, fielded the ball and fired a strike to first base a foot ahead of Palmeiro as the White Sox claimed their first World Series title in 88 years.

As the White Sox celebrated on Minute Maid Park's turf, several Astros watched. The great majority of the sellout crowd of 42,936 stayed in their seats and gave the Astros ovations. After a few minutes to compose themselves, most of the Astros went back out on the field and thanked their fans.

A season that many so-called experts predicted would end with the Astros near the bottom of the standings finally ended on October 26 at Minute Maid Park with the White Sox celebrating a World Series sweep. The Astros had fought back from a 15-30 record and became the first team since the 1914 Braves to go from 15 games under .500 to the World Series in the same year. Houston had finally brought the World Series to Texas, and the 2005 Astros will always be remembered as the team that pushed the franchise to its first NL pennant.

"Well, we started out very poorly, about as rotten as you could be for the first 45 ballgames," Garner said. "And then we found a way to turn it around. Some players started doing real well. And our pitching was pretty solid all year long, and our offense started to figure out a way to win a ballgame, and we played pretty well. I would say, as I told the team, I thought we won as a team, we lost as a team. Everybody in our clubhouse had something to do with us getting here, and it's a pretty good story, a dog-gone good story. I'm proud of those guys."

Epilogue

The World Series didn't last nearly as long as the Astros and their fans had hoped, but the high from the Lone Star State's first World Series crept into the holiday season. Throughout the Houston area and much of the Gulf Coast region Astros gear flew off the shelves as fans wrapped up and placed Astros hats, shirts, and jerseys under their Christmas trees for friends and family.

The Astros had indeed provided a lift and a shining light in a year that will go down as one of the most painful for people in the Gulf Coast region because of the destruction left behind by Hurricanes Katrina and Rita. A community that had united to provide support and shelter for their New Orleans brothers and sisters in late August and throughout September was rewarded in October with a respite from the sadness that had permeated their lives.

"Houston—and Texas—waited a long time for the World Series, and it came to us at exactly the right time," Houston mayor Bill White said. "I can't describe the tremendous lift it gave us. We showed the world in the wake of the twin disasters of Hurricanes Katrina and Rita that Houston is a city with a very big heart. Then, against big odds, the Astros took us to a place we'd never been before. The chance it gave Houstonians—newcomers and old-timers alike—to pull together was like manna from baseball heaven. We loved it."

For every three people among the approximate 150,000 New Orleans evacuees who landed in Houston after Hurricane Katrina, one Houstonian registered as a volunteer, providing a 100,000 volunteer corps that showed the world what the people of Houston are all about. The baseball gods were obviously watching, guiding a team that was left for dead in June all the way to the World Series in a feat not accomplished since 1914 by another team that had fallen 15 games under .500.

"I guess for me the biggest thing is just how proud I was of the team, just how proud I was of the guys," said Astros left-hander Andy Pettitte. "It was pretty bleak, you know, at one time. Everybody knows. You could have folded up [the] tent and packed it in. To some extent—if everybody was honest—we kind of would have looked around and said there's no way we'd pull it off. But at the same time we knew we had a pretty good pitching staff."

With Pettitte, Roger Clemens, Roy Oswalt, and Brandon Backe leading the starting rotation, Brad Lidge anchoring the bullpen and Lance Berkman and Morgan Ensberg providing the power, the Astros won their first National League pennant by displaying the grit and determination of the community they represent.

Pettitte, whose signing in Houston triggered Clemens's signing and the Astros' eventual march to the World Series, understands how a battered and proud community can rally around its baseball team. In 2001, he was an important member of the American League champion New York Yankees club that reached the World Series while the country united after the terrorist attacks on the World Trade Center's Twin Towers and the Pentagon. For Pettitte, playing for the Astros in 2005 was the equivalent of playing for the Yankees in 2001.

"Obviously we weren't hit in Houston like Louisiana or Mississippi, but the region was definitely in a need for something to cheer," Pettitte said. "It's almost to the point I was in the same way with the Yankees in 2001 after 9/11. You rally around that, and you want to give people something to cheer about. I'm really proud of the city and the way that the city handled itself, and the fans were just tremendous."

After 44 seasons of Astros baseball and 45 years after Houston was awarded Texas's first Major League Baseball franchise, it can no longer be said that the Astros have never reached the World Series. The 2005 National League champions gave their fans lifelong memories they'll cherish for years.

Texas Supreme Court justice David Medina won't ever forget the strength he received from his 10-year-old son, Vincent, after St. Louis Cardinals slugger Albert Pujols hit a game-winning three-run home run in Game 5 of the National League Championship Series. Seconds before Pujols's majestic shot, Medina and his son had been among the sellout crowd dancing in the aisles as the Astros moved within one out of clinching the World Series berth that day at Minute Maid Park.

As Pujols's home run blasted through the thick Houston air, a tear rolled down Justice Medina's cheek as they remembered the 40 years of heartbreak as an Astros fan.

"Hey," young Vincent told his father, "there's no crying in baseball."

Vincent reminded his father that only a game—not the series—had been lost. There was still hope for the Astros and their fans, and Oswalt took care of the rest two days later in Game 6 at Busch Stadium as the Astros finally reached the World Series.

"As a lifelong Astros baseball fan since I was growing up in Hitchcock, it meant everything just to be able to go to the big show," said the Texas Supreme Court judge. "It was an Astros baseball fan's dream come true after seeing so many close misses with the Astros in 1980 against the Phillies and 1986 against the Mets and 2004 against the St. Louis Cardinals."

Of all the great teams in Astros' franchise history, the 2005 one overcame the most obstacles. On paper, the 2005 Astros may not have been the strongest team in franchise history. On the field, though, they were the ones who broke through that barrier.

"I still can feel the emotion in that sixth game in St. Louis in the last three innings when the momentum was with the Astros," Astros owner Drayton McLane said. "I can remember the sheer excitement for Astros fans and our players. I can still relate to that magnificent evening in St. Louis. Seeing how proud people were in Houston and throughout Texas. I think it was just a major breakthrough for the Astros and all our fans. It was just a wonderful memory.

"I'm more determined now for 2006. Going to the World Series in 2005 lifted us far beyond where any Astros team had been or any team in Texas had been. Our desire is to continue to move forward."

About the Author

Jose de Jesus Ortiz is the national baseball writer and the lead Astros writer for the *Houston Chronicle*. Ortiz, who worked in New York from 1998 until March 30, 2001, was the primary New York Mets beat writer for the *Newark Star-Ledger* before arriving at the *Houston Chronicle* for the Astros' 2001 season. Ortiz, who has worked on both coasts and in three of the top media markets in the country, began his career at the *Long Beach* (California) *Press-Telegram*.

His story on Flynn Kyle was honored as Notable Sports Writing of 2003 in the 2004 edition of *The Best American Sports Writing*. His column admonishing the Atlanta Braves and a Georgia judge for letting shortstop Rafael Furcal play in the 2004 division series after he received a DUI conviction was honored as Notable Sports Writing of 2004 in the 2005 edition of *The Best American Sports Writing*. Ortiz has been called "one of the best baseball writers in the country because of his ability to bring the most out of the subjects he interviews," by *New York Post* media critic Andrew Marchand.

Ortiz and his wife, Megan, live in Kingwood with their daughter, Kathleen.

He has been the primary Astros beat writer since Opening Day of the 2001 season, earning the *Chronicle's* Jesse Jones Award in February 2004 for his coverage on the Andy Pettitte signing with the Astros. He also was one of four finalists in 2005 for Reporter of the Year at the *Chronicle*.

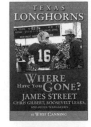